The Manpower Planning Handbook

The Manpower Planning Handbook

Malcolm Bennison
and Jonathan Casson

McGRAW-HILL Book Company (UK) Limited

London · New York · St Louis · San Francisco · Auckland
Bogotá · Guatemala · Hamburg · Johannesburg · Lisbon
Madrid · Mexico · Montreal · New Delhi · Panama · Paris
San Juan · São Paulo · Singapore · Sydney · Tokyo · Toronto

Published by
McGRAW-HILL Book Company (UK) Limited
MAIDENHEAD · BERKSHIRE · ENGLAND

British Library Cataloguing in Publication Data

Bennison, Malcolm
   The manpower planning handbook.
   1. Manpower planning
   I. Title   II. Casson, Jonathan
   658.3′01   HF5549.5.M3
   ISBN 0-07-084727-4

Library of Congress Cataloging in Publication Data

Bennison, Malcolm.
   The manpower planning handbook.
   Bibliography: p.
   Includes index.
   1. Manpower planning.   I. Casson, Jonathan.   II. Title.
   HF5549.5.M3B46   1983   658.3′01   83-18713
   ISBN 0-07-084727-4

12345 OUP 8654

Typeset by Oxford Verbatim Limited
Printed and bound in Great Britain by
Oxford University Press

Contents

Foreword

Few can claim that we have got to grips with managing manpower effectively: managing, whether as a firm or an economy, so that we can compete in terms of quality, price and delivery; ensuring that we have the professionalism in our workforces to realize the full potential of new markets and the new techniques; developing the skills to cope with change as it occurs without major disruption; providing every opportunity for individuals to develop and use their skills.

But a sound start has been made, as this book shows. Manpower management makes sense and the approach described here gets results. It is practical. It applies to the small private firm as much as to the large public corporation. It is a responsibility of every line manager or small businessman. Nonetheless, the authors start with some major obstacles. Manpower planning has a reputation for being academic, if not tedious. It has been written about for over twenty years, every new book the definitive version. It failed in the 1960s and 1970s. It belongs to the world of calculation, computers and big bureaucracies.

Many of us must share the blame for this view of manpower planning. Some still perpetuate the myths, others find it useful to use them so that they can avoid becoming subject to the discipline that good manpower management requires. A discipline that has evolved from practical experience in many sorts of organization. The early ideas of the operational research scientists who argued the need for such a discipline have been tested, simplified and remoulded to fit the realities of the work place. Today, no practising manpower planner would speak to his management colleagues of 'Markov Chains', and 'Stochastic Renewal Processes', and even were reference to be made to manpower forecasts, they would be highly qualified as to what they meant in terms of the business.

Many people have contributed to the distillation of experience which makes up this book. A number, once in the personnel function, now hold senior executive positions in firms. They were able to use the kinds of approach described in this book to reach sensible, often critical, decisions, which were not otherwise obvious, about the shape of their organizations, their recruitment and career development policies and their deployment of staff. In this way, they helped to ensure the success of their firms' business strategies. Others found better ways of handling information about people so that it made immediate sense to management, helped them diagnose problems and bring out graphically the main pressure points.

It fell to Malcolm Bennison and Jonathan Casson to set down the lessons gained from that experience. In practice, they have done much more. They realistically set down the goals that can be reached with manpower planning. They map out the ground to be covered, present a sequential form of thinking which plots a logical course through the material, whilst clearing away the undergrowth of mathematical expression and jargon which obscured the way in the past. The result is that the interested reader is taken to the point at which he can progress himself, simply by applying the lessons learned.

In 1973 Stephen Mullaly, then its Chairman, was asked why the Institute of Manpower Studies had published so little. He replied that IMS was making history not writing it. It has taken a long time but the perspective is now there. Already more is being written: on recruitment, development and career management; on measuring productivity and improving the performance of groups of people; on understanding the labour market; and on the relation of work to society. But it is this book that encapsulates the basis of the Institute's approach. It will be the starting point for operational manpower managers for many years.

CLIVE PURKISS
Director
Institute of Manpower Studies

Acknowledgements

If you the reader get benefit from this book, and as a result are more successful in managing your manpower, then you and we, the authors, must acknowledge that there are three sets of people who must be warmly thanked.

First, we would like to thank the colleagues we both worked with in the late 1960s in the Universities of Kent and Cambridge, the Civil Service and a number of companies, including BP, ICI and Shell, who were developing the techniques of manpower modelling. Their unselfishness in sharing that knowledge ensured its widest possible dissemination to those of us in companies and in the Institute who were wrestling with the problems of manpower management. They gave us an exceptionally complete set of tools.

Second, we are grateful to the managers in the companies where we have worked to test out the tool kit in the early stages and then to create the approach that is the subject of this book. Unfailingly helpful and generously supportive at the outset, companies like Royal Insurance, Prudential, Legal & General, ICI, Fiat, Dunlop, British Steel, BAT and Kodak were our experimental laboratory. They suffered the results of our failures as well as our successes. Both had to be experienced before the development of a successful approach could be completed.

Third and finally, to highlight their importance, we must thank the people who have helped in the long and arduous final task of committing all this experience to paper. Jean Randall, Jackie Bazalgette and Sherry Ryan decoded and interpreted illegible handwriting and incoherent tape recording into the final draft of the book. Our wives had to learn new skills in home maintenance and do-it-yourself while the protracted process of writing went on.

MALCOLM BENNISON
JONATHAN CASSON

1.

The objectives and nature of manpower management

Background

Manpower planning, oh we tried that in the 1960s. We used sophisticated manpower planning models to produce the company's manpower plans. The trouble was that the data were suspect and by the time that the plan had been produced it was already out of date. The last I heard was that the manpower planning model was being used by the computer operators to enliven the nightshift. They were gambling on who would be chief general manager in 1985. I am told that quite an amount of money was changing hands.

What a tragedy that the manpower planning activity that began with such promise in the 1960s should be dismissed as irrelevant by the people who now need it most, the chief executives of organizations.

During the time of preparation of this book unemployment has risen sharply, both the rates of interest and the rates of inflation have fluctuated widely and many organizations have announced major redundancies. What tragic irony that the need for better manpower management should be so great and yet the acceptability of the means to improve it is so low that many organizations omit these methods from the options they use to cope with the recession; company after company resorts to short-term manpower policies.

The tragedy is deepened by the fact that there are available practical and simple techniques to help an organization's manpower management – techniques that are relevant and useful in these times. Indeed, the same practical and simple techniques are relevant and useful in dealing with the manpower problems that result from the rapid expansion that organizations experienced during the 1960s or from the severe contractions recently experienced.

The penalties associated with failure to match manpower and organization policies are heavy in human terms. The costs of employing people have been rising more rapidly than other organization costs, and whereas overmanning five years ago might have been tolerable it is no longer the case. Organizations

1

neither generate the profits to cover nor have the reserves to absorb the increases in manpower costs temporarily, nor can they raise sales prices to offset the rise in manpower costs when rates of inflation are high. The direct result of overmanning is, at the minimum, a stop on recruitment leaving school leavers and teenagers unemployed: at the worst, redundancy among employees.

Manpower policies must be examined rigorously and answers found to such questions as: 'If we decide to reduce our research and development effort by 10 per cent over the next two years, can we achieve the staff reduction by natural wastage?' Or, 'If we stop our current capital expenditure plans and decide to close down one of our works, what will be the effect on graduate recruitment?' Even questions such as 'We are expanding at 10 per cent per annum and are concerned about the availability of future managers. Should we increase our rate of recruitment?' are being asked and need to be answered in some companies, particularly those engaged in developing the new technology of micro-electronics. To put the problem into perspective, few companies ask and answer these questions. In the vast majority of companies the questions are not asked because they are thought to be unanswerable.

The pressures to improve manpower management

Regardless of the current pressures caused by the recession, there is a developing and ongoing need to manage manpower better. It is no longer possible to achieve this objective by reacting to events, recruiting to replace high wastage, making employees redundant when there is a need to reduce costs. Since the 1960s there have been two increasing and convergent pressures on organizations to adopt a longer term approach to manpower management.

Organizations have become more complex, requiring a wider range of specialist skills in their employees. A wider range of skills means more types of employees to be recruited, and the greater the degree of difficulty in replacing such employees when they leave. Twenty years ago in a modern office there would be typists and shorthand typists. Today there are copy typists, audio typists, shorthand typists and, recently, word processing operators. If we suppose it takes about a year to train satisfactorily a good shorthand typist, we will certainly need an extra three months to add the skills required by a word processing operator. Three months must be added to the time taken to replace such an operator who leaves. When new skills are needed but take a long time to acquire, organizations often respond by creating new career streams. In doing so the size of the manpower management problem is considerably increased.

The rapidly changing technology of the last 20 years has now entered new areas of application such as clerical and administrative work, where the impact of micro-electronics on the information processing task is deep and wide ranging. Organizations find that they have skills in abundance which are no longer necessary and yet, at the same time, are short of the much needed new experience.

Employment legislation has greatly increased in recent years. Coinciding with the business recession of 1974 there has been an increased emphasis on the protection of employment. At best the legislation is seen as an attempt to give individuals protection in a field where their ability to influence organizations' decisions may be limited. At worst, it is seen as a measure which reduces an organization's ability to respond to external influences and by so doing it creates unemployment to a greater extent a little later than would otherwise be the case.

The job creation programmes of the Manpower Services Commission, the Temporary Employment Subsidy, the National Enterprise Board, initiatives of the Labour Government of the late 1970s, were a positive attempt to deal with the same problem from the opposite direction. Instead of stopping organizations from releasing surplus employees on to the labour market, they attempted to maintain employment levels by active intervention, creating opportunities directly or finding financial support to cover temporary situations.

It is now extremely difficult to reduce the size of an organization quickly and cheaply. Time can be bought by generous redundancy payments but the impact of legislation has been to slow down the process by which an organization can reduce its numbers. The current recession has increased the number of organizations resorting to 'lay-off procedures' rather than redundancies. The plain fact is that the going rate for redundancy is now so high that in a number of cases the payment of the redundancy compensation would have been enough to bankrupt the company. 'Lay-offs', the solution of the 1950s and 1960s in the stop part of the 'stop go' cycle, are now being used with increasing frequency. Those responsible for managing manpower must begin to look further ahead in attempting to foresee manpower problems.

The pressure on personnel and manpower specialists is high, the penalties for failure to provide and maintain appropriate policies are serious for the organization and for the individual. The conflicting demands of the organization in its search for efficiency, the individual in his desire for job security and to be recognized as a contributor, the State with its twin objectives of reducing unemployment and promoting investment, have made the task of a personnel or manpower specialist difficult, but nevertheless very necessary.

Early developments in manpower management

Manpower and manpower behaviour have been studied in increasing depth since the turn of the century. Beginning with Taylor's attempts to improve manpower productivity by time study, moving through the period of Frank and Lillian Gilbreth's techniques for recording motion patterns leading to work simplification on the assembly lines of the 1930s, taking in Bedaux, who made work measurement possible by introducing concepts of rating the speed with which employees work and the need for fatigue allowances, culminating with the establishment of work study functions in large organizations, epitomized by Russell Curry in ICI, there has been a genuine attempt to increase the effectiveness of manpower.

The initial work concentrated on the problems of effective utilization of manpower on the shop floor. The establishment of organization and methods of techniques in the 1960s moved the study of work into the office and clerical systems. Latterly, study of manpower has turned to the behaviour of individuals and individuals in groups. Highly motivated individuals make a greater contribution to the organization's effectiveness. To motivate individuals, studies indicate the need to give individuals objectives, to emphasize goals, to emphasize the necessity of the individual to the achievement of the organization's goals, to offer careers that have meaning; in short, the key to the organization's effectiveness is people, not machines.

The late 1960s saw the formulation into a coherent and systematic framework of many of these different approaches and added the techniques of quantification developed by operational researchers and statisticians. The banner headline of 'Manpower Planning' was given to a framework involving three sequential steps:

1. Estimate the organization's future manpower needs in terms of the numbers of people required of different skills and occupations at all levels in the organization.
2. The means by which the organization will meet these needs is now examined. In other words, how is the manpower to be supplied? To arrive at the supply the levels of wastage must be studied, the rate at which people progress through the organization must be studied, and an attempt must be made to quantify the labour markets from which the recruits are drawn. The numbers and types of people the organization is likely to have in five years' time is thus decided.
3. The gap between the needs and the supply should now be evident. Where there are insufficient people of the required ability to fill promotions, other sources of manpower must be investigated. Transfers from other parts of the organization, recruitment of experienced people directly from outside, possibly the promotion of good people from lower levels than normal; all are possible means of closing the gap. At this stage the basic levels of recruitment necessary for the organization to cover its leavers and meet its overall demand for manpower can be determined. Sometimes these calculations show that the wastage levels are not great enough to reduce the

4

number of staff to the overall demand and the organization has to consider redundancy policies.

An essential part of this framework was the statistical methods developed to assist the organization quantify the supply of manpower. Markov, linear, and renewal programming models were designed to help understand and predict the interrelated movements of employees by promotion, recruitment, transfer, and wastage within, to, and from an organization. On the demand side, considerable use was made of statistical methods to help in the prediction of the mix of skills and the numbers of people the organization is likely to need to meet possible business situations: trend analysis, time series analysis, input/output analysis, Box–Jenkins, are a few of the techniques suggested in the literature of the 1960s as being helpful in forecasting future numbers.

This framework and the statistical techniques enabled manpower policies to be developed to close the gaps: these policies were the manpower plan of the organization, and the framework and its associated techniques became known as the 'manpower planning system'. Many organizations spent considerable energy and resources in finding or developing the right manpower model to meet their situation.

Difficulties encountered in implementing the 'manpower planning system'

The framework was logical, the techniques were well founded, and the idea of a manpower planning system seemed unassailable. Yet it failed to make the impact it should have done because it contained within it an immense practical difficulty. The notion that it is possible to estimate future manpower needs, with the precision necessary to match policies of supply, is quite fallacious. Demand is particularly susceptible to changes in the outside world; wars, commodity prices, and foreign exchange difficulties cause problems in managing economies which, in turn, affect the growth rates of organizations. These external events are essentially unpredictable and so the ability to estimate the demand for an organization's manpower is suspect.

The extent of the fallacy began to show during the early 1970s. The manpower planning system was developed to help organizations with expanding manpower levels. Experience indicates that any system for forecasting the future tends to *under*estimate a change; during times of expansion too low a rate is forecast, during times of contraction the extent of the contraction is often underestimated. In general, forecasts during a period of growth will lead to manpower policies of recruitment and promotion which are insufficient to sustain the real level of growth. The organization suffers high rates of wastage, high levels of overtime working; it finds its recruitment campaigns unsuccessful and it has to resort increasingly to contract labour to meet its needs. This is the period when pressure comes on the payment systems, when demarcation disputes begin to grow. This is the period when attention is focused on the quality of promotees and recruits and when alternative sources of supply are examined. The costs involved are hidden, intangible, and unrealizable, the organization learns to live with its failure. The penalty of failure is frustration and irritation but nothing like the demoralizing and depressing effect of having too many people in the organization and having to resort to redundancy policies.

The worst situation of all occurs in the highly cyclical period, when the organization is going from expansion to contraction over a four- or five-year period. This is a situation that has pertained since the early 1970s. Many organizations experienced a major setback to growth in the aftermath of the oil crisis of 1973; many manpower policies began to be found wanting from that time. Today's conditions have brutally exposed the lack of manpower policies in many organizations, and the brittle nature of these policies in others. The realization has grown that the first part of the framework, the need to estimate the business future demand for people, is extremely difficult in a world subjected to economic cycles of varying length and unpredictable intensity.

In 1969, the manpower planners in the company that is the subject of Fig. 1.1, were considering the demand for people for the years 1970–73 inclusive. Starting with a total strength of 16 800 and taking into account the company's

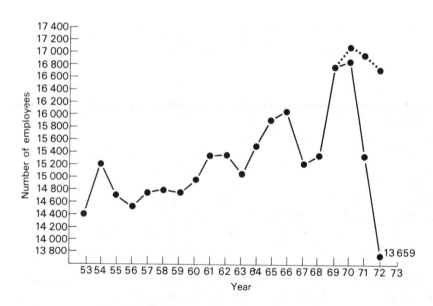

Fig. 1.1. Failure to achieve the manpower plan

investment programme, current productivity trends, results of a questionnaire asking the company's managers to define manpower needs and the sales forecasts; a peak manpower level of 17 200 was assessed for 1970 and reduction to 16 600 was forecast for 1973, the dotted line on the chart. Almost before the company forecast has been published it was wrong. The unbroken line on the chart shows the actual situation. The cumulative effect of the United States' import surcharge of 1968, the war between India and Pakistan in Bangladesh, the disruption caused by the cultural revolution in China, on a highly export orientated company had reduced sales turnover considerably. None of these events was in the control of the company, nor was any of them foreseeable at the time the forecast was made. By the end of 1973 the company's total manpower was in the region of 13 300, an error of 3 300 or some 20 per cent.

The influence of external events on manpower forecasting is deep, far reaching, and will continue to be so in future. The three months spent by the manpower planners in translating the business scenario into manpower terms were completely wasted, destroyed by unpredictable external circumstances.

Similar experiences in many organizations led to the questioning of the viability of the manpower plan. The framework was also severely criticized for the amount of time and effort involved in producing the plan. In the example three months were necessary, and our experience is that to do this in quite small organizations, in the depth necessary to assess the basic levels of recruitment for all the types of staff employed, would take one to two years. A yearly planning cycle following the steps of the framework is not feasible.

The situation can best be likened to the problem of planning a route from A to B (Fig. 1.2). A represents the organization's current demand for people; B represents the considered view of the organization, taking into account corporate objectives of their future manpower needs (the first step in the framework). Detailed plans of how to get from A to B are worked out (the second step in the framework, the supply of manpower) and in some cases there may be an attempt to evaluate the consequences of straying either side of the path by a small percentage. The organization adopts the plan and begins to move towards its objective. Before long an external event occurs which changes the business forecast for the future and, because of its magnitude, the organization needs a higher level of manpower with a different mix of skills to meet the new business situation, i.e., point C (Fig. 1.3). The organization has to scrap its previous detailed plans and begin to plan a new route from the point it has reached to the new objective C, a process which, by its nature, is again long and involved. And so the system continues. A response is required each time the forecast future of the business is found to be untrue.

Since the oil crisis of 1973 there has been the revolution in Iran removing some 3.6 million barrels of oil a day from the world market, and more recently the war between Iraq and Iran, removing another 2 million barrels of oil a day. The loss of oil production is rapidly translated to higher prices for oil which in

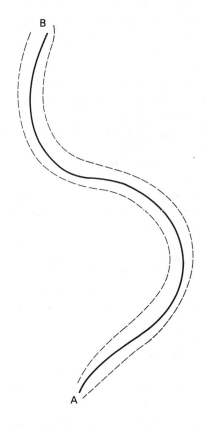

Fig. 1.2. Planning a route from A to B

turn affect the inflation rates of national economies of the West which, in their turn, affect company profitability.

The practical approach to taking manpower policy decisions

The manpower planning system must be replaced by manpower management. Instead of planning detailed routes of how to get from A to B, the practical approach concentrates on producing a map (Fig. 1.4) of the manpower configuration of the organization now and the general direction in which it believes it is heading.

It is much more important, given the impossibility of forecasting the future, to know which way to turn when circumstances change. In particular, the approach emphasizes the analysis of alternatives, linking manpower decisions

8

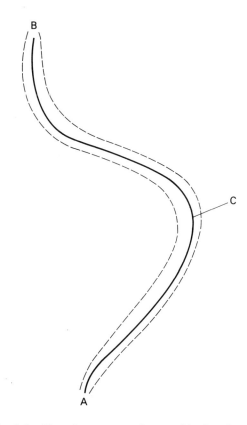

Fig. 1.3. Changing course to the new objective, C

with the factors that affect them; the organization's growth rate, its wastage, and its replacement policies. Success in manpower planning comes when organizations concentrate on identifying critical manpower decisions and providing information to help take those decisions.

Advisory work with many organizations has shown that the key to gaining acceptance of the need to manage manpower is to demonstrate that useful and realistic information will result. It is a hopeless task to try to convince a personnel manager that a manpower plan can be produced detailing the number to be recruited each year, 'O' level, 'A' level, graduate, etc., rates of promotions from level to level, how the age distribution will change, when the manager can demonstrate the manpower forecast is on very shaky grounds and in the last five years has been right only once, and that the average error is around 5 per cent in either direction.

Interest can be created if the personnel manager is shown the relationship

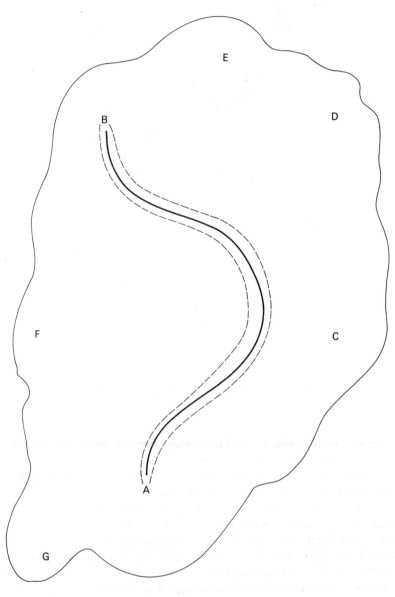

Fig. 1.4. Drawing a manpower map

between the number of recruits, the wastage rates, and the size of the organization. This leads to a better understanding of the total situation and helps to judge when a particular decision becomes critical. The knowledge that a recruitment level should be 60 per year and not 70 per year is unlikely to cause major changes in the way the personnel function operates. A change, however, from five recruits needed, to reducing the organization by five staff creates major changes in the industrial relations climate. Would a reduction in the organization's current wastage rate of 10 per cent create this situation? If manpower planning is considered as providing information via a process of analysis enabling better decisions about manpower policies to be made, greater interest will result from executives and personnel managers.

INFORMATION AND DECISION MAKING

To illustrate what is meant by providing better information for decision making, a real situation is considered. Organizations regularly experience considerable difficulty in deciding the level of recruitment of school leavers into engineering apprenticeships.

Young people are indentured as apprentices as soon as they leave school at the age of 16. A common manpower phenomenon is often noticed at the point at which employees are recruited to an organization – the induction crisis, a very high rate of leaving in the first few months of service (see Fig. 1.5). It is

Fig. 1.5. The apprentice manpower system – 1. Entry

particularly noticeable among employees for whom this is the first job, school leavers, graduates, etc. Engineering apprentices are no exception to this rule. Part of the reason for the induction crisis can be found in jobs not fulfilling employees' expectations. This will be particularly true for those who are taking a job for the first time, because their expectations of jobs are likely to be higher than those of recruits who have had previous experience. Perhaps the basic training is irksome and the employee does not have the patience to build the skills necessary for more interesting work. Three weeks spent filing a block of metal to a perfect cube may not seem relevant to a budding engineer whose interest is in designing steam turbines.

Perhaps the apprentice finds the taunts of friends earning three or four times more from their unskilled work on building sites too difficult to bear and he leaves to join them. In all jobs, in all walks of life, the induction crisis can be found and must be allowed for in planning recruitment levels.

Having survived the induction crisis, an apprentice is likely to stay for the remainder of his term. Every day that he or she remains, an apprentice increases the chance of completing the four-year term. Each day completed is an investment; to leave before the full term is to get no return on the investment. Nevertheless, during the remainder of the period there will be some losses. Ill-health, accidents, disablement are some of the reasons. The family might move to another locality and it may not be possible for the apprentice to remain with his employer. This type of wastage is difficult to predict but fortunately the rate is low.

At the end of the fourth year, in fact the end of the apprenticeship, another common phenomenon is noticed (Fig. 1.6). A significant proportion of the people who complete their apprenticeship leave the organization that has trained them. This phenomenon is to be found whenever a long training period comes to an end and it has a particularly long tradition in engineering. The idea of the journeyman going out into the world to apply his new found knowledge in a wider range of situations was one that was still to be found in the engineering industry until 10 years ago. Now organizations value apprentices trained by themselves too highly to let them go elsewhere. Nevertheless, it happens; the rate at which it happens must be evaluated and used when calculating the level of apprentice recruitment.

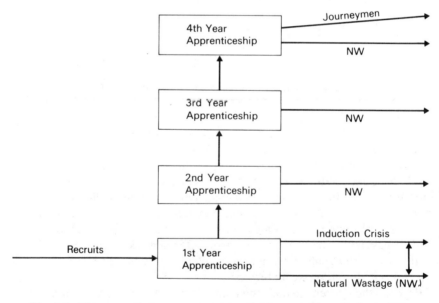

Fig. 1.6. The apprentice manpower system – 2. Manpower flows during training

Engineering apprentices, during the first year of their apprenticeship, are allowed day-release to attend school for technical training. Some of them do well in their first-year examinations and are then allowed to continue studying for the remainder of the apprenticeship. The ones who fail revert to a normal apprenticeship. Technical training continues during the second, third, and fourth years of the apprenticeship, and by the time the apprenticeship is completed, the apprentices are extremely well qualified and often enter the design office as designers or draughtsmen (Fig. 1.7). It should be noted now that this is the first time in the structure that it is possible to recruit fully trained designers and draughtsmen from the labour market. An organization does not need to get all its designers and draughtsmen by training apprentices.

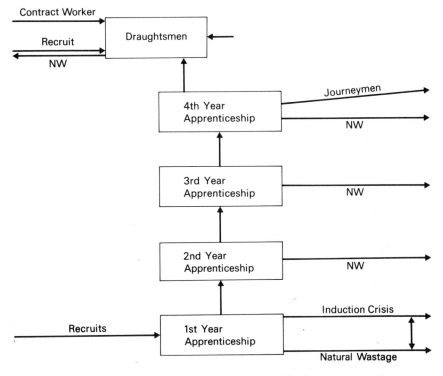

Fig. 1.7. The apprentice manpower system – 3. The draughtsman option

At the end of the fourth year, apprentices who have not gone through technical training or who do not leave the organization become craftsmen within the organization, and again it should be noted that an organization does not need to get all its craftsmen from training its own apprentices but can recruit them directly from the labour market either as permanent employees or on short-term contract (see Fig. 1.8).

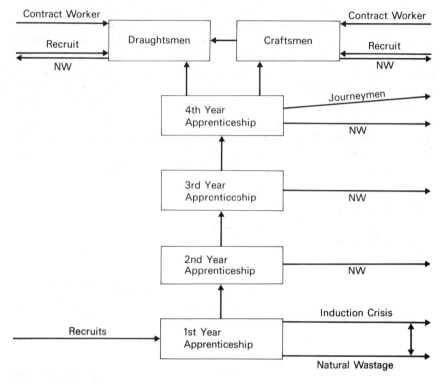

Fig. 1.8. The apprentice manpower system – 4. The craftsman option

To complete the picture, draughtsmen, designers, and craftsmen can become supervisors, and there is often a flow from the craftsmen ranks into the design and draughtsmen ranks in order to keep up the level of practical experience in the design office.

THE PRINCIPAL MANPOWER FACTORS AFFECTING DECISIONS

Looking at Fig. 1.9, it can be seen that the level of recruitment of school leavers into apprenticeships is governed by a number of factors. Clearly, a crucial piece of information in determining how many apprentices should be recruited is the estimate of the number of jobs at the draughtsmen and craftsmen levels the organization needs in four years' time: the demand for manpower. Much can happen to an organization's manpower levels over a four-year period. How many people in 1976 would have forecast the revolution in Iran with its consequent impact on the world economy?

In determining the number of school leavers recruited into an engineering apprenticeship scheme, attention must be paid to the numbers of apprentices,

14

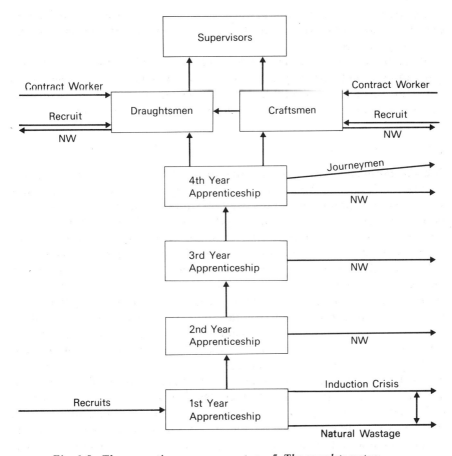

Fig. 1.9. The apprentice manpower system – 5. The complete system

draughtsmen, and craftsmen who will leave the organization during the four years over which we are trying to plan. Predicting the rate of loss from an organization is a complex process. Induction losses, losses after training, the natural wastage from the system, and retirements, all must be taken into account.

The third factor, affecting the level of recruitment of school leavers into apprenticeship, is the replacement policy of the organization. An organization relying on attracting skilled craftsmen ready trained from other organizations in the labour market will require no school leavers. On the other hand, an organization may meet all its requirements for craftsmen and draughtsmen from within its own apprenticeship ranks, since its particular technology or type of business is specialized or demanding of such high quality standards that it can only ensure it meets these by being responsible for the training of all its

15

skilled people. This organization will need to fill all the vacancies that it has or expects to have in four years' time in its draughtsmen and craftsmen ranks from its own apprentices.

These three factors, the level of demand, the rate of loss from the organization, and the replacement policy, are common to almost all manpower problems and recur so frequently that the assessment of these three factors has become a major part of an effective approach to manpower management.

THE ELEMENTS OF THE APPROACH

Drawing the manpower system   In order to ascertain the information needed to decide the level of school leavers recruited as apprentices, the manpower system for the apprentice recruits had to be drawn. Until the set of boxes and flows representing the way that manpower behaves from recruitment as an apprentice to the final supervisory level in the system had been drawn, it was not possible to specify the information needed to help with that decision.

Drawing the manpower system for any problem is the key to identifying the manpower decisions that have to be taken and the influences on those decisions. Where employees enter the organization a decision is required: what level of recruitment is needed to fill the number of expected jobs and to allow for wastage? Where two types of manpower can be considered for the same job, decisions must be taken as to how much of each type of manpower is best able to fill those jobs. For instance, promotion to supervisor can come from either the craftsmen or the draughtsmen ranks. Filling all vacancies at supervisor level by promotion from craftsmen would debar the most technically qualified, technically knowledgeable employees (the draughtsmen) from those posts. Filling vacancies at the supervisor level exclusively from the draughtsmen would reduce the level of practical experience among the supervisors. The organization will establish a proportion from each of the two flows that it feels is consistent with its current circumstances. The proportion may change from time to time. It is imperative that the organization realizes that it is exercising a choice and does so consciously. Wherever two boxes draw on manpower from the same box, choices have also to be made on which of the two boxes has priority.

Defining the manpower system is the first and crucial step in the approach to successful manpower management.

Key indicators of manpower problems   Adding a few easily obtainable facts about manpower to the manpower system will give an indication of current and future manpower problems. This is the second step in the approach. A start can be made by adding to the diagram of the manpower system the numbers of people in each of the boxes and the average numbers of people moving along each of the flows over the last year. Immediately, the manpower system is brought to life. A sense of scale is derived, and an organization may be revealed to contain a very high proportion of people at the lower levels feeding up to a very small number of people at the top of the hierarchy, an indication that promotion flows are going to be slow and the chance of promotion quite low. In a system that has a number of streams that feed to a common box at the top of the organization, the preferred stream for promotion can easily be seen.

These perceptions can be enhanced considerably by drawing the manpower system to scale so that boxes are directly in visual proportion to each other and the widths of the flows connecting boxes are also drawn in proportion to each other (see Fig. 1.10).

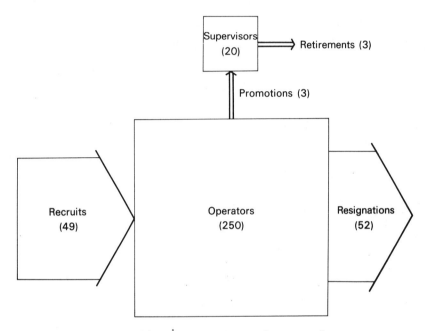

Fig. 1.10. A manpower system drawn to scale

In this simple system of operators and supervisors, it is clear that the problem is one of replacing the wastage that occurs and not of finding candidates for promotion.

The age distribution of employees or the length of service distribution is easy to obtain and will give a vivid picture of the experience profile within the organization and some clue as to the general outlook for careers. Since it is difficult to change the characteristics of an organization's manpower quickly, the age or length of service distribution will provide a clue to the past patterns of growth in the form of age or length of service bulges.

Finally, a manpower system can be viewed as a career hierarchy. Translating the age distribution into a career profile by calculating the percentage of staff in

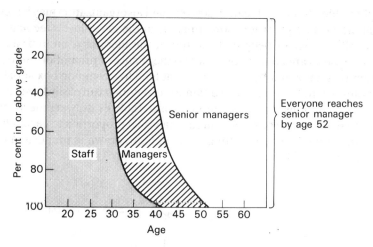

Fig. 1.11. Career progression diagram – career stream I

each level at particular ages or lengths of service will enhance the organization's perception of the problems it may have within that career structure. The speed of promotion and the proportion of people promoted to any level are clearly visible. Figures 1.11 and 1.12 show how different are career prospects in two career streams within the same organization. In Fig. 1.11 100 per cent of the people who have remained with the organization have reached senior manager by the age of 52. In Fig. 1.12 only 40 per cent of those who have remained have reached senior manager by retirement age.

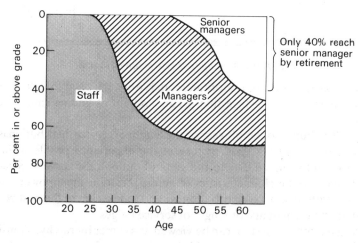

Fig. 1.12. Career progression diagram – career stream II

18

Summarizing the information required for key indicators:
– Stocks in each box at the beginning of the year.
– The flows into, out of, and between each box during the previous year.
– The age distribution.
– The length of service distribution.
There are few organizations that do not have such information readily available.

Estimating the demand for manpower in the future   It has already been stressed, and it is central to the approach that has been adopted, that it is not possible to forecast accurately the number of people required in any future situation. Nevertheless, the attempt must be made, since the impact of growth or contraction on manpower policies is considerable. The key to success is not to produce minutely detailed forecasts of the manpower system in five years' time, but to identify likely business changes and consider each projected change in terms of its impact on the manpower system. Experience indicates that the important variables are the capital expenditure plans of the organization in terms of opening or closing production units (in service organizations opening or closing down services), and changing technology. Experience shows that once managers' thoughts are concentrated on specific events, they are quite good at estimating the manpower effect. The problem is that they are never certain whether these events will happen. They can, however, monitor whether decisions to increase or decrease capacity are being taken and, therefore, adjust manpower policies to suit.

Quantifying the rate of loss from the organization   An organization's policies of manpower management are heavily influenced by rates of loss. Plans to expand an organization are severely constrained by the high loss rates which go with expansion: plans to reduce an organization are dependent on how fast the organization can run down by natural wastage. Redundancy is a policy of last resort in most organizations, due to the inhibiting legislation that affects the decision to use it. There is evidence that many organizations do not understand how wastage behaves, or even how to measure it, and take wrong manpower decisions as a consequence.

It is important to break wastage down into the different types that exist.

The induction crisis   Once the rate of leaving is related to length of service, it becomes clear why Murphy's law applies to an organization's attempts to change its manpower levels. The risk of leaving is high when length of service is low. Figure 1.13 illustrates the relationship. An organization that is expanding has a high proportion of its people with low lengths of service and can expect high wastage, an organization attempting to reduce its numbers by reducing its recruitment levels, thereby reduces the proportion of people with low service and the number of people leaving will fall.

19

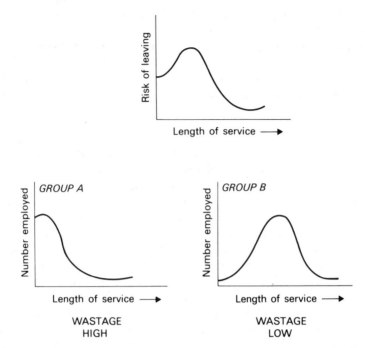

Fig. 1.13. The effect of length of service patterns on wastage levels

Natural wastage Generally, the level of wastage reduces after the induction crisis (which can last as long as the first two years in some organizations). There is a strongly held belief that the rate of natural wastage responds to the level of morale within the organization. This is broadly true but there is an overriding factor that operates first: the level of vacancies in the labour market for the occupation under study is a much more important variable. Comparing patterns of wastage for the same occupations over a period of time shows that there are considerable variations in the pattern of leaving from one year to the next. Further examination has shown that it is strongly linked to the labour market. The change in survival patterns (a way of measuring the retention of employees in the organization) of accountants from 1973 to 1977 is shown clearly in Fig. 1.14.

If the survival pattern of accountants that was found in 1973 was applied to a group of 100 accountants for the rest of their working lives, only 22 per cent would have survived to retirement age and half of them would have gone by four years of service. Contrast this with the 1976 survival pattern which shows that nearly 70 per cent would have survived through to retirement. Continuing the measurement into 1977, the pattern indicates that this has changed yet again and the survival pattern is now similar to that of 1973. Other information

20

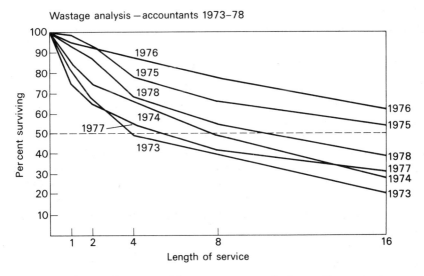

Fig. 1.14. *The impact of the economy on survival rates of accountants*

indicates that there was an over-supply of people in the accounting profession in 1975 and 1976, probably related to the numbers passing the accounting examinations early in the 1970s. This type of cycle in which the level of wastage from the organization varies with the state of the external job market occurs frequently.

Retirement   Retirement can be predicted with a reasonable degree of accuracy. Retirement rules are usually based on age or length of service or a combination of both. Once the rules and the ages and lengths of service of employees are known, retirement can be predicted. Sickness, death, and the wish of some employees to retire early will affect the prediction. One organization was astonished to find that only half of its employees within 10 years of retirement survived to their official date of retirement. It is important to study the age or length of service distribution in the organization. Many organizations expanded their craft activities immediately after the war. A high proportion of craftsmen are now about to retire.

A number of other factors affect levels of wastage. Among these must be included:

(a) occupations;
(b) whether an employee is in his or her first job;
(c) age of employees;
(d) travel-to-work patterns.

In measuring and predicting the outflow of the organization, an attempt must be made to evaluate their importance.

Manpower decision making cannot ignore the ways that people are replaced in the organization. Often the choice is prescribed by company policy. One organization may have a policy to recruit direct from school and to fill jobs at higher levels by promotion. Other organizations use a combination of direct recruitment and internal promotion. Taking employees into the lower levels of the organization and, after training, moving them to higher levels as experience is gained, probably enables an organization to have a tighter control over the standards of competence of employees. External recruitment, on the other hand, may have benefits since those recruited contribute new ideas developed in different circumstances.

Only subjective assessment can really determine which policy is best in which situation. It is important, however, to evaluate different combinations of these since they affect manpower decisions significantly. Data on the types and quantities of people recruited from year to year are relatively easy to obtain but those concerning promotion present a greater problem. Few organizations collect records which summarize promotions from year to year. Often such information is limited to that which can be found in dossiers of individuals and as such is difficult to summarize. Techniques such as career progression diagrams, which have already been illustrated in Figs. 1.11 and 1.12, are one way of obtaining this type of information.

Summarizing the information required to analyse any replacement flow we need to know the following points:
- The type of people, in terms of age, length of service, qualifications, etc.
- Whether the flow has priority over other flows.
- What proportion of the total inflow into the box this particular flow represents.
- Whether the flow is a push or a pull. Do people move in response to a vacancy in the group into which the flow goes, or do people move into the group when they have reached a standard of some sort in the group from which they are moving.

DRAWING THE MANPOWER MAP

At this point in the approach, the manpower system has been defined, key indicators and manpower problems have been examined, an estimate has been made of the number of people needed by the organization to meet these objectives and how this might vary, the rates of outflow have been measured, the replacement policy operated by the organization has been assessed. The remaining task is to bring these factors together in a way that helps the decisions. It is at this point in the approach that resort is made to the doyen of the manpower planners of the 1960s, the mathematical manpower planning model. The model brings together the factors, the information about the factors, and the decision into a quantitative scenario. In essence the model is a liberating process in the approach to manpower planning, since it allows the ability to answer questions of a 'what if' nature. What would happen to the supply of craftsmen if we reduced our apprentice intake to 20 per year, is a typical example. Because of the speed and the simplicity with which the current models work, many different combinations of factors can be processed and their influence on the decision evaluated.

THE MANPOWER MAP – AN EXAMPLE

Drawing the manpower map can best be illustrated by looking at another actual example, a decision concerning the number of graduate recruits needed over the next five years.

The manpower system was drawn, a very simple one sufficing, the organization believed in recruiting a number of graduates to meet its basic requirements and, having decided what that number was, shared them out among the disciplines that needed graduates in a way that was consistent with current priorities. It did not believe that graduate recruitment should be based on estimating the requirements of each separate group of graduates – engineers, scientists, etc. Information about the people in the manpower system was obtained independently and this indicated that there were about 1800 management jobs and that the managers could be divided into those who had graduate qualifications and those who had entered the organization as school leavers and had been promoted to management.

Information about the future demand for managers in the organization was difficult to get. When asked about the future growth rate of the organization there were blank looks. 'It is extremely difficult to estimate,' said one of the personnel managers. 'It all depends . . .'. When this reaction is encountered a successful way to continue is to change the question and ask what decisions about the future business the organization is considering at the moment.

Decisions about capital expenditure and about technological change have to be taken some years ahead. Unless such a decision is under active consideration it is unlikely to come within the ambit of the normal five-year planning cycle over which graduate recruitment is considered. It appeared that the organization was considering the building of a complete new plant. This made the task of estimating the manpower changes in the future much easier. Thought had already been given to the size of the plant and an analysis of existing plants gave a very reasonable estimate of the number of managers that would be required. If the new plant were to be built, it would require an additional 1 per cent of new managers each year for the next five years. At the same time, the organization was considering whether or not a number of old plants should be closed down. The two decisions were, in reality, independent although the betting within the organization was that if the new plant was built the old ones would be closed down. Since the plants considered for closure were known, the reduction in manpower numbers was easy to arrive at. Analysing the effects of the closure showed that it would reduce management numbers by about 1 per cent per annum for the next five years.

The benefit of examining key indicators was shown when the rate of outflow from the organization was considered. A study of data on leavers over a five-year period showed a significant variation closely correlated with the economic situation over the previous five years. Rather than average out this fluctuation it was decided to use the extreme cases when considering loss rates. The highest wastage pattern found in the previous five years, the lowest found during that period, and an average of the two was used in the analysis. The indicators also showed that the graduate managers had a very much higher rate of outflow than non-graduate managers and it was, therefore, imperative to consider the two groups separately in arriving at the likely losses from the organization.

In attempting to assess the replacement policy of the organization, the problem of lack of data was shown all too clearly. There was information about the number of people recruited and it was possible to get the age distribution of the graduates who came in. Getting information on the people promoted into the management level with experience from within the organization was impossible. Subjective judgement had to be relied on and the manpower analyst found that the organization felt its most efficient management profile occurred when 70 per cent of all the vacancies were filled by graduate recruits and 30 per cent were filled by promotions from below. Again, an attempt was made to push this policy to its extremes. Realistically it was felt that the organization could manage if over the next five years it recruited only graduates, or alternatively if it filled 50 per cent of its vacancies at management level by promotion from below. A manpower model was used to quantify the relationship between the demand, the loss rates, and the replacement policies and was used to work out the number of recruits required for each situation. Figure 1.15 shows the results of the analysis.

If the new plant was built and the old plants were not closed down and the rates of wastage were high, then 100 graduates would be required to maintain the current replacement policies. On the other hand, if the organization closed down the old plants and had low wastage with its current replacement policy, it would only need 30 graduates per year. In this way the contours of the map are sketched in.

The big difference between these two possibilities developed another of the ideas incorporated in the approach to manpower management.

Numbers of graduate recruits required.....

Level of wastage	Replacement policy		Expansion or contraction in number of management jobs		
	% RECRUITED	% PROMOTED	+ 1% p.a.	0	− 1% p.a.
High	100	0	151	127	104
	70	30	100	84	69
	50	50	66	55	45
Average	100	0	97	78	58
	70	30	68	54	40
	50	50	48	38	28
Low	100	0	78	60	43
	70	30	57	41	30
	50	50	41	31	22

Fig. 1.15. A manpower map of graduate recruitment levels

The difference between 100 recruits and 30 recruits is so great that it led to the consideration of what else might have to change if the level of this decision had to change by this amount, and so arose the idea of illustrating constraints on decision making on the map. A number of constraint points can be found. For instance, when the organization stops recruiting there is every chance of redundancy. The point at which no recruits are required is clearly important to identify. In this example the lowest level of recruitment is around 20 and the point of zero recruitment occurs when the rate of reduction of management jobs approaches 3 per cent per annum.

Another constraint is encountered when training is considered. Large numbers of recruits tie up a lot of resources in training and assimilating them into the organization. In this example, the managers felt that the organization could handle 60 graduates per year but above that level there would be difficulty in training and assimilating them into the organization. To mark these areas the map has been shaded.

A third constraint occurs when the organization is trying to recruit more graduates than there are available on the labour market. This organization did not have a high reputation among graduates and examination of previous records showed that it had never been able to recruit more than 100 per annum. Points on the map, combination of circumstances requiring more than 100, have been cross-hatched. The remaining points of the map have been left blank because there are no apparent constraints.

USING A MANPOWER MAP

At the outset the organization clearly expected that the new plant would be built; that the old plant would be closed down with no effect on the number of management jobs; that its wastage would remain at the average level of past years; and that it would be able to maintain its present replacement policy. It would, therefore, need 54 graduate recruits per annum.

Suppose, however, that its forecasts are wrong. Suppose the decision is taken after all to build the new plant but not to close down the old ones. Suppose this is a surprising political decision. Suppose too, that since the organization is increasing the total amount of employment in the area, high wastage could ensue.

It can now evaluate the way that the level of graduate recruitment should be increased to meet the new circumstances. It finds that it has a problem. To satisfy the new situation it would need to recruit 100 graduates per year. If it maintains its present replacement policy it will need more graduates than it can probably recruit on the labour market. This problem can be resolved by increasing the promotion from non-management ranks and filling a higher percentage of vacancies by promotees. However, even when promotion from below is pushed to the maximum and 50 per cent of the vacancies are filled in this way, there remain problems of training and assimilating the remaining graduates since more than 60 per year would be required.

This situation is one for which the organization will need the maximum warning in order to develop alternative policies – possibly to increase training resources; certainly there will be a need to identify employees who are promotable. If, by some chance, the organization manages to contain the wastage rate to the average level experienced in the past, there will still be problems. There will still be a need to recruit 68 graduates but by increasing the promotion from below, the problem can be managed.

By looking at decisions in this way, by mapping out the manpower system and bringing together information about the factors that are important, the organization gains some idea of the direction in which it should change its policies when external events change unexpectedly.

Developing manpower strategies

It was stated at the beginning of this chapter that there are really two facets to the approach that has been developed. One, the solving of specific manpower problems has been dealt with in great detail. The second part of the approach stresses the need to develop a strategic view of manpower. Although adequate techniques, as described earlier, exist for dealing with individual manpower problems, the danger is that a good solution to one manpower problem could be detrimental to other manpower policies the organization wishes to follow. Unless the organization has a clear idea of priorities and the relationship between different aspects of manpower policies, in other words a strategic view of manpower, it risks suboptimization in solving individual problems. This need to consider manpower strategically is particularly important when an organization's manpower level is inconsistent with its business needs, during slumps and booms. All too often organizations attempt to solve their problems by a series of short-term measures. The short-term responses can be divided into two groups; in the first group, where the manpower levels are too high, the organization moves through a series of steps:

- It avoids cutting the manpower levels.
- It reduces manpower numbers by natural wastage effected by bans on recruitment or partial bans on recruitment by requiring signature of a director or senior manager.
- A 10 per cent reduction is effected all round in the manpower numbers.
- A programme of induced wastage is introduced.

When manpower levels are too low and the organization is expanding rapidly, the short-term response is:

- High overtime levels.
- Frenzied recruitment campaigns.
- Panic over wastage.
- Training capacity exceeded.
- Increasing use of contract labour.
- Distortion of the pay structure.
- Hoarding of manpower.
- Expansion of the service functions.

Organizations that avoid getting into such crises in the first place or show themselves to be successful in getting out of them, have one thing in common: an appreciation of the need to think strategically about manpower. Different approaches to this will be discussed in a later chapter but the key again to developing and maintaining manpower strategy is to enhance the information that is kept about manpower and the way that it is related to business information.

2.

Defining the manpower system

The successful development of this approach to manpower management outlined in Chapter 1 depended on overcoming two fundamental obstacles. The term 'manpower', while it is a useful shorthand to encompass the whole of the human resources of an organization, is too wide and all-embracing. The manpower resources of an organization are a many faceted diamond or a hydra headed monster depending on your political viewpoint. Although the beginnings of a trend towards single status for all employees can be deduced at this time, there are many divisions that can be discerned in the way that an organization differentiates between its employees in its policies for recruitment, promotion, transfer, and loss. The reasons for the differences might be technical: only certain employees have the technical background that fits them for some of the jobs within the organization. There may be geographical boundaries, the more decentralized an organization is geographically, the less easy it is to move employees between locations. The reasons may be political: an organization explicitly or implicitly may regard people who have entered by a particular route the only ones suitable for filling certain jobs in the organization. In many cases, the restriction is on the basis of entry qualifications. An analytical basis for dividing an organization into its basic manpower groups is required.

A considerable amount of work has been done on the problem of breaking manpower down into useful categories within the organization for the purposes of manpower management. Job classification systems have been studied by the Manpower Society, the Local Authorities Conditions of Service Advisory Board and the Local Government Industry Training Board, and by the Institute of Manpower Studies (IMS), in conjunction with Shell and British Gas, when developing its system of occupational classification (IMSSOC). This approach to manpower management draws on that work at three different levels. At one end of the spectrum it uses the broad occupational boundaries and functional splits, through the understanding of the need to study the activity to which a person's work is directed and precisely what is performed by a manpower group in fulfilling that activity, to the use of the finest level of detailed multi-axis job classifications.

In defining the manpower system of an organization, the experience of IMS advisers in helping many companies over a number of years indicates the need to start by dividing the organization into its basic manpower groups before proceeding to the investigation analysis and exploration of particular problems of manpower management.

Broad manpower structures

A common problem for all management techniques that require an analytical approach in the early stages, is that experienced by practitioners who get into too much detail at too early a stage in the investigation. Whether it be method study, operational research, value analysis, too detailed descriptions of the problem at too early a stage lead to preconceived solutions based on wrong premises. The problem solver has to stop and start again. This is particularly the case with the study of manpower management since the manpower of an organization can be looked at from many viewpoints. To avoid this it is strongly recommended that, first, the broad manpower structure of the organization is sketched out to provide perspective. It helps enormously when work is being done on a manpower problem to be able to see where one particular group fits into the whole. A recent study of an organization showed that the recruitment levels had been calculated on the premise that the career staff in an insurance company were a self-contained group employed solely in the branch network of the company. In reality, a considerable number of the personnel at the head office were found to have come from the branches. This fact was totally ignored in setting recruitment levels so that the organization consistently under-recruited. A broad sketch of the overall manpower system revealed that recruitment levels needed to increase to allow for head office recruiting many of its specialized staff from branches.

The task of describing and defining the overall organization manpower structure is a relatively simple one. The manpower structure tends to follow the broad organizational divisions and we can represent whole functions by a single box. While no two organizations have the same manpower structure, there are broad similarities that have allowed the classification of manpower structures at this level into three broad groups.

MANUFACTURING ORGANIZATIONS

In manufacturing organizations, except those producing many diverse products, the singleness of purpose of the organization leads to similar manpower structures. The manpower system is usually hinged around the manufacturing department. The central function will comprise production, with its ancillary and closely related functions of engineering, split into construction and maintenance, and process development.

Hierarchically there are usually two broad groups to be found in each of the functions, the career staff of the function and the non-career staff. The flow of career staff will be generally into the support functions of engineering, process development, possibly research, where the latest technical skills of the new entrants and the experience they have gained in the organization can be used quickly. Figure 2.1 illustrates how this would look, drawn as a manpower system.

The second group comprises the commercial functions including marketing, distribution, supply, customer relations. It should be noted that there are often strong links to the technical support function, whose personnel are needed to help with customer queries. Again there is a broad distinction into two basic groups of people, the professional group of people who often enter as commercial trainees, and a clerical group below them. There is usually a considerable flow from the clerical group into the professional group, much more than would be typically found for the non-career staff in the production group functions. Manpower flows in this group would tend to be from the general trainees into a specialist area within which most people will remain, gradually gaining more expertise in their specialism with little cross-linking or transfer from one stream to another.

The general managers of the commercial functions will often be drawn from the separate functions, experience of a particular function being secondary to management ability. For instance, a manager whose basic experience is marketing could be promoted to head of distribution. It is probably best to represent this, in a broad manpower system, as a single box. Figure 2.2 is an example of the commercial manpower system.

The third of the manpower groups is more a collection of individual functions with little movement between them. In this group will be finance, personnel, management services, etc. Each will tend to be self-contained, taking in its own professional staff who will remain in their professional capacity as depicted in Fig. 2.3.

If the manufacturing organization has a number of production sites, then the manpower system for the non-career staff will tend to be restricted to the particular site at which they are employed, whereas career staff will tend to move from site to site, as will the professional staff of the marketing group and of the administrative functions.

The research, development, and technical functions manpower systems are interesting. Some will be organized along branches of scientific knowledge and others along product lines; the balance will depend on the organization. The manpower analyst will need to examine this boundary before finalizing the

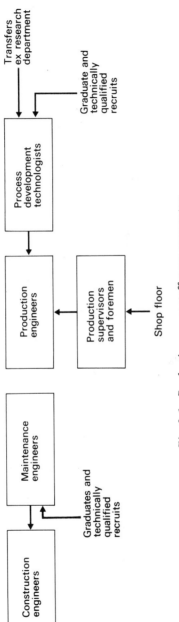

Fig. 2.1. Production career staff manpower system

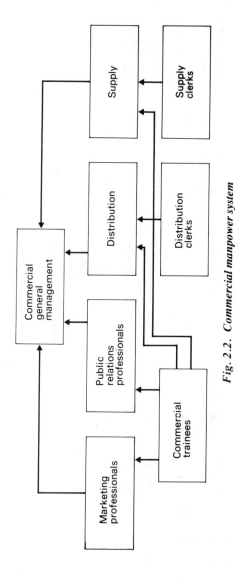

Fig. 2.2. Commercial manpower system

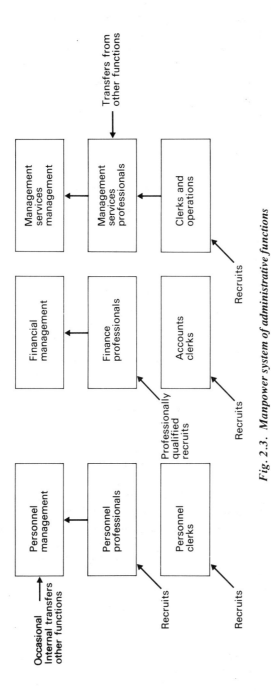

Fig. 2.3. Manpower system of administrative functions

broad system, but should always bear in mind that the flows between these groups will be high. A new product being developed may need the expertise of a group of scientists to solve a problem. The company whose system is depicted in Fig. 2.4 makes plastic widget die casting machines and engineers and chemists are the main disciplines needed in these functions. They are trying to develop a machine with greater throughput; this involves studying the machinery itself and the way the plastic deforms under pressure. The characteristic of this manpower system is the large number of flows.

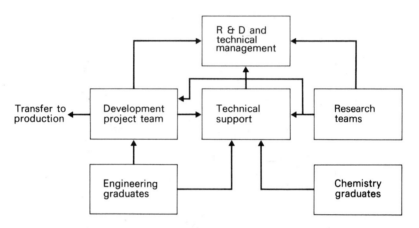

Fig. 2.4. Research, development, and technical manpower systems

A particular problem of manufacturing organizations occurs when they are organized on a matrix basis. It has been the fashion of recent years to overlay across the normal functional type of organization the second organization which tries to bring together the different functions towards specific business ends. The manufacturing organization may produce a wide range of products and, therefore, will organize business groups along product lines. This is much more an organizational boundary and not quite so much a manpower split, since the people who are drawn together to form the business area team will tend to look to their own individual functions for their manpower management. For instance, an accountant in a business area group will tend to look for his promotion within the accounting function. It does, however, open the general management of such an organization to a rather wider set of contenders than would be the case in the non-matrix organization. The manpower system in Fig. 2.5 represents this by separating off the people who are in the business area management part of the organization as a box of potential successors for general management.

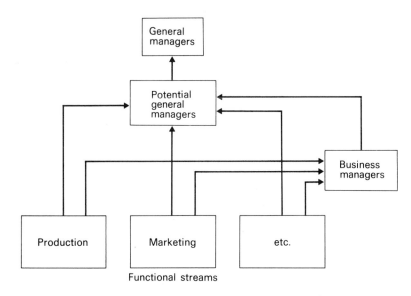

Functional streams

Fig. 2.5. The general management part of the manpower system of a matrix organization

In the main, non-career staff fit easily into a broad manpower system in their own functions. An organization's clerical and typing resources, although they may be present in every function, are likely to be recruited for the overall organization and then allocated to functions, allowing the analyst to represent them as one box. A typical manufacturing manpower system of a broad nature would look as in Fig. 2.6.

COMMERCIAL SERVICE ORGANIZATIONS

One of the common features of organizations supplying commercial services to the general public is that they are spread geographically, either throughout the whole of the country or in a local area, and are organized into branches. This tends to lead to a manpower structure easily subdivided into distinct groups. The first and most obvious is the group in the branch structure itself. Remembering that the main objective is to work at a broad level marking out the main manpower groups, it is probably sufficient to differentiate within the branches between career staff and non-career staff. In some organizations everybody who enters a branch will be considered as career staff, in others there may be very different selection criteria. In those organizations where everybody has the opportunity to follow the full career, it is worth identifying the level in the structure where it is decided which individuals have that potential by making a distinction at that point. In banking type organizations, where the tradition is

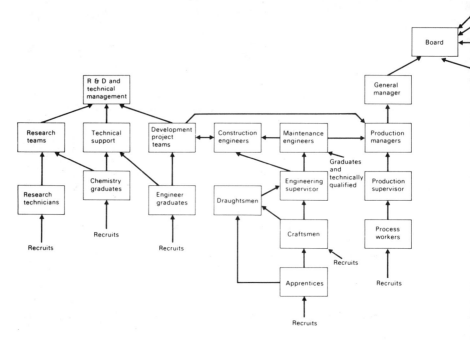

Fig. 2.6. A broad manpower system for a typical manufacturing organization

for anyone who enters to be able to reach branch manager, a useful point of identification is to find out those who have passed their institute exams. As a general rule, only those who have the appropriate provisional qualification can go on to become manager. Within the branch structure, there may be specialisms among the career staff, but these too are best ignored at this level of the analysis (see Fig. 2.7).

The second group that ought to be shown as a separate entity is the head office specialist functions. The nature of the commercial services is that the success of the organization in offering, selling, and maintaining such services is dependent on people in the organization who have built up many years of experience in this particular type of service. For instance, in the London offices of insurance companies there are underwriters who are responsible for fixing the price of premiums to guard against unusual losses; the business is competitive and its profitability depends on the experience and expertise of the underwriter in the head office. Such people have spent many years building up their experience, either in the head office function from the beginning, or having started in the branch insurance structure. The number of functions offering different specialities at head office will depend on the organization and the exact commercial services that it wishes to offer. The main manpower features

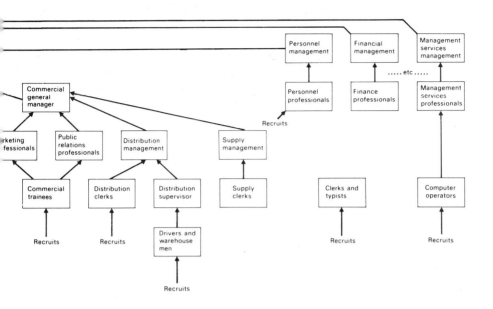

Fig. 2.6. (Continued)

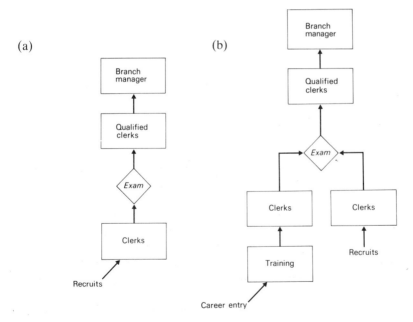

Fig. 2.7. A manpower system detailing branch staff in commercial service organizations.
(a) All enter at lowest level. (b) Two stream entry.

of such functions are best represented by a single box of professional staff. Clearly, there will be another manpower group which supports them consisting of clerical and support staff within the organization who are unlikely to move from the clerical and support group into the professional group (see Fig. 2.8).

As with the manufacturing type of organization, there will also be a group of functions whose role is administrative. Again, accounting, finance, management services, personnel, will be typical of the functions that would be included under this heading. Again, each of these specialisms will tend to be separate with its own group of professional staff.

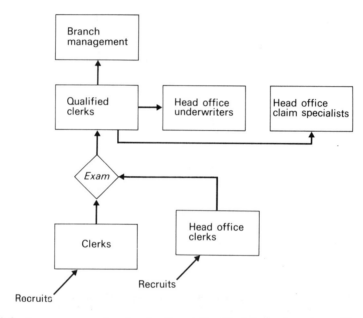

Fig. 2.8. A manpower system showing the relationship between branches and head office

Within this structure the flow of professional staff will tend to be into the branches for training in the basic industry, moving on either up the branch structure or into the head office specialist functions. Occasionally there may be transfers from either the branch structure or the head office specialist functions into those administrative functions where technical knowledge is not required such as personnel, corporate planning, etc.

One of the more intractable problems in drawing manpower systems occurs when this type of organization is extremely large and has superimposed on the branch structure a regional administration. Some of the banks and some of the insurance companies have regional head offices which are a microcosm of the headquarters head office function and contain within them some of the specialist and administrative functions. In drawing the manpower system, it is best to include the people who are in the regional headquarters in either the branch structure, if they are performing roles similar to that of the branch staff, or in the head office manpower group in the case of the specialisms, both technical and administrative (see Fig. 2.9).

PUBLIC SERVICE ORGANIZATIONS

Under this heading we are leaving out the manufacturing public services such as British Steel, British Gas, the electricity industry, and concentrating on sectors such as education, health, and local authorities. In drawing the manpower systems of organizations under this heading, the typical structure contains two basic groups. The first group contains a number of separate professional streams which have little movement from one stream to another. In the local authority, traditionally there are series of separate departments: surveyors, architects, social services, the works department, etc. The chances are that when a head of one of these functions is required, the authority will advertise and people within that professional group elsewhere in the country will tend to apply. The chances are that a replacement will come from outside the particular authority. The same thing is true of health authorities where administrative, professional, and technical staff are concerned. The manpower system for this type of function will consist of a single box of professional staff with a box of clerical support staff below it, but again there will be very little movement from clerical and support staff to the professional staff. There will be almost no movement between each of these streams.

Running alongside this professional structure will be the similar type of administrative functions found within the manufacturing type of manpower system and within that of commercial services comprising finance, personnel, management services, etc. It is interesting to see that unlike the previous two types of manpower systems, these specialisms will continue right up to the head of the function. In manufacturing and in commercial services there tends to be an executive group drawn from each of the functions that manage the organization. To some extent the best people, irrespective of function, are chosen for that executive. In the local authority and the health authority situation, the executive group is often a committee of the heads of the functions.

Detailed manpower structures at the problem-solving level

Manpower mangement in reality is concerned with two sets of problems. Given some idea of the future size and shape of the organization, information is

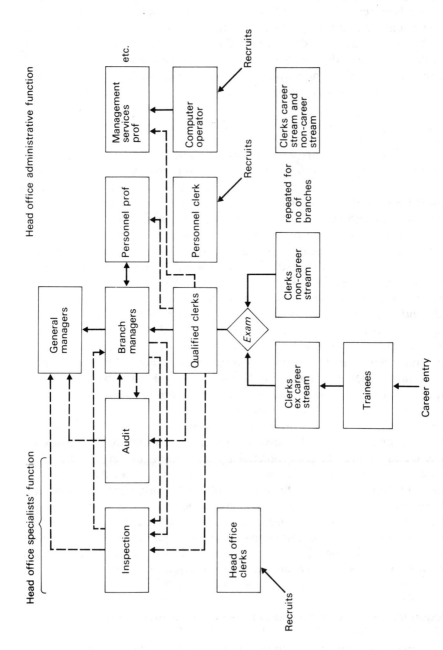

Fig. 2.9. A broad manpower system for a typical commercial services organization

needed about the manpower flows that will be necessary to offset the loss of people from the organization, to replace people promoted within the organization by either recruiting from outside the organization or by transferring people from other parts within it. The second group of problems concerns the situation where the organization wishes to know what the impact of changing one of its policies with regard to manpower flows is likely to be on the size and shape of the organization. Perhaps a shortage of a particular skill in the labour market means that the company must increase promotion to offset losses. In doing so, it is concerned whether the increased promotion flow will distort the organization's manpower structure.

Both cases are concerned with the stocks and flows of manpower. In essence, the idea of bringing together information about manpower for decision making means identifying the different groups of people within the organization and quantifying the manpower flows among, into, and out of those groups. When an organization has a problem that it wishes to investigate, its first task will be to define the set of stocks and flows that make up the manpower pertinent to this particular problem. The degree of detail to which the stocks and flows are drawn will be very dependent on the problem itself. Where overall recruitment levels are concerned, it might be as simple as a single box representing total manpower with one flow out representing the loss rates and one flow in representing the recruitment.

On the other hand, an organization that is trying to balance the different recruitment levels of school leavers, technically qualified people from further education, and graduates, may find that it has to construct a very complex manpower system in order to be able to solve that problem. The process by which manpower systems at this level are defined is essentially subjective, depending on the manpower planner's experience in the work and the analytical skill which is brought to the problem.

It is the experience of the authors that when an organization is asked for its manpower system the organization chart will be offered in response. In general, experience shows that the organization chart is a long way from the manpower system, reflecting as it does, the political and organizational reality rather than the manpower groups to be found within the organization. A much deeper and more searching look has to be brought to bear, using the organization chart as a starting point, by discussion with people from within the organization who have information and knowledge that allows the picture of the manpower system to be built up. To do this the manpower planner must widen his circle to include line managers, heads of functions, as well as personnel specialists. A useful group for starting such a discussion would be the person responsible for recruitment into the organization, a senior training man, a line manager of the particular manpower group that is under discussion, the manager responsible for management development, and the specialist within the organization who has access to personnel information. The latter is a most useful person to have since the discussion often gets bogged down as to whether a particular flow is relevant or not. Ready access to a source of information about such a flow can save considerable time.

The process by which such a team will work can only be subjective. There have been attempts in the past to draw manpower systems by building them up from information about all the movements that have taken place in the organization over the previous historical period. These experiments have been very time consuming and have usually finished up with manpower systems which are far more complex than they need to be, since many manpower movements take place which do not represent policy and can only be described as noise in the system. It appears to be much quicker and more effective to sit the team down and begin the discussion of the problem and attempt to draw the manpower system using a few simple guidelines to aid the discussion. These guidelines have been built up over a number of years of trying to draw manpower systems and, although the general order which they follow seems to be best, it is not imperative that this order be followed. Indeed, during the discussions that will take place, there will inevitably be some backtracking as new information and new thoughts are encountered.

ENTRY POINTS

Although many organizations say that it is possible to recruit from outside at all levels in the organization, in practice there are well defined entry points for recruitment. Over a period of time an organization will have attempted to identify from where it gets its best recruits, at what ages, with what qualifications, and will try to maximize the number of people brought into the organization along those routes. As a consequence of these years of experience, considerable information is usually to be obtained about the points of recruitment and the type of people recruited. Among the entry points that are commonly found are 16-year-old school leavers, technically qualified people at 16 and 18, and graduate entry. If one is looking at a manpower system of a multifunctional organization it is as well to look for the points of entry from other functions within the organization. For instance, there may be a clearly defined pathway from a technical function to manufacturing after people have gained four or five years' experience in the organization.

GROWING GRADES

In drawing manpower systems, there is often a tendency to equate a box of people with a grade if the organization uses grades to denote its hierarchy. It is rarely the case that a single grade in an organization will encompass a complete manpower group. It is much more likely that a manpower group will cross several grades. An example is the way that an organization will use its grades to

42

help motivate employees immediately after they have been recruited. As will be seen later, organizations lose considerable numbers of the employees that they have just recruited. This high rate of loss is often countered by moving people quickly through a series of grades immediately after recruitment in order to help them feel they are progressing. In such a group of grades there should be a guarantee of emerging at the top of them since not to do so implies a mistake in selection at the time of recruitment.

SIGNIFICANT JOB STEPS

Taking this idea of linking together different grades into manpower groups to represent different levels in the hierarchy, experience shows that a number of critical levels can be identified. The concept that the team should be looking for is at what point does a significant change in a job take place. These points are not necessarily marked by grade boundaries: sometimes the organization's perks are a better means of identifying them. Look for instance for the introduction of company cars, top-hat pension schemes, life assurance schemes, service agreements, sabbatical leave, etc. Movement from one significant job step to another reflects a real increase in an individual's responsibilities and status. A selection process is usually involved. Six job steps have been identified which will cover 90 per cent of all manpower systems.

1. **Training** Unless there is a very good reason for doing so, it is not worth while separating trainees into more than one box. Where separation into different boxes occurs, this usually reflects different wastage patterns. This point will be expanded later in the chapter.
2. **First job** Movement out of training to the first job in an organization clearly is a significant job step. The first jobs that are found in many organizations have some common characteristics. The scope of the job is limited; the employee will not do the full range of work that others did, priorities will be decided by supervision, the progress of the work will be closely monitored.
3. **First level of responsibility** The next level of responsibility occurs when the constraints of the previous level are removed. The individual becomes responsible for his own priorities, the progress of his work, and the full range of work is done for the first time. Here we find the professional or a practitioner in most of the functions. If we were looking at a personnel function the personnel officer out of training with responsibility for offering a personnel service to a group of departments would be an example. If we were looking at process workers in a chemical plant, we would be identifying that group of workers who are fully responsible for plant operations.
4. **Supervisory responsibility** Clearly a significant job step occurs when an individual becomes responsible not only for his own work but also for other people's work as well. Here we would include section leaders, assistant

foremen, employees who are responsible for the work of groups of people within a functional strain.

5. **Management responsibility**   The distinction between management and supervision is a difficult one to draw but management tends to imply the balancing of conflicting priorities and pressures, probably between different groups of workers. A supervisor will probably be responsible for a group of people doing the same task, a manager is almost certainly responsible for different groups of manpower doing different tasks.

6. **General management**   The same problem of definition between manager and general manager occurs as has been found in distinguishing between supervision and management. A pragmatic way of deciding is to classify general managers as those who are looking after more than one function.

SIGNIFICANT JOB STREAMS

It is important to differentiate in a manpower system between the different streams that exist. Different streams may have different standards of entry or promotion chances as against other streams. Sometimes a distinction is not obvious.

One of the more difficult to handle is that where the professional group divides into those who become the management of the function and those who become increasingly expert and specialized in that particular professional function. The situation occurs in research departments where some of the research chemists will be eventually developed into managers, yet others will continue doing research work but bringing greater and greater expertise to it.

A similar parallel situation occurs in the insurance industry where an insurance professional can become a highly skilled underwriter whose contribution to the business and its profitability is critical, or else, starting from the same stream of underwriters, he can become a manager of underwriters.

In many organizations there is a common entry point for all the streams and then the organization begins to subdivide into specialities and the manpower system follows parallel tracks until it begins to converge again when the senior executive levels of the company are chosen from the managers of the specialisms.

THE REAL BOUNDARIES OF THE SYSTEM

Most organizations contain a number of intersecting manpower systems covering different groups of people. It is important to define the real boundaries between the systems. They may not coincide with the physical, locational, or organization divisions within the organization.

A typical problem is where to draw the boundary between the head office manpower system and the unit in the field. Organizationally, they may be separate entities. In manpower terms, we find that the headquarters or the head office draws considerable numbers of its staff from the units, thus there is a manpower flow from one to the other.

In an organization geographically separated into a number of manufacturing sites, there is a tendency to think of each site as a complete manpower entity, yet there will be people in those sites who do not belong to the manpower system of a particular site but whose manpower system transcends all sites. Take, for instance, the personnel function. On each manufacturing site there could be a personnel officer. In all probability the personnel officer will not be part of the works manufacturing manpower system. He will be unable to take on manufacturing responsibilities because of his lack of technical training. His manpower system will be found to flow between the manufacturing sites, gradually getting to higher levels and possibly moving on to head office or to the headquarters personnel function at a later date.

PUSH AND PULL FLOWS

The full implications of a manpower system cannot be understood by looking at the stocks or the groups of manpower and the way that the manpower flows from one group to another. It is just as important to look at how a flow takes place.

Two situations are found. People move to fill a vacancy. Someone at a higher level in the organization leaves, a vacancy is created which is filled from a number of sources; by transfer from another part of the organization, by promotion from below, or recruitment from outside. In other words, a person is *pulled* into the vacancy. The other situation happens when a person moves from the box because a certain standard of performance has been reached or some other criterion attained. The organization may require that an employee cannot hold a chief clerk's position until he has passed his professional banking or insurance exams. It may be that people move from the probationary grade into the first real job that they do when they have spent one year in the probationary grade. The concept here is of a *push* out of the manpower group that they are in to another when some defined criterion has been met. The relevance of separating flows into these two will become more easily understood later in the chapter.

Checking the manpower system with data

Having considered all these points and incorporated them into the manpower system, the team that has been considering the problem will have got about as far as it can go using subjective discussion as the vehicle for drawing the system. From this point on, we have to examine hard data:

45

(a) to take us further in our analysis and definition of the manpower system;

(b) to judge whether our perception of the manpower system exists in reality.

Information should be sought about the stocks and flows as they have been suggested and each flow on the manpower system that has been drawn checked to see whether it has, in fact, occurred in the past and also to find where there are significant flows that have occurred that were not postulated in the manpower system. The manpower system must be adjusted according to what is found. Care must be taken to avoid reflecting chance aberrations and one-off events from being incorporated into the manpower system. Experience shows it is almost always possible to demonstrate that at least one person has moved via the most unexpected route possible.

At this stage, it is very important to distinguish between groups of people who have different wastage rates. For technical reasons, during the process of quantifying the manpower stocks and flows, it is imperative to separate groups of people who have different wastage patterns. Each box that has been drawn on the system must be tested to see within it whether there are differences in behaviour, differences due to different qualifications, different sexes, etc.

During the course of the discussion you might have found that members of the team had reservations as to whether it was possible to define any manpower system at all since the jobs that became vacant in the organization were freely advertised and any employee could apply. The view may have been expressed that with such freedom it is impossible to define a system. It is not so much who applies for a vacancy that determines the manpower system but who is eventually chosen, and although there may be a very wide field of people who apply for vacancies there may be very distinct criteria in terms of who is chosen to fill the vacancies. In practice, the widespread notification of vacancies internally is no barrier to being able to draw a manpower system.

The practical use of the guidelines

Before applying the guidelines to a complex problem their application can be shown by a reference to the manpower system for apprentices that was built up in the first chapter. Looking at that system reveals three entry points: school leavers into the apprentice training school; experienced draughtsmen and designers into the design office; and experienced craftsmen into the craftsmen box (see Fig. 2.10).

The significant job steps that are to be found demonstrate one of the situations where it is useful to split the training box into more than one. The apprentice training box is split into four boxes representing each of the years in the system. This is absolutely necessary since there are very different patterns of leaving throughout each of the four years of the apprenticeship. The middle

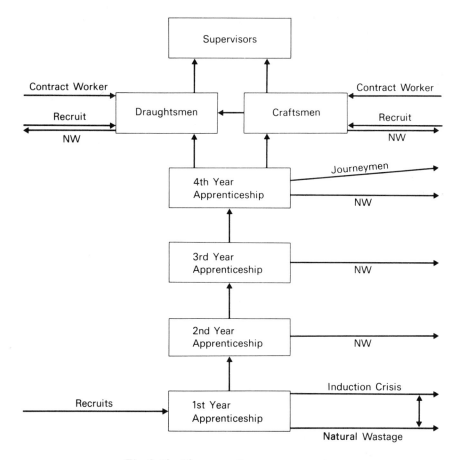

Fig. 2.10. The apprentice manpower system

two years show the least difference but we needed to differentiate between the second and third year since we need to know the exact number of people in the fourth year in order to calculate the wastage from that year. It was not necessary to separate the craftsmen and draughtsmen ranks into two boxes representing people in their first job and people exercising the full level of responsibility in their jobs, since the time taken to move from the one to the other is very short. The other significant job step distinguished is that of the supervisory responsibility. The need to consider significant job streams and the real boundaries of the system can be demonstrated by the fact that the design office has had to be included in the manpower system. At first sight, a man-power system that is looking at the craftsmen within an organization will content itself with looking at apprentices, the craftsmen, and the supervisors of

47

those craftsmen. Because a significant number of the apprentices undergo technical training and become well qualified, the organization moves them into another stream, that of the design office. Thus the real boundaries of the manpower system have to be expanded to cope with this and we can see that there are, in fact, two job streams available for apprentices. Both push and pull flows are to be found within the example. People enter the apprenticeship at the bottom and move out of each box at the end of each year into the next box and, finally, those who are left at the end of the fourth year and who stay with the organization move into the craftsmen box or the design box, dependent on the level of technical qualifications that they have. Movement from designers and craftsmen to supervisor is a pull and only takes place when a vacancy exists in the supervisory ranks.

THE FAILSAFE INSURANCE COMPANY – CASE EXAMPLE

On being asked for its manpower system, this organization brought out the organization chart shown in Fig. 2.11.

The group of staff that the company was concerned with were the professional staff in the branch insurance system. The organization chart shows that

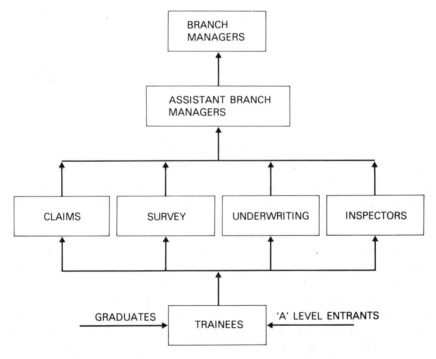

Fig. 2.11. Drawing a manpower system – 1. Organization chart

there is an entry from school leavers, 18-year-olds, and a separate entry for graduates from university level into a training scheme. Movement from the training scheme occurs into one of four functions: claims, survey, underwriting, and inspectors (the latter sell the insurance). Employees can progress up each function and eventually become assistant branch managers and finally managers of branches.

Following the guidelines as previously specified and looking first at the entry points into the organization, there was general agreement among the team of people conducting the analysis that the main entry was definitely into the training scheme from school at 18 years old and from graduates between the ages of 21 and 23.

There was a difference of opinion as to whether the company recruited experienced insurance professionals trained by other organizations. It was clear that some had been recruited in the past and it was also clear that far fewer were being recruited by this route currently. It was decided to add an arrow to the bottom of each of the functions to represent movement in of junior people at the bottom of the functions from other insurance companies, people with a little experience. There was very decided agreement that the company never

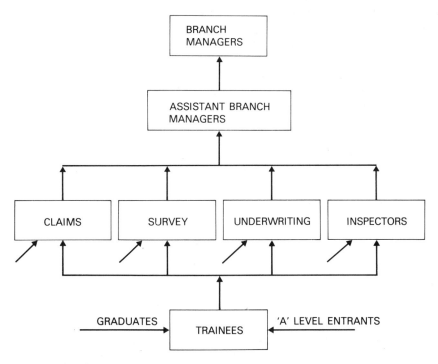

Fig. 2.12. Drawing a manpower system – 2. Entry points

recruited its senior section heads, assistant branch managers, or branch managers from outside the company. The organization chart was amended as in Fig. 2.12.

WHY TRAINEES WERE GRADED

At an early stage in the discussion, grades were put against each of the boxes and considerable discussion took place as to why the trainees were graded from grade 2 to grade 6. What was the point of grading trainees. After all trainees were trainees! The response was that in the past the organization had experienced very high loss rates from the training scheme. The loss had been so high that the company had investigated why it was taking place. The results of the investigation indicated that the training period was too long, about five years for a person entering with 'A' levels, and some three years for a graduate entering from university. The exit interviews showed that the feeling grew among some trainees that they were not progressing and the resulting disappointment caused them to become dissatisfied and leave. The recommendation was made and implemented that the company should grade progress during training to help individuals feel that they were progressing and getting somewhere. Accordingly, grades 2 to 6 were allocated to the training scheme.

Some of the members of the team expressed the view that this had only solved the high levels of wastage among the people towards the end of their training and that these high levels persisted among groups in the first two years. It was, therefore, decided to mark that for later investigation by drawing a dotted line between grades 3 and 4 in the training box, as in Fig. 2.13. When the manpower system had been drawn for the first time, data would be obtained to check whether this difference in wastage patterns existed. Clearly the company used the grading system as we have described on page 42 – 'Growing grades'.

The discussion continued and the group attempted to define the different job steps that were to be found. On movement out of training the trainee, whether he was in the claims, underwriting, survey, or inspectorate function, was given a job that was closely prescribed and well monitored by supervision. The person moving into claims would only deal with a very limited type of claim, the new inspector would probably only sell a particular type of business that was easy to deal with.

DISTINCTIONS BETWEEN GRADES

This phase did not last very long and as soon as a vacancy existed at the next level the person in grade 7 moved into grade 8 and undertook the full level of responsibility in whichever function he was. Not only was this significant job step marked by a change of grade, but it was also marked by the person qualifying for one of the company's perks. The company gave a mortgage to its

50

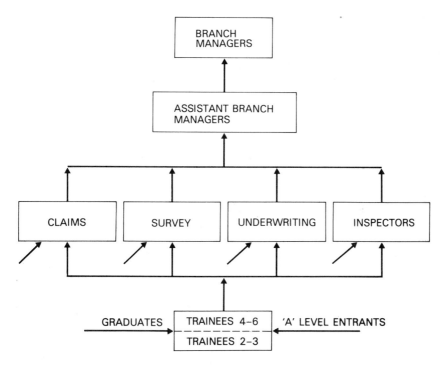

Fig. 2.13. Drawing a manpower system – 3. Growing grades

employees who wished to purchase houses at a highly subsidized rate. This had the effect of reducing wastage significantly and locking people into the organization. Therefore, since the full capabilities of an individual were not demonstrated until he had been moved out of training and into a job for the first time, it was felt unwise to lock people in before the company had decided that it wished them to stay and before they themselves had decided insurance was for them. The granting of a reduced rate mortgage was only given when a person moved into a grade 8 vacancy.

Considerable time was spent by the team on looking at the difference between grade 8 and grade 9 jobs, and the conclusion was arrived at that the only difference between the 8 and 9 graded job was that the grade 9 job tended to be in a slightly bigger branch. The job evaluation scheme had points awarded for the size of the branch in which the employee worked. It was not necessary to go from a small branch to a large branch, people moved from grade 7 to grade 9 on occasions when vacancies occurred in large branches, and from a manpower point of view, there was no difference between people in grades 8 and 9: both were fulfilling the full level of responsibility in their functions.

Grade 10 marked the first level of supervision within the organization. At

51

grade 10 the professional became a section head, responsible for looking after a group of professionals working in the claims area, etc. Again, the difference between grade 11 and grade 10 was due to the size of the branch and it was felt that these two grades should be grouped together as section leaders.

On the organization chart grades 12 to 16 were designated as assistant branch managers. They were clearly managers with wide ranging responsibilities and could not be classed as supervisors.

The final significant job step was assessed to be that of branch manager. A branch manager is much more like a general manager than the manager of a function since he covers a wide range of commercial services. Often a difficulty is encountered at this point in the analysis. In many commercial services' organizations the branch sizes vary considerably and an assistant branch manager job in one branch can be a much bigger job than the branch manager of a small branch. In some organizations we have found ourselves making artificial manpower boxes, i.e., 'branch managers (large branches)' as the top box with a box below labelled 'branch managers (small branches) and assistant branch managers'.

Alternatively, we might have decided to differentiate between the boxes by having all the branch managers in one box together with the assistant branch managers of large branches, leaving only assistant branch managers of small and medium-sized branches in the box below.

Each of these situations must be decided on its merits. The key is to look at the promotion pattern judging the frequency with which people move from assistant branch manager to branch manager and back to assistant branch manager in a large branch and so on. In this case, the branch sizes were reasonably big and the situation did not occur in which a man who was an assistant branch manager went to branch manager of a small branch then went back to assistant branch manager in a large branch. There was a clear distinction between branch managers and assistant branch managers enabling separate boxes to be used in the manpower system. After grouping the grades into significant job steps the manpower system begins to emerge from the organization chart and can be seen in Fig. 2.14.

A very interesting and significant fact emerged from the discussion of how the manpower system should reflect the supervision and management boxes. One of the tests of whether a box is a management box or a supervisory box is to examine whether it covers more than one activity.

In looking at the assistant branch managers' jobs in the company, two distinct types emerged. In most branches one assistant branch manager covered claims, underwriting, and survey; another assistant branch manager covered simply sales. This led to the question of whether the assistant branch manager of sales was really a supervisor or not since he tended to stick within the sales function. The view was expressed very strongly by the team that the assistant branch manager sales was much more senior than the assistant branch

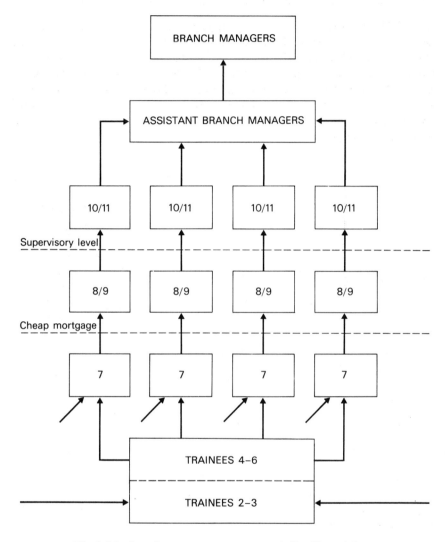

Fig. 2.14. Drawing a manpower system – 4. Significant job steps

manager services. Pursuing this line of enquiry and trying to ascertain the reasons why he was felt to be more senior, revealed the fact that in general only assistant branch managers (sales) progressed to branch manager and that it was very, very unusual for assistant branch managers of the services side of the company to become branch managers.

Figure 2.15 shows the self-fulfilling prophesy that had been created. Only the best of the trainees were chosen to be inspectors. The reason was that the inspectors tended to have the widest knowledge since, in order to sell insurance, they had to have some knowledge of claims, survey, and underwriting. In the past the inspectors had been the natural candidates for branch managers' jobs since their job knowledge was wider. Gradually the pattern had built up of moving the best people from training into inspectors and making them eventually branch managers.

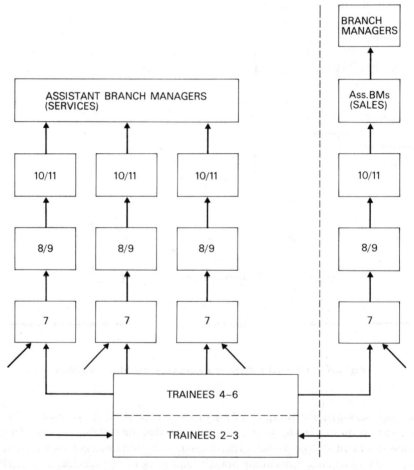

Fig. 2.15. Drawing a manpower system – 5. Job and career streams

The organization chart showed an equal chance for people in the claims, underwriting, survey, and sales areas of becoming branch managers. In reality the inspectors had a very much better chance and there were two broad streams within the system. Between claims, underwriting, and survey, there was considerable movement. The vacancy for an underwriter could easily be filled by someone from claims. The vacancy in the claims professionals could be filled by an underwriter or a survey professional. Most of the jobs were information processing type jobs, requiring broadly the same knowledge and experience. On the sales side, however, this was very different. To sell insurance required quite different qualities.

This concentrated attention on the branch managers and where they had come from in an effort to prove whether this was exclusively the case or not. Some of the members of the team were concerned as to what happened if the organization made a mistake in its assessment of people in training. Perhaps some late developers only showed their true potential when they had been moved into the services side of the business where, theoretically, they had little chance of becoming branch managers. What did the organization do with these people with ability?

It transpired that there were two routes by which they could eventually become branch managers. One route progressed up the services function to assistant branch manager and then at the level of assistant branch manager transfer was possible into the sales function where skills in managing a team of salesmen were more important than selling skills. The second route was more indirect. There was a considerable flow out of both the services and the sales streams, into the head office functions and some returned from head office as assistant branch managers or as branch managers later in their careers. In this way, Fig. 2.16 shows that the real boundaries of the system have been pushed out to include a considerable part of the head office function.

RECRUITMENT NEEDS

This is a particularly interesting point to note since the recruitment levels had traditionally been set to fill the needs of the branch manpower system. In reality a considerable proportion of people were going from training directly into the head office functions. Recruitment levels had been underassessed for a number of years as a result. The team considered the impetus of the flows: which flows were push and which flows were pull. As can be seen from Fig. 2.17, movement in at the bottom of the organization from outside was a push, and movements from training into the first jobs in the inspector stream, in the services stream, and into head office were also a push, as was movement back from head office into the assistant branch management level. All the other flows in the system were pull flows, people only moving when vacancies existed.

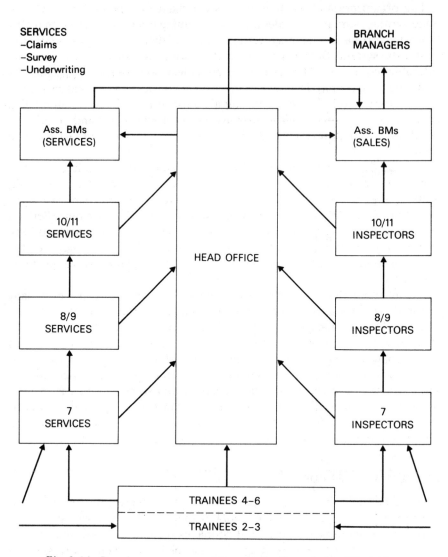

Fig. 2.16. Drawing a manpower system – 6. Real boundaries of the system

The most surprising of these flows was a push flow of recruitment into the organization. In reality the organization did not calculate its recruitment needs to fill the vacancies that it had in any one year. It had a general view of the number needed within the system, but it based the number it recruited on the quality of the people who came forward. Its general target for recruitment for

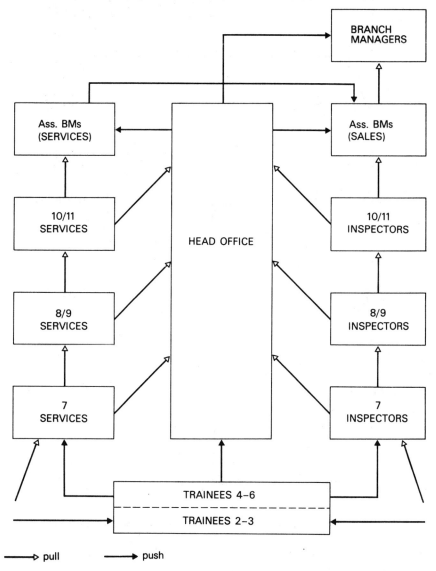

BRANCH MANAGERS

Ass. BMs (SERVICES)

Ass. BMs (SALES)

10/11 SERVICES

10/11 INSPECTORS

8/9 SERVICES

8/9 INSPECTORS

7 SERVICES

7 INSPECTORS

HEAD OFFICE

TRAINEES 4–6

TRAINEES 2–3

pull

push

Fig. 2.17. Drawing a manpower system – 7. Identifying flow types: push and pull

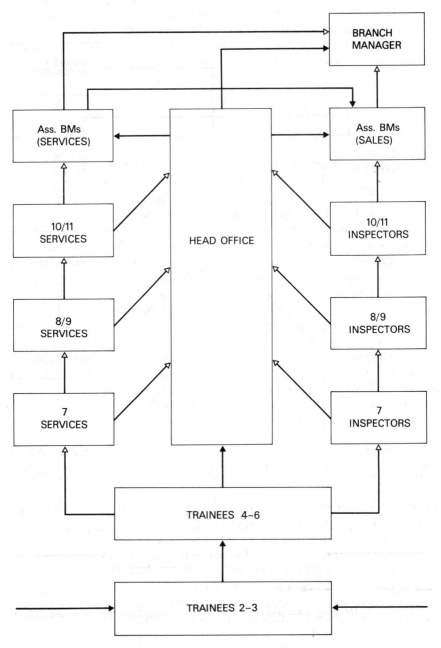

Fig. 2.18. Drawing a manpower system – 8. Final manpower system

graduates was about 35. If, in a particular year's recruitment, only 20 good graduates accepted offers, then it only recruited 20. If, in another year, the quality of graduates was better and it made 40 offers which were accepted, then 40 would be recruited. Thus, people were pushed into the system as recruits dependent on the quality of the people coming into the labour market.

WASTAGE BEHAVIOUR

The team could go no further as a result of subjective discussion, and its perceptions had to be checked by getting information about what had actually happened in the organization. Since the organization did not have a personnel information system at that time, this was a difficult task and clerical effort was only available to examine one previous year's manpower flows. In general, an examination of the year's flows confirmed the manpower system except in two specific items. The trainee box was shown to include two sets of wastage behaviour. As had been suspected at an early stage in the discussions, trainees in grades 5 and 6 had much lower wastage behaviour than trainees in grades 2, 3, and 4. Accordingly, these two boxes were separated. There was a small but very significant flow direct from the assistant branch manager services to branch manager. It transpired that the good people could and did get promotion to branch manager from the less favoured functions, but although it could happen it did so to a much lesser extent than promotion from the inspector stream. The manpower system was amended to reflect this in Fig. 2.18.

Finally, an examination of previous recruitment data which were readily available, showed that recruitment of experienced people into the organization was extremely low and to all intents and purposes could be left out of the system. The final manpower system, therefore, looks as in Fig. 2.18.

Summary

A disciplined, patient attitude to this step in the approach will pay substantial dividends. The practitioner should not rush to his drawing board and sketch manpower system after manpower system. Seeking the opinions and advice of experienced managers, line as well as personnel, and drawing the system at a broad level first in order to understand the relationships between the different manpower groups, are early steps to be followed.

When eventually the detailed manpower system is drawn, question it closely and check its validity with data where this is practicable.

3.

Indicators of manpower problems

A considerable industry in this country significantly contributing to job creation, is the industry of company watching. Six days of the week, each of the main daily newspapers will sustain at least a page of comment about the financial state of companies, from broad analyses covering whole industries to the minute examination of a particular company that happens to be under scrutiny. On Sunday, the remaining day of the week, the level of activity does not diminish; it increases, if anything, since at least two of the major Sunday papers devote a complete section of their paper to business affairs.

These commentators are using a series of indicators, developed over many years by the accounting profession, to look at the financial and economic health of organizations. The balance sheet, cash flow statements, profit and loss accounts, quarterly, half-yearly, and final results, all provide useful information that allows financial commentators to dissect the financial structure of the company and monitor its health, warning the public when danger signs become apparent. The profession is continually improving its indicators; the rapid rates of inflation over the last 10 years have shown the need to allow for inflation in cost-accounting systems.

The manpower health of a company does not receive the same degree of attention. Take any company's annual report and compare the amount of space allocated in that report to the financial health of the company with the space devoted to comments on manpower. The amount of space that is given to manpower in annual reports is increasing but it occupies such a small percentage that any increase appears to be large. A cynic would remark that the current interest in manpower and this increase in its reporting is only a temporary phenomenon fuelled by the rapidly rising cost of manpower and the fact that it is one resource by which an organization can reduce its costs.

It should not be forgotten that the accounting profession has been developing its measures for many years. Prior to the 1880s there were spectacular failures of companies and public outcry forced the development of better financial indicators. The study of manpower in organizations is much more recent and there has not yet been time to develop the same powerful indicators, but the process has begun. Manpower planners in organizations who have noted the difficulty of communicating aspects of manpower policies to senior managers, have been developing more powerful ways to represent manpower problems, and to show the impact of manpower problems on other company problems. One or two general indicators of manpower problems are gradually becoming established.

In one of our largest organizations the manpower planning function has been established for some six or seven years. The philosophy of the group from the beginning was close to that recommended by IMS, the idea of looking at manpower decisions and bringing together information needed to help take those decisions. The organization used up-to-date methods and in general its work was extremely successful, but it never seemed to fire the imagination of the very senior managers in the organization. Its impact seemed to remain where the problem was, with those managers who were concerned about the problem. For instance, if it was looking at the recruitment of financial accountants, its report would be welcomed by the chief accountant of the organization and would be used by him to change his manpower policies, but the work in general did not register with the chief executive of the company as being a useful practical tool.

This was true until one year the organization produced a simple statement describing the company's manpower under a number of headings. These reports were called 'manpower profiles'. They split the organization up into its manpower components, drew it up as a set of boxes and flows, produced simple age structures to show the amount of experience there was in the company's employees, and reported on the main manpower flows into and out of the company. The organization is heavily regionalized and at first this was done as an experiment in one of the regions. Its impact on the chief executive of the region was electric. It provoked more questions back to the manpower planners than they had anticipated and was immediately followed by all the other chief executives clamouring for their region's manpower to be subjected to the same treatment.

Although there are not many similar cases, this is not an isolated example. Other organizations are developing a similar approach to bringing aspects of manpower policies to the attention of the decision makers. It is the purpose of this chapter to bring together a number of such attempts to provide indicators of manpower problems that can be derived quickly and simply from readily available information and that have been shown to have impact.

Using the manpower system as an indicator

Manpower planners recognize that the act of drawing up a manpower system and reducing the complexity of an organization's manpower to a set of boxes and flows, provides insight into the type of problems an organization might be facing. Having drawn manpower systems many times in a wide range of organizations, one is continually surprised at their impact on the managers that have been used to help define the manpower system. At the end of the process the manager may sit back and say 'Well I have always had a feeling that the rate of promotion within the function that I control is not only determined by my policies. I can now see that a very important factor is the production function.' What he is seeing is that his function, the technology function, is used as a training ground by the production department for its future managers and that a significant percentage of his young professionals move into the production field. Although he knew that this was happening, its impact was so clearly demonstrated by drawing up the manpower system that he gained new insight.

The drawing of the manpower system indicates where manpower decisions must be taken. At every 'entry point' into the system there must be a decision on how big or small the level of entry is to be. Where there is a flow from one box to another, the conditions under which that flow occurs must be defined. Sometimes it is a very simple decision to replace a vacancy in the box above by an individual from the box below. Even in this simple case, decisions must be taken on the type of people who will satisfy the criteria for the move. What sort of people do we promote? How much experience do they have in total within the company or within the box which they currently occupy?

Wherever there are two flows or more into a box, decisions must be taken not only on the sort of people who move along those flows, but additionally, on the weighting that the organization gives between the two flows. In Fig. 3.1 how does the company decide when a vacancy occurs at the assistant branch manager level whether this should be filled by a person promoted from the section leader ranks or someone taken and transferred from head office?

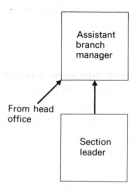

Fig. 3.1. Highlighting manpower decisions – 1. Choosing successors

Wherever there is more than one arrow leaving a box, again decisions have to be taken on how the people who are leaving the box are apportioned between the boxes to which they are moving. Figure 3.2 shows that trainees, on completion of training, can move into one of four functions: claims, underwrit-

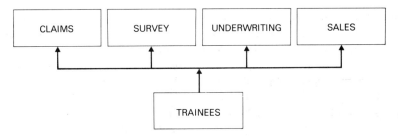

Fig. 3.2. Highlighting manpower decisions – 2. Choosing career paths

ing, survey, or sales. How does the company decide to apportion trainees between these functions?

A quick glance at a well drawn manpower system will instantly reveal the manpower problem areas within that system. Looking at Fig. 3.3, depicting in a manpower system the technical, production, and engineering functions of a manufacturing company, reveals that the problem group for the company will undoubtedly be the production operating managers. At this point in the system there are flows in from supervisors, from technical functions, and from the engineering function, clearly indicating that this box is crucial to the career and promotion structure of a number of functions.

DRAWING THE MANPOWER SYSTEM TO SCALE

For many years manpower systems were always represented by rectangular boxes of the same size, and flows by a simple arrow from one box to another. The practice seemed satisfactory until, by chance, a system was drawn with its boxes drawn to scale and the width of the flows shown in proportion to each other. This particular example concerns the study of the manpower problems of primary school teachers in part of the United Kingdom. The manpower system was defined as four boxes, head teachers, assistant head teachers, teachers (male), and teachers (female). The separation of primary school teachers into males and females on the manpower system was necessary because these two groups were known to have very different wastage patterns. The diagram, when drawn, looked as in Fig. 3.4.

This manpower system was not questioned until the data relating to it arrived on the desk of the analyst, who could not help but notice the very high ratio of primary women teachers to primary men teachers. The ratio was so weighted towards women that the analyst felt that instead of giving insight into the manpower problems, the manpower system was misleading. The manpower system was redrawn as in Fig. 3.5 but this time with the boxes to scale and the width of the arrows representing the flows proportional to the number of people moving along that flow. The impact was startling. The very large number of women teachers to men teachers was apparent as was the large

63

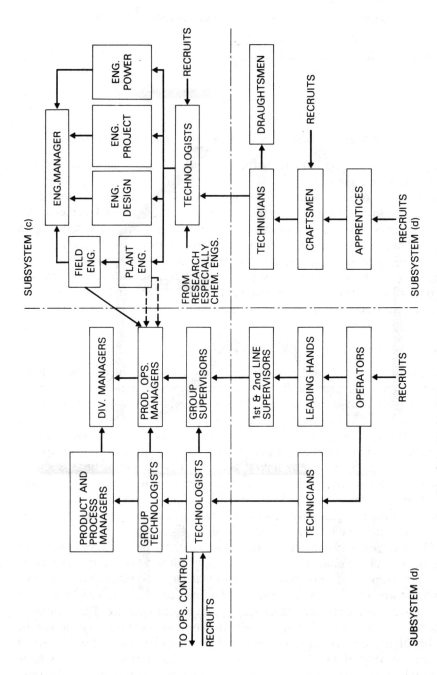

Fig. 3.3. Highlighting manpower decisions – 3. The crucial group

64

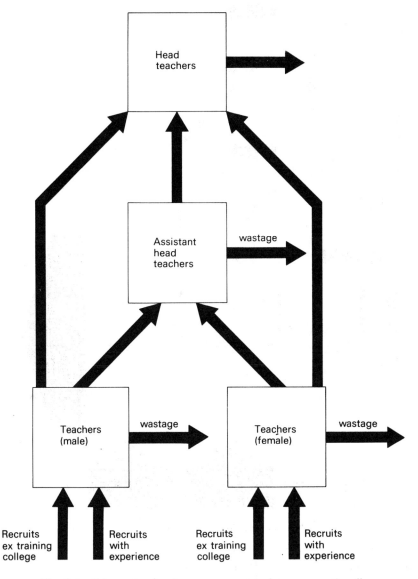

Fig. 3.4. Primary teachers' manpower system drawn conventionally

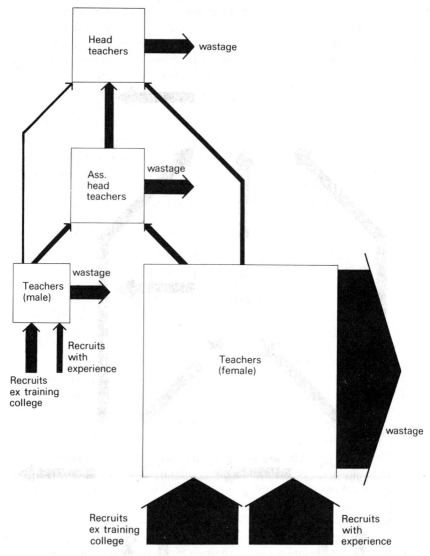

Fig. 3.5. Primary teachers' manpower system drawn to scale

number of teachers compared with assistant head teachers, and the very high rates of loss of primary school female teachers.

The redrawn system shows clearly that one of the major problems of the education authorities is the replacement of women primary school teachers. There appears to be high outflow, and recruitment comes from two sources, teachers coming from training schools and teachers who have experience. Those teachers with experience may be coming from other areas within the

United Kingdom or could be returning to the profession after a period of absence to have families. The reason for doing the study in the first place was to estimate the number of training school places required at teacher training colleges. Drawing the system in this way shows that an important piece of information in that decision is the percentage of primary school women teachers who leave and eventually come back to the system after having had children.

The information needed to draw a manpower system to scale is simple and is usually readily available within the organization. A simple way of proportioning the boxes to each other is to take the biggest box, calculate the square root of the numbers in that box, and use this to determine a square of appropriate size. In general, squares are easier to compare visually than rectangles since if one is using rectangles, care must be taken to keep the ratio of length to height of the rectangle constant.

In drawing the flows between boxes in proportion to each other, some trial and error will be necessary. Sometimes the scale chosen to represent the width of a flow creates a flow wider than the box into or out of which the flow takes place. In drawing up the primary teachers' manpower system to scale, the first flow to be drawn was the wastage of head teachers. The width of that flow, when drawn in proportion to that of the wastage of head masters, was much wider than the box drawn for the primary school women teachers. A simple way to reduce but not eliminate this is to find the largest flow and then ensure that the scale chosen to represent it produces a flow which is smaller in width than the box into which or out of which it flows. In peculiar circumstances, a small box on the manpower system may still end up with the flow into or out of it being bigger than the box itself. If this happens it is a simple matter to rescale and redraw the system.

In organizations that are growing or declining rapidly, the analyst may have difficulty in deciding whether to use the numbers at the beginning or at the end of a particular year, or even the average numbers employed during the year. One way to get over that problem is to draw the boxes to scale at the beginning of the year and then extend or reduce the boxes to show the situation at the end of the year.

In Fig. 3.6 we can see the substantial growth that has taken place over the year and how the relative size of the two boxes changed. Drawing the manpower system to scale clearly shows problem situations such as a very large box taking its promotees from a much smaller box, indicating the probability of extremely good promotion prospects which could lead to shortages of staff available for promotion. Large boxes feeding very small boxes indicate poor prospects of promotion.

In Fig. 3.7 we see that we have a small box between two larger boxes. This could indicate that the residence time within that box could be very short if the organization is expanding.

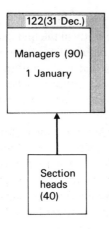

*Fig. 3.6. The effect of growth in numbers on
a manpower system*

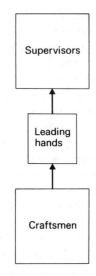

*Fig. 3.7. A scaled manpower system to
indicate promotion rates*

QUANTIFYING THE FLOWS ON THE MANPOWER SYSTEM

For even greater insight into possible manpower problems, indicate the numbers in each box at the end of the year and show on the flows the number of people who have moved along that flow within the preceding year. Comparing the flows into a box with the flows out shows whether the box is expanding, contracting, or maintaining its size. If this is done throughout the manpower system, it is easy to see where the manpower pressure in the organization is.

The age distribution

Two sales managers were considering the results of a series of manpower forecasts produced by the manpower planner in the organization at their request. Their main concern in asking for the forecast was to get some information on the levels of recruitment that would be necessary to meet the expansion in production capacity that the organization was planning, its consequent effect, and the number of salesmen required to sell the higher production levels and the new products that were to be produced. They were pleased to find that their subjective opinion on numbers of recruits that would probably be required had been more or less vindicated by the results of the manpower planning model, but were suprised at the change in the shape of the age distribution forecast by the manpower planning model.

The manpower planner pointed out to them that their present age structure had two distinct bulges in it. One immediately before retirement and the other between the ages of 20 and 30. In five years' time, according to the model, the age structure would be much flatter with a higher percentage of older people in total. 'How would this affect their manpower policies?' he asked. His question was idle curiosity to some extent but also he was curious to hear their subjective opinion about the shape of the age distribution since a number of manpower planning colleagues had been talking about the age structure, and what was its ideal shape, at a recent meeting. He was quite unprepared for the diametrically opposed views that the two sales managers took.

The first said that he welcomed the change in age structure most warmly. 'A higher percentage of older sales representatives would be beneficial, leading to a much more stable pattern of sales.' He had found that the judgement of the older, more experienced representatives enabled them to get business that would remain with the company. It was very rare for a contract signed by one of these older representatives to be lost. He was beginning to lose count of the number of times he had unsuccessfully attempted to rescue contracts obtained by younger sales representatives who, by their energy and determination, had pressed a customer into signing. The customer had subsequently thought better of the idea and in many cases even the experienced sales manager had been unable to stop him changing his mind about the contract. The chiding words of the production manager on the need to have long production runs and not be continually chopping and changing production plans, were becoming tedious. He welcomed the change to an older age structure.

The second sales manager said:

'Potentially this is a very serious situation. I was already concerned at the large number of people above the age of 50 and was considering taking more advantage of the early retirement package, and now you are telling me that the percentage is going to increase considerably over the next five years. I know that the production manager grumbles when we change the production plan but you give him a choice between changing the plan and increasing the occupation on his plant, and he will tell you very quickly that no profits are made until plant occupation is around 80 per cent. The higher level of sales comes from the younger sales representatives, of that I am quite clear. Young, keen and energetic, they are not easily put off, will get round more outlets in a day, and are more determined in talking to customers. I'll accept a few ineffectual rescue acts; it's the volume that counts. We must do something about

69

reversing this trend and getting, somehow or other, a larger proportion of the staff in the next five years at the younger end of the age structure. Now let me see, what have I done with the latest set of rules on the company's early retirement provisions?'

In suggesting that the age distribution can be used as an indicator of manpower problems, we do not expect to be able to satisfy the question that is often asked, as to what is the ideal age distribution most suited to the set of tasks that the organization has to do. We have no idea whether a 40-year-old production manager is better than a 55-year-old production manager. Little research that is generalizable has been done in this field. What we are suggesting is that a careful study of the age structure of an organization will reveal a considerable amount of information from the past patterns of growth of the organization; it will indicate potential problems in providing careers within a structure, and suggest the need for an organization to be re-examining recruitment policies for the next five years.

THE CURRENT AGE DISTRIBUTION

What can be said about the organization with the age structure shown in Fig. 3.8?

Immediately it can be seen that the largest percentage of people are in the age range 45 to 55. What can be inferred about the organization's manpower policies from this age structure? One set of policies that will produce such an age structure is an organization that recruits the bulk of its people in their early twenties and had its main expansion as an organization some 25 to 35 years ago. It could be the result of manpower policies that recruit people right the way across the age structure with very high losses in the people at the lower end of the structure, people below the age of 35, or it could be the result of recruitment policies spread over the age range 20 to 35 in an organization that has been steadily declining. In making each of those interpretations, recourse has to be made to other information about manpower policies within the organization. Beyond saying that it is an old or a young age structure, very little interpretation is possible without some knowledge of the recruitment and wastage distributions by age. Once these are obtained much wider interpretation of the impact of the age structure on policy is possible. By comparing the peak of the age distribution with the recruitment age range, it is possible to infer something about the growth period of the organization. The only way that an age distribution, peaking at age 50 can occur in an organization that only recruits between the ages of 20 and 25, is for it to have expanded between 25 and 30 years ago. An organization with an age structure which has a very high peak between the ages of 25 and 30 and yet has extremely high wastage rates at those ages, must be expanding and recruiting large numbers of people at or below those ages.

70

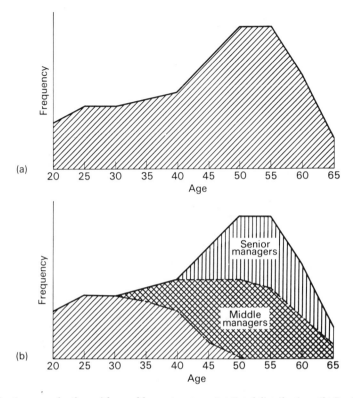

Fig. 3.8. *An organization with an old age structure. (a) Total distribution. (b) Broken down by level*

THE AGE–GRADE DISTRIBUTION

Further insight into the type of manpower problems is afforded by the simple expedient of breaking the age structure up by grade (Fig. 3.8a). In this example we see that not only is the age distribution peaked between the ages of 45 and 55 but a very high percentage of the senior posts are filled by those over 45 within the organization. Very few of those aged 45 or less have ever reached the middle manager grade. Does this mean that the company will have severe shortages of managers when the current senior staff retires over the next 10 years?

In the example depicted in Fig. 3.9 we see an age structure that is very young.

When we impose grade distribution on top of Fig. 3.9a we notice that a large percentage of the senior posts are held by a group of people between the ages of 30 and 35. Does this mark a change in the company's policy? Is this a new departure, the promotion of much younger people to senior manager? What

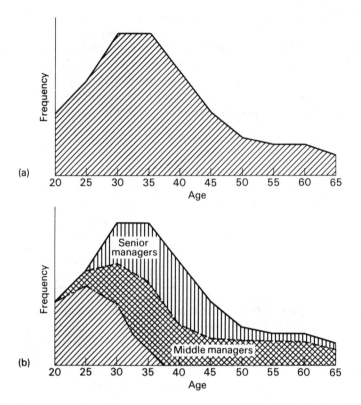

Fig. 3.9. An organization with a young age structure. (a) Total distribution. (b) Broken down by level

happens to promotion if this organization is not expanding? Will those people who are promoted to the top of the organization at 30 to 35 stay for 25 years, and what will the company do about the promotion blockage that results?

It should be reiterated at this point that grading is not the only way of expressing the level within the manpower structure. It is just as easy to use salary bands, or groups of job titles.

THE STEADY STATE AGE DISTRIBUTION

The previous two sections have shown the interrelationship that exists between the age structure, the organization's recruitment policies, and the patterns of wastage from it. This interrelationship can be used to produce yet another indicator.

Take the idea to its extreme unreality. An organization is neither growing nor declining. It recruits all its employees at the age of 20, it has no wastage and

72

they all retire at the same age, 65. What will be the shape of its age structure? It is easy to see that it will be a rectangle (see Fig. 3.10). Each year the organization will recruit the same number of people as retire. As well as being a rectangle, that age structure will never change, since those who leave are replaced by the same number who start and because the people within the structure age by one year, the gaps left by those retiring are filled by those the year before retirement and eventually gaps are created at age 20 for the recruits.

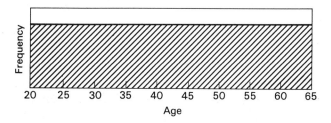

Fig. 3.10. Steady state age distribution – 1. Starting point

Suppose that the organization does not recruit everyone at age 20 but spreads the recruitment over the age range 20 to 25. What effect will that have on the shape of the age distribution? It will still be flat after the age of 25 but the numbers will increase from 20 at a steady rate up to the age of 25, reflecting the spread of the recruitment (see Fig. 3.11).

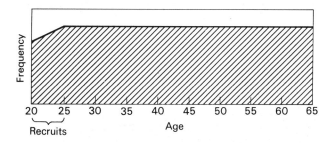

Fig. 3.11. Steady state age distribution – 2. Adding in recruitment over an age range

More realistic assumptions about retirement, allowing for the increasing number of people are reflected by retiring between the ages of 55 and 65, the age structure of our hypothetical company beginning to slope downwards after the age of 55. The basic age structure is still flat between ages 25 and 55, but this plateau is a little higher than it was to maintain the constant number required to allow for the spread recruitment and retirement (see Fig. 3.12).

Wastage tends to be higher among younger people. (This will be returned to

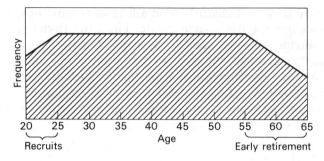

Fig. 3.12. Steady state age distribution – 3. Introducing early retirement

in a later chapter.) The wastage data showed that the rates are highest between the ages of 20 and 35 and after that age they reduce to much lower levels. For our age structure to keep on replacing itself without any change in the numbers employed, means that we have to compensate for the wastage by increasing the number of people recruited. Since we lose a large number of people between the ages of 20 and 35, there will have to be a substantial increase in recruitment levels, but also we must not forget that there is some loss after the age of 35. These losses, too, must be accounted for in the recruitment intake and since intake is only between the age of 20 and 25, a high peak will be created within the age distribution at age 25. The height of this peak will be dependent on the rates of wastage. How fast and how far this peak reduces will be dependent on the rates of wastage up to the age of 35. From that point onwards, the rate of decline of the age distribution will slow down since the wastage rates after 35

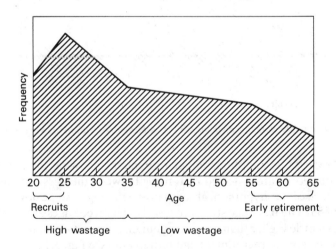

Fig. 3.13. Steady state age distribution – 4. Taking account of wastage patterns

are very much lower. There will be a gradual decline in the age structure from 35 to 55 at which point the steepness of the slope will increase again, reflecting that additional wastage of early retirement. This age structure, too, will be self-reproducing (see Fig. 3.13).

Finally, remove the last obstruction to reality by allowing the organization to expand or contract. What happens to the shape of the age distribution in the steady state? If the organization is expanding at 2 per cent per annum then each year it must recruit 2 per cent more people than it loses. It only recruits between the ages of 20 and 25 and, therefore, it must increase that recruitment to allow for the increased growth and the wastage that will come from those recruits. We find, therefore, that the peak of the age structure increases before the age of 25 to accommodate this (Fig. 3.14).

The higher the rate of expansion, the more the peak increases. An organization that is contracting continually does not need to replace employees and recruitment can be cut back between the ages of 20 and 25 to allow the organization to contract by the requisite amount. It must be remembered that since the wastage is highest between the ages of 20 and 35, the reduction in the number of recruits will have an impact on reduced wastage. We find a very radical change takes place in the shape of the age distribution under con-

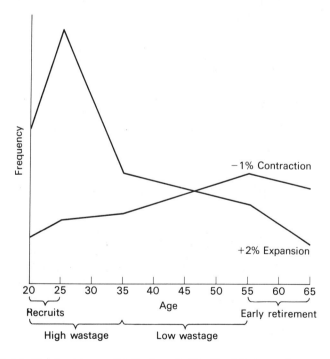

Fig. 3.14. Steady state age distribution – 5. Finally adding growth or contraction

traction; a typical curve would look as in the 1 per cent contraction curve in Fig. 3.14.

For any given recruitment and wastage distribution (including retirement) and growth rate, there is a steady state age distribution that the organization will arrive at if it maintains the same recruitment and wastage patterns. In itself, it is not a very helpful concept. No organization will ever get to the steady state, nor do we think, as some manpower planners do, that the organization should change its policy towards the steady state, since a steady state is unlikely to be reached. By comparing it, however, with the current age structure, blockages and shortages in the structure begin to be revealed. Let us take the case of an organization that has the age structure shown in Fig. 3.15.

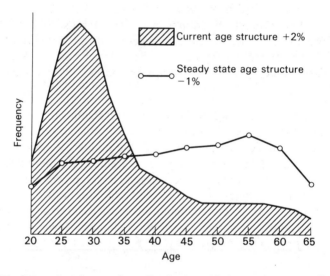

Fig. 3.15. Comparing the actual age distribution with the steady state age distribution

Here the organization has a high percentage under the age of 35, most of whom are in the bottom level. Its recruits are between the ages of 25 and 35 and the wastage is also concentrated within that band. The company expects to decline at a low rate of 1 per cent per annum. We can calculate, using the recruitment distribution, the wastage distribution and the assumption of −1 per cent growth, the steady state age structure. If we then compare this with the current age structure we see that an organization with those recruitment policies and that wastage pattern would have a much flatter age structure concentrated towards the older end of the distribution. This is quite unlike the current age structure.

By experimenting with the growth rate, we find that the organization's current age structure will be much more suitable for an organization that has been growing at 2 per cent. We can begin to see that if the future for a company is one of decline, even at the slow rate of -1 per cent per annum, it appeared to have far too many people at the young end of the age distribution. In other words it is going to find it impossible to give promotion to this bulge of younger people unless it has a high growth rate.

It is in this way that the steady state age distribution is useful. By using it to compare with our current age structure, we can get some idea of the difficulties we may be called upon to face under different conditions of growth or expansion.

The reader will have begun to observe that our preoccupation with the age distribution is not because we think that there are particular ages at which people perform best, but that the age distribution, given an understanding of the recruitment pattern and the wastage rates by age, expresses something about build-up of experience within the organization. Once a particularly shaped age distribution is established, it is hard to change in the short term. Supposing that the organization does not like an age distribution with a peak around the age of 45, indicating significant promotion blockages, and wishes to change it. How does it change it? It could recruit significant numbers of people at each end of the spectrum but that would entail a considerable increase in costs, unless it reduced the population in the middle. We will see, when we consider the wastage rates normally to be found, that the wastage rates of 45-year-olds are among the lowest to be found in manpower groups. Policies of induced wastage might have to be followed and these, too, are very complex. The practicability of quickly changing the age structure is very limited and, therefore, we find that an age distribution changes slowly and the changes represent changes in the experience profile of an organization.

The length of service distribution

In the previous example, the assumption has been that the organization recruits people in a well defined age band. In the example quoted the range is 20 to 25. We can say, with a degree of certainty, that a 45-year-old man in an organization will have between 15 and 20 years of service. Where recruitment takes place within a very narrow age band then the age and length of service distribution are very closely correlated. There are organizations, however, where this is not the case and recruitment can be spread over a very wide age band, and the close relationship between age and length of service does not exist, therefore, that age distribution is not such a good measure of the experience profile of the organization.

In these cases, it is much better to use the length of service distribution as the indicator of manpower problems, in the same way as the age distribution has been used previously in this chapter. The steady state length of service distributions can be caculated and used in the same way, and similar inferences can be made from length of service distributions which have peaked at different points on the length of service range.

A difficulty arises in using the length of service distribution. Since most retirement rules in organizations are based on age, it is easy to see from the age distribution the numbers of employees likely to retire over the next few years, and an assessment can be made of the loss of experience within the organization and how that might have to be replaced. Supposing that our organization recruits people between the ages of 20 and 40 without any noticeable preference between those ages. Suppose, too, that the organization retires people at the age of 65. There is now no correlation between the age and length of service, a person with 20 years' service could, assuming that the retirement age is 65, retire within 5 years or not until 25 years have passed. We shall see later that this can cause problems in attempting to quantify manpower problems.

The career progression diagram

It is possible to use age or length of service and level in the organization as an indicator of the speed with which employees progress through the organization's structure. This is an extremely useful and valuable tool for highlighting blockages and shortages, as well as being the best way yet developed of presenting information about career progression in a precise and visually stimulating way. The technique was developed by Roger Morgan at the University of Cambridge in his work on career planning, in the 1960s.

It is important in learning how to interpret a career progression diagram to know how it is calculated. Let us reduce the calculation to its barest example (see Fig. 3.16).

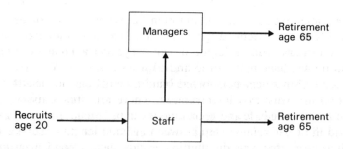

Fig. 3.16. Calculating career progression curves – 1. Manpower system

Two measures are needed to calculate the career progression diagram – a measure of level in the hierarchy whether it be grades, salary bands, or job titles, and a measure of time in the organization; here age or length of service is equally acceptable with a proviso that if age is used then the distribution of recruits must be within a narrow age band. These data can be found within every organization and are usually very easy to collect.

In this organization, we only have two levels, management and staff. We also recruit at the age of 20 and retire people at the age of 65. Age can be used, therefore, as a measurement of time in the organization.

Begin the calculation by laying out in a table the number of people in each level at each age. In Fig. 3.17 we can see that in our hypothetical examples we

Age	20	21	22	23
No. of managers	0	0	1	3
% in and below	100	100	100	100
No. of staff	24	35	28	17
% in and below	100	100	97	85
Total	24	35	29	20

Fig. 3.17. Calculating career progression curves – 2. Calculations

have no managers below the age of 22, 1 aged 22, 3 aged 23, and so on. The number of staff at age 20 is 24, at 21 is 35, at 22 is 28, and so on. For each age, we calculate the percentage of people in or below each level as a percentage of the total for that age. Take an example: what is the percentage of people in the staff level or below at the age of 20? The total number of people aged 20 is 24 and the total number of staff aged 20 is 24, therefore, the percentage of the 20-year-old age band in or below staff is 24 out of 24 or 100 per cent. Now let us try the calculation at age 23. At age 23 we have three managers and 17 staff, a total of 20. The percentage of 23-year-olds in or below staff is 17 out of 20 or 85 per cent. The number of people in or below manager at age 23 is 3 managers plus 17 staff, i.e., 20, out of a total of 20 in the age band, therefore, the percentage in or below the managers is 100. It does not take long to realize that the percentage in or below the top level in the structure is always 100 per cent.

To reinforce the principles involved in the calculations, let us add an additional box to our structure called trainees. Figure 3.18 shows that we have 10 trainees at 20, 12 at age 21, and so on until by age 25 we have none.

The method of performing the calculation is identical to our first example. First of all calculate the total number in each age band. For each age band we start at the bottom of the structure and calculate what percentage are in or

Age	20	21	22	23	24
No. of managers	0	0	1	3	5
% in and below	100	100	100	100	100
No. of staff	24	35	28	17	27
% in and below	100	100	97	87	85
No. of trainees	10	12	7	4	2
% in and below	29	25	19	17	6
Total	34	47	36	24	34

Fig. 3.18. Calculating career progression curves – 3. Calculations for a three-box manpower system

below that level. At age 20 we have 10 trainees, and a total of 34 people in the age band, so the percentage in or below trainees is 10 out of 34 or 29 per cent. The percentage in or below staff at age 20 are the 24 staff and 10 trainees or 34 out of 34, again 100 per cent. Having established the principles of the calculations, in Fig. 3.19 we plot the percentages that we have calculated.

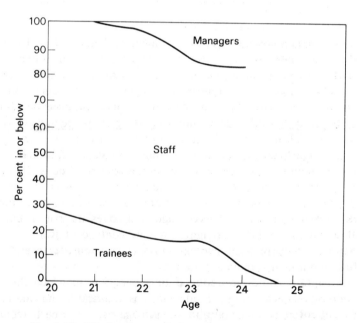

Fig. 3.19. Plotting the curves for a three-box manpower system

In using and interpreting these diagrams, every manpower planner must be aware of the basic caveats.

1. They are percentage diagrams and as such show relative position at each age not the absolute numbers. Two principal points follow from this reservation. Because the percentage of trainees falls from 22 per cent at age 20 to 7 per cent at age 24, it does not necessarily mean that the number of trainees has fallen – indeed the number of trainees could actually have risen across that part of the age band – but that the number of staff has risen more over the same age range and, therefore, as a percentage, the percentage in or below trainee falls.

2. The effect on the calculation of having very small numbers as the total for any age is the next point to be borne in mind. Big changes can occur in the percentage of people in any level from age band to age band, if the numbers in the age band are fluctuating wildly and are also small. If we only have two people in an age band, and they are in two different levels, then the percentage in or below one of the levels will be 50 per cent. This effect tends to be more noticeable at the older end of the age distribution, when ill-health and retirement often reduce the numbers to very small amounts.

Bearing those two points in mind, how can we begin to interpret these diagrams and use them as indicators?

Let us start by considering some hypothetical interpretations of the diagram (Fig. 3.19) we have just calculated. This particular diagram could be obtained in the situation where, at age 20, we recruit into our organization both 'staff' and 'trainees'. This must be the implication of having two levels represented at the lowest age. At age 21, the organization does not recruit trainees but simply recruits a few extra 'staff'. This has the effect of increasing the percentage of people in or below the 'staff' level and decreasing the percentage in or below the 'trainee' level.

At age 22, the organization recruits a 'manager', some additional 'staff' but no 'trainees'. This has the effect of increasing the percentage in or below 'trainee' further and for the first time showing some 'managers' on the graph.

At age 23, more 'managers' are recruited but recruitment of 'staff' and 'trainees' has now stopped. The percentage of 'trainees' has now dropped to 19 per cent and there is little change in the percentage of 'staff' within the organization, but there is an increase in the percentage at age 23 of the population that are 'managers'.

So this diagram could be obtained in a company in which there is no promotion from 'trainee' to 'staff' and 'staff' to 'manager'. The change in the relative frequencies simply being the result of increasing the percentage of people recruited at the higher level as the age increases.

In a similar way, it could be shown that the decreasing percentages of trainees and staff produced by this diagram are simply the result of trainee wastage. In this case the company recruits all its trainees age 20 and as the numbers in training waste away, it recruits 'staff' and 'managers' to fill the gaps.

Although the diagram can be produced in these two rather peculiar ways, the most usual cause of the percentage of people at the lower grades declining as the age increases is promotion into the higher grades. This interpretation can be asserted with a degree of certainty when the recruitment and wastage patterns of the organization are also known. If in our previous example we stated that it was the company's policy to recruit only at staff and trainee levels at age 24, then we can see that the reduction in the trainee level is either caused by promotion from trainee to staff, or by the wastage from the trainee grade. If we are further told that wastage of trainees is insignificant after the first year, then the fall in the percentage that are trainees from 19 per cent at age 22 down to 0 at age 25, is the result of promotion. Since managers are not recruited at all, the increase in managers' percentage from 22 onwards again must be the result of promotion from staff to manager.

The career progression diagram is an excellent tool which uses very simple and easily obtainable data to show information about the career progression of an organization.

THE INTERPRETATION OF CAREER PROGRESSION DIAGRAMS

Having made the point that interpretation of the career progression diagram cannot satisfactorily be made without a knowledge of the recruitment and wastage pattern of the organization, and for the moment accepting as the norm that recruitment tends to be concentrated in a narrow band in the lower age ranges, and that wastage too is higher in the lower age ranges, reducing as age increases, we can begin to make some general points about the career progression patterns of the organization.

First, the number of grades represented at the lowest age range reveals facets of the organization's recruitment policy. If the career progression diagram shows that two grades are present at the lowest age, as in Fig. 3.19, then we can say with certainty that the organization recruits into both 'staff' and trainees. It could be that the organization recruits people with different qualifications, bringing the people with the lower qualifications in as trainees and those with the higher qualifications as 'staff'. It could be that the organization not only recruits directly into the bottom level but also from another manpower system within the organization at the next grade above. Even if the career progression diagram shows only one level to be present at the lowest stage, it does not necessarily mean that the organization only has one point of entry, i.e., at the bottom of the organization. An entry point could occur at higher levels in the organization, but this may or may not necessarily show on the career progression diagram, as we shall see later.

Second, and generally speaking where the percentage of people in a given grade reduces rapidly as age or length of service increases, this indicates that promotion is taking place over that age range. Where the change in the percentage takes place within a narrow age band, i.e., where the line representing the grade boundary between two grades is very steep, then promotion for some reason is being concentrated in a very narrow age or length of service band. Figure 3.20 shows that staff get promoted to manager mainly between the ages of 30 and 35, although it can occur anywhere between 25 and 40.

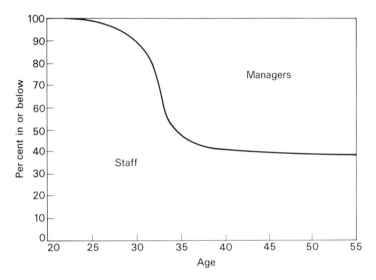

Fig. 3.20. Interpreting career progression diagrams – 1. The basics

Third, where the grade boundary lines are close together and are also steeply inclined, it indicates that the residence time in a succession of grades is very small. When the lines flatten out, it indicates that residence time is increasing, i.e., the percentage of people in or below a given grade is not changing rapidly with the age or length of service. In Fig. 3.21, we see that there is very rapid promotion up the grading structure for the first three grades, the lines being close together and steeply inclined, but from grade 3 on the lines become less steep and wider apart.

The boundary between grades 1 and 2 in Fig. 3.21 is so steep that it never flattens out and eventually, by about the age of 35, the line has reached 0, in other words, nobody remains in grade 1 after the age of 35. The inference is that everyone who is recruited to that grade and remains in the organization will be promoted to grade 2 before the age of 35. If we look at the next boundary, we see that it has reached the 10 per cent level, the line begins to flatten out and then does not seem to change at all. How should we interpret this situation? Given the 'normal' wastage and recruitment patterns, we can say that by the age of 40 only about 10 per cent of the people will remain in grade 2. Alternatively it can be said that 90 per cent of all those recruited who stay in the organization will reach at least grade 3 by the age of 40.

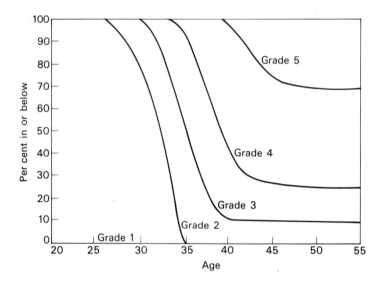

Fig. 3.21. Interpreting career progression diagrams – 2. Speed of promotion

We can continue in this way moving up the levels in the system, looking at points at which the lines flatten out, and reading off what proportion of people are likely to reach those levels by retirement age. We can begin to answer many of the questions that personnel, in particular recruitment specialists, have been asking for many years. The typical question of a graduate seeking employment with an organization, is 'What are my career prospects?' It has not in the past been very easy to tell graduates what the career prospects were, but by plotting the career progression diagram, we can say things like 'Well, 10 per cent of the people who join us and remain with us in the research function reach the top of the organization.' Alternatively, we could say 'If you join us, you can expect to have attained manager by the age of 45.' A third answer to that question might be '10 per cent of those who join us become heads of functions before retirement, another 20 per cent reach the assistant manager level and you can guarantee to have become a senior professional by the age of 38.' The proviso is that the present pattern of wastage continues into the future.

One or two problems to be found in interpreting the career progression diagram are considered in this section of the chapter.

In Fig. 3.22 it can be seen that by the age of 40 the percentage in the second grade, having stabilized around the 10 per cent level, begins to increase rapidly and by age 45 to 50 has reached 30 per cent of x. After that point it begins to fall away again back to the 10 per cent level that was reached before.

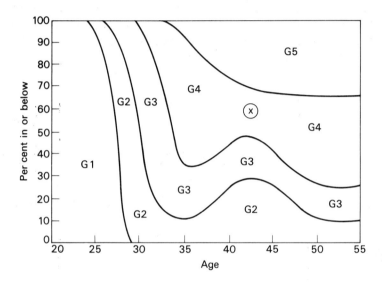

Fig. 3.22. Interpreting career progression diagrams – 3. Explaining a bulge

What could possibly be happening here? The percentage in grade 2 rises rapidly, but are we sure that it is grade 2 that has increased or could it be that grade 4 has decreased? Remember that a career progression diagram, because it uses percentages, measures relative change. Can we think of any possible likely explanation why people in the fourth grade should begin to reduce rapidly from the ages of 40 to 50, i.e., the point marked x in Fig. 3.22. Could this be the point at which people transfer from this manpower system into other manpower systems in large numbers? Could it be that people in the fourth grade originally joined at the bottom of the organization but on a fixed term contract, and the contract is running out when they have reached about the fourth grade around the age of 40? There could be some interesting parallels here in the armed services. In the officer ranks there are clearly determined outlet points once certain ranks have been reached.

If these possibilities can be discounted by our knowledge of the organization or by examining data, and if we discount the rather frivolous and academic

85

suggestion that there has been mass demotion, we must look to a second entry into the organization at grade 2 between the ages of 40 and 50. This is the usual explanation. The organization recruits young, well qualified people in at the bottom of its management manpower system and they move up the system quite normally, it promotes, however, people with lesser qualifications, but with high levels of experience into the bottom of the management structure.

Looking at Fig. 3.23 and concentrating on the top two levels, we see that movement from assistant manager into management begins around the age of 40. By the age of 50, about 10 per cent have moved into the management level and this percentage stays constant until about the age of 55 when the percentage in the top management grade begins to increase again and seems to carry on increasing until retirement at 65.

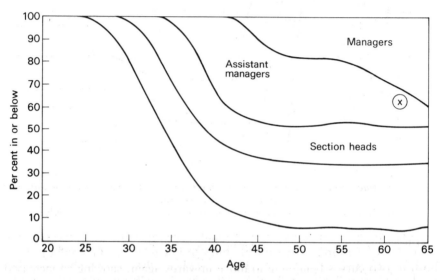

Fig. 3.23. Interpreting career progression diagrams – 4. Early retirement effects

A quick glance at the organization's promotion records should show whether much promotion takes place between the ages of 55 and 65. Sometimes it will be confirmed that there is this second promotion age. The diagram is then clearly showing the existence of a high flying group whose members are promoted earlier than the main group.

If the data do not show evidence of promotion between the ages of 55 and 65 into the top management grade, then the clue to the explanation is usually to be found by looking at the levels below top management in the career progression diagram. We often find that what is happening is that the people who feel that they are not going to make it to the top jobs begin to take early retirement from about the age of 55 onwards. In fact, what we are seeing is not an increase in the number of managers, but a decrease in the number of assistant managers. The point marked x in Fig. 3.23 shows the ages at which assistant managers are retiring early.

Yet another problem of interpreting the career progression diagrams can be seen in Fig. 3.24.

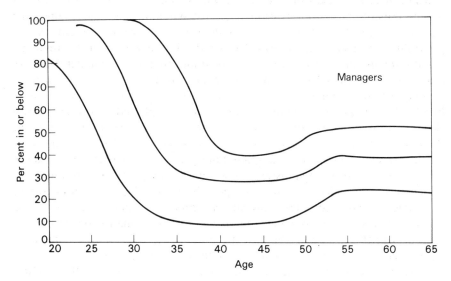

Fig. 3.24. Interpreting career progression diagrams – 5. Changes in the organization structure and growth rates

Here we have an apparently normal diagram with the curves moving smoothly downwards at reasonable rates to low points and then not just the bottom two curves beginning to move upwards again, showing an increased percentage below these boundaries, but almost all the lines do so, and then they steady at this higher level until the end of the age structure.

The most likely thing happening here is a major change in the organization's career policy. In the past it may have had a different career structure which allowed a smaller percentage of people to reach the management levels. In Fig. 3.23 we see that this used to be about 50 per cent. This policy has now been replaced by a new policy, probably generated from a new structure, that has a higher percentage of people getting to the next level, so we see the curve showing the grade boundary between the bottom two levels to be flattening off, not at 50 per cent but at 40 per cent. As well as being caused by a change in the structure, this often happens when a company experiences a rapid change in its growth rate. It finds that in the past it has only needed to get a small proportion of people through to top management, because it was not growing very rapidly.

87

When a period of growth occurs it needs people at the higher end of the system to manage the expansion. Unless it recruits outside the organization it will find that the previous recruitment policies have been geared to the level of managers needed for its lower growth rate and, therefore, it will have to begin to take less experienced levels of the younger people to meet the new need. This pressure pushes the career curves downwards.

Manpower planners in smaller organizations sometimes have difficulty producing sensible career progression diagrams. When they plot the results of the calculation, they find that the grade boundary curves fluctuate wildly. As has previously been suggested in this chapter, this is due to the fact that there are small numbers of people in the different grades that they use and a change of one or two can be a 50 or 66 per cent change if there are only two or three people at that age band. To get over this problem a number of analysts have banded together their data into five-year bands and plotted the career progression diagram at the end of the bands. Undoubtedly this removes some of the fluctuations that were experienced, but there is a danger of hiding some of the significant change points in the grade boundary curve. A better way, experience shows, is to use a statistical smoothing technique to smooth out a line which has been calculated at each age. Unfortunately, the best smoothing formulae are rather complex to use and take time to calculate. The Institute has included packages in its collection of computerized manpower techniques to deal with this problem. The next two graphs (Fig. 3.25) show the impact of using such a smoothing technique to plot the career progression.

You can see from a comparison of the two that very little of the essential changes in the flows of the grade boundary curves is lost by the smoothing, but the random fluctuation or noise is well controlled.

To summarize, experience shows that the career progression diagram is a very powerful visual tool for displaying to managers a complete picture of the career policies within the organization. This was brought home very strongly in a project where the IMS adviser was having considerable difficulty getting data showing how long people were staying in the different grades in the organization. The managers found that promotion tended to be rather sporadic in the organization, varying wildly from year to year and they found it difficult to make subjective estimates. In desperation the analyst drew a career progression diagram from some of the data. The personnel officer in the organization responsible for the management development scheme was quite surprised at how clearly it indicated the policy that the company had built into its management development scheme. For the first time he could see that it took about 15 years for a man to become a manager, after having completed training. He said 'I have been criticized heavily by our branch managers because the personnel development scheme does not do what it was intended to do. Here for the first time I have objective evidence that it really does work. Could you hold on a minute while I get my manager in? I would like him to see the diagram.'

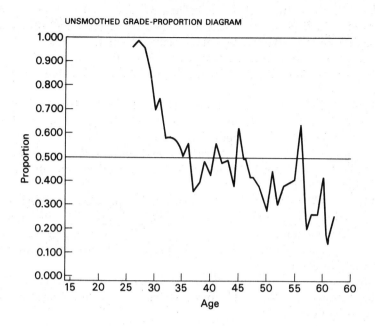

UNSMOOTHED GRADE-PROPORTION DIAGRAM

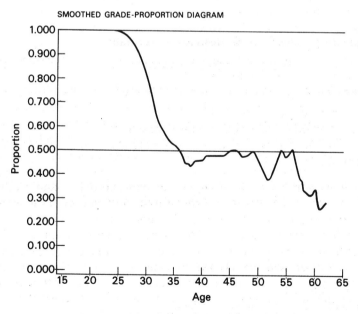

SMOOTHED GRADE-PROPORTION DIAGRAM

Fig. 3.25. Smoothing a career progression curve

Two minutes later he returned with the manager and the analyst was asked to explain the diagram, how it was calculated, and what it showed. This was followed by a five-minute discussion between the personnel officer and his manager about the effectiveness of the management development policy. They said that it was so interesting that they sent for their superior and again the analyst was asked to explain how the diagrams were calculated and what they meant.

The finale of the final act in this play shows the analyst sitting quietly on one side, while five people, from the head of personnel down to the personnel officer responsible for management development, discussed for 15 minutes the implications of what the career progression diagram was showing them. Until that time they had not been able to discuss objectively the effectiveness of operation of the scheme.

This shows the great value of drawing career progression diagrams in that they present a very good visual picture of what is happening in the organization in a way that most managers can understand. The wide ranging discussion that then takes place about policies is, in the eyes of most manpower people, extremely valuable.

If the managers in the organization for whom the career progression diagram has been drawn say 'Well, I did not know that . . .', then the analyst has done his job thoroughly enough.

A case study – the Failsafe Insurance Company

THE CONCERNS OF THE ORGANIZATION

Company has been expanding   New systems are improving efficiency:

– Should manpower levels fall?
– Can reduction be achieved by natural wastage?
– What is the impact on those with potential: can career prospects be maintained?

The first steps are to determine the manpower system appropriate to the problem (see Fig. 3.26). In the case of this example, these are described in Chapter 2.

ANALYSIS AND OBSERVATIONS

Numbers employed
– Trainees reduce by one-sixth in year.
  Is company planning for effect of new systems?
– Services sector growing, inspectors contracting.

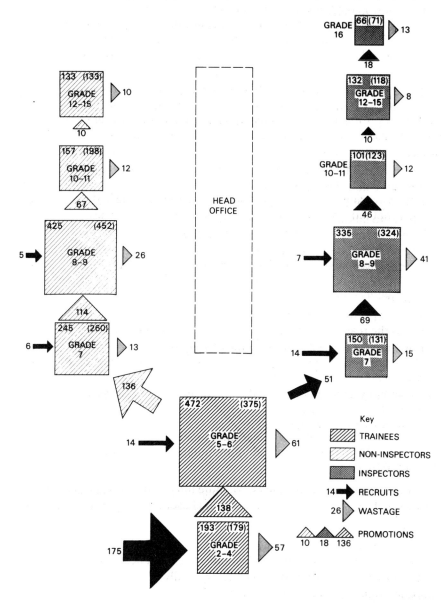

Fig. 3.26. The Failsafe Insurance Company – 1. The manpower system to scale

Why? New systems are expected to reduce service staff.
Inspectors are salesmen and generate new business, why reduce?
- Inspector management grades

Grade	Year start	Year end
16	66	71
12–15	132	118
10–11	101	123

Total number of managers increases yet number of inspectors decreases.
Number in grades 10–11 increases by 20 per cent.
Policy? At beginning of year more grades 12–15 than 10–11.

Flows
- Tremendous losses of trainees in first two years (30 per cent).
  Selection and training policy?
- Below grade 12 inspectors are almost twice as likely to leave as service staff.
  Losses to labour market of experienced salesmen.
- Low recruitment levels of experienced staff.
  85 per cent of recruits enter as trainees.
  Surprise to management?

Prospects
- Trainee promotion automatic to grade 7.
  Is this the reason for the large number of promotions to grade 7 on the service side?
- High promotion rates from grade 7 to grade 8 – 50 per cent of grade 7 promoted.
  Is promotion automatic since the rate on each side is the same?
- Promotion rates above grade 9.
  Short promotion ladder?

INSPECTOR DEVELOPMENT

The next step is to concentrate on the more important of the problems revealed by the analysis. The inspector stream was chosen for the following reasons.

- Inspectors generate revenue.
- Inspector numbers are falling.
- There appears to be very high loss rates of experienced inspectors.
- The management structure is changing rapidly.
- Suggestion of promotion blockages.
- The impact of the new systems on this stream is not clear.

So far limited, easy to get data have been used. To go further requires the examination of the inspector stream in detail (see Fig. 3.27).

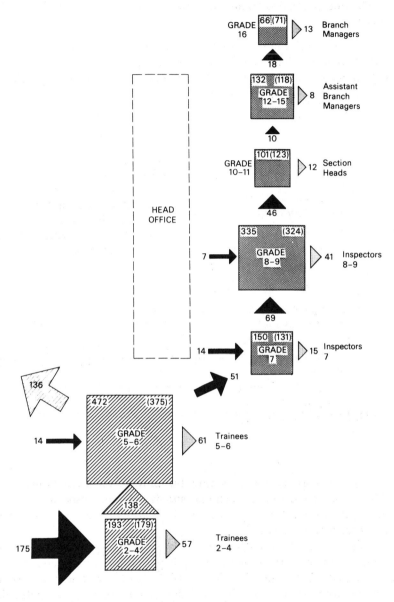

Fig. 3.27. The Failsafe Insurance Company – 2. The inspector stream

93

This structure with high numbers below the age of 35 is typical of structures to be found in rapidly growing organizations.

The one year's data analysed show a decline in the number of inspectors. Is this because:

(a) the training scheme is not producing sufficient inspectors;
(b) there are high rates of loss of inspectors; or
(c) management policy is to reduce numbers as a consequence of the introduction of new systems? (See Fig. 3.28.)

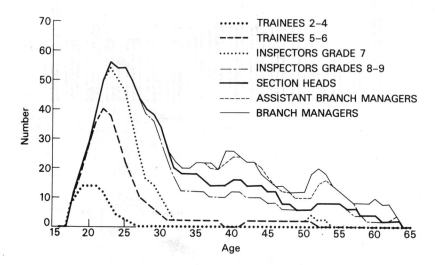

Fig. 3.28. The Failsafe Insurance Company – 3. The smoothed age/grade distribution

Detailed analysis of wastage rates by age was done throughout the structure. All but one band showed a similar steady diagram. Inspectors 8–9 showed a markedly different pattern with very high losses in the age range 28 to 31 and early retirement around 58.

Matching this knowledge with the career progression information, it can be seen that the majority of losses are of experienced people (see Fig. 3.29).

For any given wastage patterns and policies of recruitment, there is an 'ideal' age distribution (see Fig. 3.30). The dashed lines show two such distributions – one representing 4 per cent growth with its need for younger people, the other representing 2 per cent decline. The actual distribution suggests that 4 per cent growth has been the growth pattern to date.

94

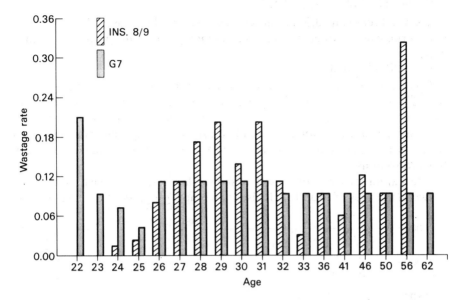

Fig. 3.29. The Failsafe Insurance Company – 4. Comparing wastage rates of inspectors

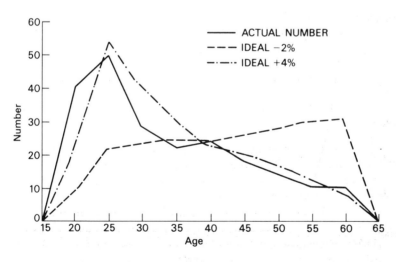

Fig. 3.30. The Failsafe Insurance Company – 5. Comparing the actual age structure with the ideal age structure for 4% growth and 2% decline

The seven areas (Fig. 3.31) represent the seven grade bands.

A vertical line cutting through several shadings shows the proportion in each band.

For example, at age 40:

No one is a trainee 2–4, about 10 per cent are trainees 5–6 or inspectors 7, 40 per cent are inspectors 8–9, 15 per cent are inspectors 10–11, 30 per cent are assistant branch managers 12–15, and 5 per cent have made it to the top.

Near-vertical lines indicate very rapid promotion, e.g., movement through the first three grades for people less than 25. Near-horizontal lines indicate very few promotions.

The career progression diagram shows that salesmen reach grades 8–9 between the ages of 24 and 32. It also shows rapid progression to that point, the

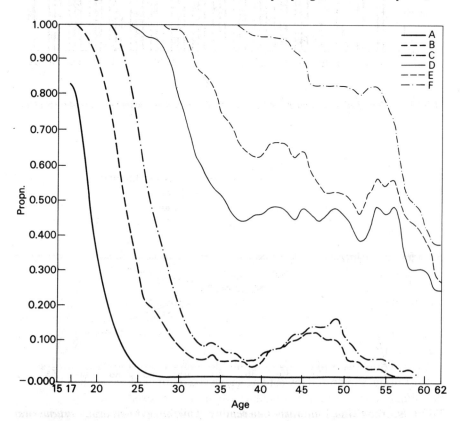

Fig. 3.31. The Failsafe Insurance Company – 6. Career progression diagram for inspectors. A = trainees 2–4; B = trainees 5–6; C = inspectors grade 7; D = inspectors grades 8–9; E = section heads; F = assistant branch managers

lines below are close together and steep. The boundary in the diagram marked 'D' is that between inspector 8–9 and section head. About 50 per cent of the total numbers do not progress beyond this point.

High wastage rates of experienced inspectors in an organization that has been expanding suggest that expectations are being frustrated.

The diagram (Fig. 3.32) explores future career prospects for inspectors by comparing the number of section head jobs needed to *maintain* not improve career prospects for inspectors under different conditions. The unbroken line shows that the number of section head jobs would have to increase from 101 to

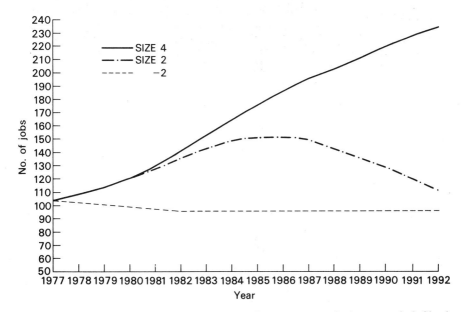

Fig. 3.32. The Failsafe Insurance Company – 7. Career prospects for inspectors 8–9. Size 4 = 4% expansion, size 2 = 2% expansion, size −2 = −2% expansion

about 230 if the organization were growing at 4 per cent per annum. Even 0 per cent growth, the middle line, shows that the number of section head jobs would have to increase for a time to maintain career prospects due to the bulge in the age structure.

As the company is planning to reduce numbers as a result of the new systems it is installing, the dotted lowest line shows the number of section head jobs it is planning to have. A major imbalance can be seen to exist.

This exercise was done with data readily available in most organizations and with techniques advocated in this chapter. The approach highlighted facets of the organization's manpower problems which were difficult to appreciate beforehand.

Summary

As more and more organizations practise our approach to manpower management, commonly occurring manpower situations will be identified and more indicators of manpower problems will be created to highlight them at an earlier stage, hopefully before they have become major manpower problems.

Nevertheless, for the moment, the manpower system, drawn to scale, the age distribution, and the career progression diagrams are powerful indicators of potential problems. Furthermore, their pictorial nature creates a visual impact which seems to be effective in helping senior managers reduce the time needed to comprehend the complex nature of manpower problems. Decisions result more often and more quickly as a consequence.

4.

Key influences on manpower planning – relating manpower to the business

A key influence on all the manpower decisions that an organization has to take is the number of people that the organization expects to employ, at its different levels and functions in the future. Decisions about recruitment levels, about career policies, are fundamentally affected by the numbers of people that the organization expects to employ. The approach to manpower planning suggested by this book has as its central theme the need to avoid an overdue reliance on forecasting the future accurately, and to spend more time on monitoring how factors that influence manpower decisions change, by having paid more attention to the information that is required in taking manpower decisions, the organization should be able to change its manpower policies to meet the changing conditions.

This chapter tries to help the understanding of this extremely complex problem by structuring it into four sections.

- The conceptual problem of relating manpower levels to business decisions.
- The process by which managers can be helped to assess future manpower levels by visualizing a variety of business scenarios.
- The techniques that can be used to quantify manpower levels.
- The processes used by organizations to build manpower levels into their corporate plans.

The conceptual problem

What went wrong with the manpower planner's forecast in the example in Chapter 1, when instead of the organization reaching a target of some 16 700 at the end of its forecast period, it was actually down to 13 000? The problem was that the organization failed to expand its sales as it forecast it would. Events in the external world in places like Bangladesh, China, and the United States stopped its sales targets from being reached. Equally, the organization may have failed to forecast a major change in technology; in today's conditions, especially in the fields of electronics, the rate of change of technology is very rapid indeed. It may have been that the manpower planner overestimated the number of people required to do the tasks and meet the objectives, and the organization found it did not need so many people to achieve its production levels.

In reality the task of forecasting the future number of people required in the organization is an extremely difficult one and from the outset it should be recognized that there are two forecasts that are required. Figure 4.1 shows the fundamental problems involved.

The first problem is to forecast what is going to happen to the nature of the organization over the period that we are concerned with. Will the organization stay where it is (the horizontal arrow) or will it decline? The impact that

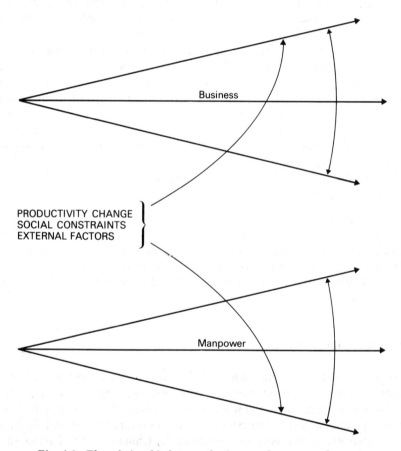

Fig. 4.1. The relationship between business and manpower forecasts

changes in the organization have on manpower levels is so fundamental that this question must be asked and to some extent answered before the next question – how many people do we need to meet the projected changes in the organization in the future? – can be answered. For any given state of the organization, the manpower levels themselves can increase, remain the same, or decrease; the exact relationship between them is determined by the way that producitivity will change over the period of the forecast. One problem is that productivity is often defined far too narrowly and concentrates purely on labour productivity.

ASSESSING THE CHANGE IN THE LEVEL OF PRODUCTIVITY

Horse power per man   Looking at some of the other factors influencing productivity shows how difficult it is to estimate its change over a period of four or five years. In the late 1950s there was considerable discussion among economists and politicians as to why British levels of productivity were much lower than their counterparts in the United States. The discussion at that time seemed to concentrate on how much more efficient and better were the tools that the United States' worker had to aid him in his tasks than those of the British worker. Whereas the British worker seemed to have to rely on muscle power, the American worker had a wide variety of powered tools to help him. A United States' car worker on an assembly line would probably have pneumatically operated spanners to tighten the nuts and bolts, whereas his British counterpart would still be relying on hand-held spanners. In United States' engineering factories the movement of materials would be on conveyor belts or electricity-powered trucks whereas in the UK the 'tradesman's mate' would supply the horse power, carrying the material manually or on a hand-powered truck.

Capital expenditure   A major influence on productivity is the level of capital expenditure. Two organizations making the same product could have levels of productivity that are very different. Yet within these organizations an examination of manpower productivity would show no difference in the rate of working or the attendance levels of individual workers within the two organizations, the high level of productivity in one emanating from a more up-to-date process plant.

Work organization   A company had for many years operated an incentive payments scheme for the skilled craftsmen in its workshop. Over the years the scheme had been debased and it was the general opinion among management that the incentive payments had no impact on productivity since the times for doing jobs were out of date and were overestimated. The company decided to remove the incentive scheme and replace it with a flat-rate day payment. The new system of payment had been in operation for a few months when, to its astonishment, the management found that the productivity in the engineering workshops was significantly lower than it had been under the incentive scheme. Investigation revealed that the incentive scheme had had an effect on productivity, but in quite a different way from that which the work measurement people anticipated. The administration of the scheme required the craftsmen to submit job cards, containing details of the job and the standard time allowed, in order for the bonus to be calculated.

Over the years the practice had grown up that the men limited the amount that they earned from the incentive scheme to about 40 per cent of their base rate, or in work study terms, a performance rating of about 120. The standard times were slack enough to allow the craftsmen to earn much higher levels, but the self-limiting of earnings was done to avoid drawing the attention of the work study department to the blatant slackness of the scheme. The men felt that by limiting themselves in this way, the standard times would not be revised. Throughout the course of a week, the craftsmen put the engineering jobs through the different machinery in the workshops and collected the cards, and at the end of the week they shuffled through the total number of jobs that they had done and sorted out jobs with standard times calculated to reach 120 performance.

These cards were submitted to the work study department and the bonus duly paid. If for some reason the work flow within the workshop was disrupted and work was not getting to the craftsmen, then they had no opportunity to collect the tickets that they required. The craftsmen were very quick to tell the supervisor that the work flow was reducing and work was brought up to the machine. Human nature being what it is, when the work was there it was put through the machine. After the incentive scheme was approved, although the job tickets were retained to help progress the jobs through the workshop, they were no longer needed for payment purposes. When the workflow in the workshop was disrupted, there was, therefore, no incentive for the craftsmen to tell the supervisor that there was a shortage of work, since they did not need the tickets to collect the bonus payments. The foreman was not told of the shortage of work, and productivity fell very rapidly. The organization had to improve work organization to bring the productivity level back to its original level.

Changing technology   Currently this factor is a major influence on productivity. Major changes in technology are affecting levels of productivity. Technological change has been going on at a high rate since the Second World War, but its speed and impact have increased in the last few years. Whereas to re-equip a steel mill might take a construction programme of two years, costing millions, with a 25 per cent saving in people, micro-computer technology can be applied to the office within one or two months and have a greater impact on productivity.

Motivation Attention paid to better motivation of workers in the organization often leads to a significant improvement in productivity. Many organizations have studied the work content of jobs of their workforce and tried to make them much more satisfying and interesting to the job holders. Plenty of research evidence exists to show that workers in well designed jobs perform better. The effects of these types of productivity improvement programmes, however, take one or two years to have an impact on productivity levels.

There are, of course, other factors influencing productivity but it can be seen from considering the five above that the task of forecasting an organization's productivity levels over the period involved in any manpower forecast is going to be difficult. We have to look at capital expenditure plans, how we intend to change working methods, and how we might improve the morale of the work-force over that period. Not only are we involved in attempting to decide *which way* the changes will have influence, but also we are attempting to estimate *how deeply* the changes will affect productivity.

SOCIAL CONSTRAINTS AND UNCERTAINTY

Let us suppose for a moment that we are successful in the two tasks that must be done if we are to assess manpower levels in the future accurately, mainly to forecast in which direction the business will change and secondly, for that business change, to guess how productivity levels could alter over the same period.

A large organization held a meeting of its technical experts throughout the world to discuss the way that technology might change. At the end of the three-day conference the experts came to the conclusion that if they applied known technology to the whole of their production process they could reduce manpower levels within the production function by 93 per cent. What is the chance of that coming about? The answer is almost certainly none. This is especially true in a climate of unemployment and recession. There are social constraints which will influence decision making of this sort. The problem of accurately forecasting future manpower levels has increased yet again. Not only do we have to forecast the direction in which the business might change, and the productivity levels that will be achieved over the forecast period, but we also have to assess the social constraints that apply to the organization that might modify its business plans.

Finally, let us bring in one of the points that was made at the beginning of Chapter 1. Any forecast of the future, no matter how well it interprets business change, productivity levels, or social constraints, will be subject to the chance and uncertainty of the modern world. There are very few organizations that are not affected in some respect by the recessions or booms that take place in world economy.

Having reinforced, perhaps to the point of appearing somewhat paranoid, the difficulty of attempting to forecast future manpower levels, any manpower planner in an organization will nevertheless have to make the attempt. He will be called upon to operate at two levels.

Visualizing manpower/business scenarios

Many of the problems that the manpower planner deals with do not concern the total manpower of the organization but only a part; for example, the number of recruits required by the research function or an estimate of the fall in promotion prospects in production as a result of reduced manpower levels. Here we need to assess the number of people required for each box in the manpower system.

Over the last five years an approach has been developing that is of practical value. The essence of the approach is not to look for precise forecasts but to discover the main changes in the organization that are under consideration and might affect the numbers to be employed in the manpower system. The approach concentrates on looking at changes already being implemented or that are possible over the next few years, and attempts to assess the minimum and maximum impact of the changes on manpower.

Changes in an organization's structure, in its product range or in its technology take considerable time from the point at which the idea is first mooted to their implementation in the organization. A good way to proceed, therefore, is to find out all the things that the organization has underway and additionally is considering doing, because these will be the changes that will be implemented within the next five years. If something is not currently under consideration, then the chances of it being implemented within the next five years are extremely remote.

The success of the approach depends on bringing together decisions that have been taken and changes that are under active consideration and estimating what the effect on the manpower system will be, by looking at each of the boxes of the career structure in turn. This approach is difficult to visualize conceptually, but becomes much clearer when an example is followed through.

THE CLAY BRICK COMPANY

This case study concerns a medium- to small-sized organization producing high-quality facing bricks for the building industry. It was a highly successful organization that had grown over a number of years. Not only did it have plants all over the United Kingdom but had taken over companies in Europe, particularly in Belgium and Holland, and recently had acquired a company in the United States. Its ability to expand its market share and acquire other companies was based on the very high quality of its products which in turn was due to its policy of employing good quality technologists and future production managers. Its policy, as can be seen from the company manpower system (Fig. 4.2), was to have a mixed career development policy. A number of its engineers and production managers came from its technology stream but a significant proportion were externally recruited.

The most important factor to be taken into account in determining how many technicians and technologists the company should recruit, is the level of business and size of the company expected in the future. Prior to this case study, an IMS adviser would attempt to get two broad estimates of the expected increase or decrease in staff over the next few years. Managers would be pressed to give a subjective assessment of the maximum rate of increase or the minimum rate

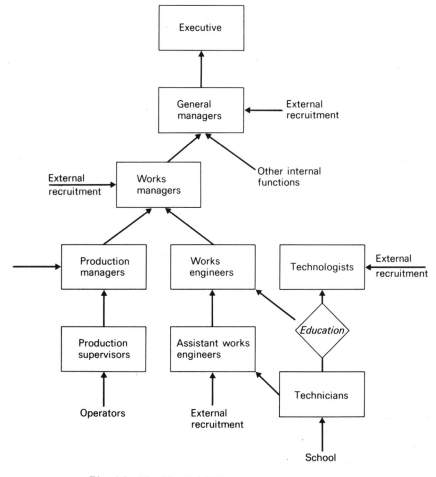

Fig. 4.2. The Clay Brick Company – manpower system

of decrease in numbers to be employed. Similarly he would press for a subjective assessment of the minimum rate of expansion or maximum rate of decrease that could be expected.

In this case, the personnel manager was not prepared to give overall subjective estimates of the change in the numbers to be employed. He felt that there were far too many factors for an assessment to be made. Equally, suggestions made by the adviser were turned down. It looked as if there could be no further progress on the problem of assessing technician recruitment levels, since this piece of information was so crucial. Since the difficulty appeared to be bringing together all the factors that affect future numbers to be employed, it was decided to examine these one by one, and attempt to assess their impact on future numbers and, finally, having considered all the factors, to bring them together in an overall conclusion. It was felt that this could most easily be done by examining the current concerns of the senior executives and attempting to evaluate the impact on numbers by considering in turn each box in Fig. 4.2.

There was first a short discussion to gather together the concerns of senior management. Currently under consideration were decisions about the opening of new brick works on completely new sites. The company was wondering whether to expand its production capacity by acquiring other organizations in its field of business. The success of the company in the past had built up its cash reserves and the senior managers were concerned that this cash should be put to the best use. Should they diversify out of bricks and into ceramics as well? What could they do about the high rate of technological change that was beginning to affect the brick industry. The new company it had acquired in the USA, while managerially extremely effective, was technically very much inferior to the parent company and the transfer of technologists to the American company was under active review.

It was decided to consider first those issues which would have a minimum effect on the numbers to be employed in the career structure, and those that were easiest to implement, gradually working up to the more unlikely issues and those with a much greater impact on the numbers employed.

The no-change situation   What is likely to happen to the numbers employed in the career structure if the company does not implement any major changes and carries on producing from its existing resources with its existing technology? Is this likely to affect the number of general managers required or the number of works managers? Hardly, the number of general managers is a function of the organization's philosophy, while the number of works managers is a function of the number of works that the company has. In practice, increasing business from existing resources utilizing spare capacity is unlikely to create management jobs, but if the company's spare capacity were to increase as a result of a decline in the market, there could be pressure to reduce management jobs to cut expenses. In this particular case the company is anticipating a steady and unspectacular growth in its share of the market over the next five years and the consensus view is that the numbers employed in the career structure would not change for this reason.

Increasing production capacity   Increasing production capacity by buying new equipment for existing plants, building a new plant, or even building a complete new site are ways that the existing capacity can be increased. Each of these will have a different level of impact on the numbers to be employed in the career structure and again it was decided to look at them in order of increasing impact on numbers employed. Increasing capacity by buying additional equipment would prove to have little effect on the manpower levels. Supposing that the restriction on present capacity was the equipment used to take away the bricks once they had been produced; the company decided to buy additional fork-lift trucks to do this. The maximum impact on this management structure will probably be limited to a slight increase in the number of supervisors required. It is highly unlikely to increase the works managers, works engineers, and so on.

If the company decided to build a completely new plant on one of its existing sites, the impact on the career structure would be greater. Depending on the size of the plant to be constructed, there might have to be an increase in the technologists, the production supervisors, the engineering strength at the assistant works engineer level, and certainly a production manager to be responsible for the new plant. A case for increasing the number of works managers could be made if the number of existing plants was at the limit that the current works managers could control. Consequently, the management structure might be reorganized and an additional works manager needed. Only subjective judgement can be used to assess that requirement.

Expanding existing capacity by adding a completely new site, implying that more than one plant is to be constructed, will have an even bigger impact on the numbers to be employed. Since each site requires a works manager, and each plant on the site will require its complement of managers, engineers, technologists, etc., large additions to numbers of employees will be necessary. Again, it is unlikely to affect the number of general managers unless the company feels the demands on general management will be so increased that it would be better to reorganize and increase the number of general managers. Perhaps it might decide to reorganize the company into northern and southern users and appoint a general manager to head each area.

Experience shows that assessing the impact on numbers of changes in capacity is relatively easy. Once the organization is able to say whether the increase will come from new equipment, a new plant, or a new site, valid comparisons with its existing levels of employment can be made.

It is not so much a question of how many people the new plant will employ that causes the uncertainty. That estimate can be made with a reasonable degree of accuracy. The uncertainty arises from the difficulty of forecasting whether the new plant can be built or not.

A similar pattern of reasoning can be followed when considering decreases in existing capacity, i.e., the closing down of equipment, the closing of plant, or even the closing of sites.

Acquisition/divestment There are a number of issues to be considered when attempting to assess the effect of acquisition or divestment on numbers employed. On acquiring a new organization will the company replace the whole of the acquired staff with its own staff? Will the staff who have been taken over with the new company wish to stay?

In considering this problem it was easy for the manager of the company with whom the adviser was working to make very clear distinctions. No, the company did not have an automatic policy of replacing all the staff taken over. In previous acquisitions, if it felt that the management of the organization was good, it would simply install its own general manager. The impact on numbers of acquiring organization A or B or C would be done in this way, affecting only the general manager level. On the other hand, if organization D or E were acquired, where the management was extremely bad, considerable numbers of managers from the existing organization would have to be moved in to make the company viable. In companies F and G, if they were taken over, the problem would be different in that the total management of those companies would probably resign since they were family companies and the effect on numbers would be considerable.

The lesson is clear. The difficult problem of assessing the effect on numbers of acquisition or divestment is considerably eased by breaking it down into practical situations. Managers can then use their judgement and make reasonable assessments.

In general, one of the motivations for acquisition is the opportunity it provides to economize on overheads and, therefore, unless the previous management is totally unsatisfactory, or if the organization is a family-run business, it is unlikely that a significant increase in the numbers employed will result from acquisitions. The number of managers required could increase temporarily during the period of assimilation that follows the acquisition, but that effect tends to be short lived.

The impact of divestment on numbers can be considered by a similar process. Is the company planning to sell the current staff along with the company? In other words, does the organization that is buying the company want the current staff, or is it planning to utilize those current staff in other parts of its business? It may decide to divest itself of one business in order to make space for it to move into another area. In doing so, it may wish to retain the current staff for the new venture.

The key to assessing the impact on future numbers to be employed is to ask these specific questions. A company's acquisitions or diversifications take a long time to plan and implement. Unless it is an extremely large organization, the act of acquisition or divestment will use up considerable management resources and the number of times it can do this in a five-year period will be strictly limited. Questioning managers to assess the actual impact on numbers employed should use the technique of maximums and minimums. The maximum case could represent the takeover or acquisition of a company that was a family-type business in which the whole of the management pulled out and would have to be replaced from the acquiring company's own management structure. The minimum situation might be found where the company took over an organization with a very sound management structure and only replaced the general manager.

Diversification Diversification, as its name implies, is the acquisition of a company in a field of business other than the parent company's. The effect on numbers employed tends to be considerable when an organization diversifies. Even when diversifying into a closely related field, in this company probably from brick making into ceramics, it will be short of the expertise used in the new business and will retain the existing management of the new business initially, therefore limiting the immediate effect on its own management career structure. In the long run, however, alternative career paths are open to the managers of the organization and managers in the acquired organization. Again, diversification will absorb the effort of a large number of managers in the parent company and the number of times that this can be done during the five-year planning horizon will be small.

Technological change The impact of technological change on the numbers to be employed in a career structure is very varied. Take the case of the technologies employed in the company. If the change in technology is such as to make redundant the company's existing technology, then it may find that its demand for technologists reduces very rapidly indeed. The current classic example is that of organizations that manufactured control systems in the 1950s, which were based on electromechanical methods of operation, relays with circuit-breakers, etc. The move into electronic systems of control has demanded knowledge of new technologies. In many cases it was possible to retrain existing technologists but inevitably there will be a strong demand for an increase in the numbers of electronics people and a sharp reduction in demand for people with an electromechanical control system background. The chances are that this type of technological change would only affect the professional, the supervisory and first line management groups, since detailed knowledge of the technology will not be required among the middle and senior managers.

The impact of a change in technology on the numbers to be employed in the

109

other career structures of the company will be insignificant unless the change in technology allows such a significant improvement in productivity that it is possible to restructure the organization and close down some of the production units.

In the case of this brick company, the limitation in the past on the size of the production unit was the physical problem of baking the bricks to an even quality. Since it was making facing bricks, quality levels were of supreme importance and to get the even heating that gave good quality bricks, the company used a small-sized kiln. Control systems had developed over the years and improved the control of the heating zone within the kiln. It was now possible to double the width of a kiln and thus make a big increase in its volumetric capacity, without affecting the quality of the bricks. In its future production plans the company postulated the possibility of opening a brand new plant with all the new technology employed, using a very large-sized kiln, on its biggest deposit of clay.

Two production scenarios resulted. If the market continued to expand, the company could open the site and leave its existing production sites operating with a steady increase in production from the new site to meet the market expansion. In this case the numbers to be employed in the career structure would be considerable. At least from works manager down there would be an increase in numbers. Whether additional general managers were required would depend on how the new works was integrated into the company's total structure. If a new regional grouping was formed as a result of opening the new site, then additional general managers would be required.

If the market did not expand, then the company would open the new site and close down two of its smaller and less efficient works. This would mean a reduction in numbers to be employed in the career structure, again from works manager downwards, and possibly there might be some regrouping regionally which could reduce the number of general managers required.

Behavioural factors Over the last 15 years, close attention has been paid by organizations to the number of managers employed. A considerable amount of work has been done by behavioural scientists to determine the conditions under which managers perform best. The optimum length of lines of communication has been studied and spans of control of subordinates have been researched. Since an important part of the career structure is the management levels within it, there may be changes in the numbers to be employed in future for these behavioural reasons. As an organization grows, the career structure tends to grow from the bottom, the number of professional staff is increased until the supervisor finds that he is dealing with too many professional staff and additional supervisors are created. This addition carries on up the management chain. It is difficult sometimes to determine at which point this will happen, but allowance should be made in an expanding career structure for this effect. Not only the number of people to be employed in each box must be looked at, but also from time to time the organization may question the number of levels that it has established. It may decide that an alternative to adding more supervisors to a manager is to create an intermediate level between supervisor and manager, an assistant manager for instance. Unfortunately, this type of change can take place quite quickly from the idea to its implementation in terms of change in the organization. It will not be so easy to predict over a five-year period and possibly all that can be done, using the approach of questioning current preoccupations of management with regard to the career structure, is to look at the next two years.

The approach just described tends to establish the number of people to be employed over the next five to ten years by asking a series of questions about aspects of the company's future plans. It relies on the fact that a lot of the

		Production						Technical		
		GM	WM	WE	PM	AWE	SUPV	PE	FT	OT
M	**UK**									
I	Internal expansion	0	0	0	1	1	3		0	
N	Acquisition	0	1	0	0	0	0		0	
I	Technical change	−1	−1	−1	−1	0	−5		−2	
M	Diversification	0	2	0	0	0	0		0	
U	**Rest of World**									
M	USA	0	0	0	0	0	0		0	
E	Holland	0	0	0	0	0	0		1	
F	Belgium	0	0	0	0	0	0		1	
F	Selling expertise	0	0	0	0	0	0		1	
E	TOTAL	−1	2	−1	0	1	−2		0	
C										
T										
M	**UK**									
A	Internal expansion	1	1	1	3	2	13		1	
X	Acquisition				−10	unspecified mostly plant				
I	Technical change	−1	−1	−1	−1	0	−5		−2	
M	Diversification	0	0	21	18	unspecified mostly plant				
U	**Rest of World**									
M	USA	0	8	0	0	0	0	1	2	1
E	Holland	0	0	0	0	0	0		0	
F	Belgium	0	2	0	1	0	0		2	
F	Selling expertise	0	0	0	2	0	0		2	
E	TOTAL	0	10	0	5	2	8	1	7	1
C										
T										

GM: general managers; WM: works managers; WE: works engineers; PM: production managers; AWE: assistant works engineers; SUPV: supervisors; PE: productivity engineers; FT: fuel technologists; OT: other technologists.

Fig. 4.3. The Clay Brick Company – business scenarios showing different manpower needs

influences on numbers to be employed are the result of changes of an organization's technology and production capacity that take a long time from the idea being thought of to its implementation. By looking at decisions that the company has taken over the last couple of years and looking at the decisions that are currently occupying the minds of the senior executives, it is possible to track down possible changes in numbers. By examining each box in turn and questioning how this particular change will affect this particular box and using the technique of minimum and maximum answers, it is possible to arrive at a table that describes how numbers in the career structure might change in the future (see Fig. 4.3).

Techniques for quantifying manpower levels

In the previous example the main aim was to help the manager understand the relationship between manpower levels and the different business situations that could be encountered by the organization in the near future. All the manpower levels resulted from subjective assessment and the organization may decide that the level of accuracy needs to be improved before the manpower policy decisions, which are consequent on fixing manpower levels, can be assessed, i.e., recruitment levels, the number of managers with potential who need training and development. Techniques exist which can be used to improve the level of accuracy.

WORK MEASUREMENT

The most direct way to assess manpower requirements is to measure the amount of manpower that is required to perform the activity. There are three broad sets of work measurement techniques in use.

Time study   The most well known, some would say notorious, is the technique known as time study. A trained observer breaks down the job to be measured into small component parts and observes a number of workers performing the tasks, an allowance is made for the speed with which different workers work, in order to arrive at a standard time, to which is added an allowance that recognizes the degree of physical effort required for the job and allows an additional time for relaxation or recuperation. Time study is very costly, involving the observer repeating his observations a number of times. Although the concept of rating is used and although work study observers are trained to detect the different rates at which people work, there can be high variations between observers in the times that they finally arrive at for the job. Of course, the time value that is arrived at is only good for the job method that was observed, and for the tools and techniques used in the performance of the job. If these change radically, then the time is no longer appropriate.

A particular problem is encountered when measurement is used as the basis of an incentive payment scheme. It is in the interests of those who are receiving the incentive payment to obtain a bigger time than is necessary at the outset, by building into the working method unnecessary activities which, once the job has been timed, are not performed. If the job has been correctly timed in the first place, strong incentives are created to find unofficially better ways or short cuts to the job method in order to reduce the time taken to do the job. This does not always show itself in very high bonus payments, since workers often use the slackness that has been created in the times to spread the work out over the shift, working at only a moderate level and yet getting a high bonus payment.

One work study observer had timed a job of filling sacks with a powder in a warehouse, and had observed over a number of months a very steady level of performance from the men in the warehouse of about 60 bags per shift. He was astonished one day to find that the work record sheet showed that one operator claimed to have done 150 bags. The observer was currently conducting a running battle with the warehouse on the subject of over-claiming of output for bonus purposes. Down he went to investigate, only to find that the men had anticipated that he would be questioning the level and the 150 bags that had been claimed were there for him to inspect. It seemed that the team of men who had worked in the warehouse had had a severe disagreement and one of their number had been so upset at this disagreement that he had decided to leave, but in a resentful mood he decided to pay back his colleagues and this he did by showing that it was possible to fill 150 bags during a shift's work.

The observer, to his chagrin, found that when he had timed the job the men had convinced him that they were using the largest possible scoop to transfer the powder from the drums into the bags. He found that they had a much larger scoop constructed privately in the engineering workshop which filled the bags in approximately half the time. Needless to say, the job was retimed using the larger scoop. Job times established by time study usually become obsolete within one to two years of their being set, and unless the organization is very efficient, the chances are that the jobs will not be retimed straight away.

The costliness of work measurement by time study can be reduced by producing standard data. Jobs which are repetitive or jobs which are themselves made up from very common activities can be measured by the use of data. In most cases a number of different observers will time the same jobs over and over again until they are satisfied that they have reached a good value for the jobs. These will then be written down as standard data. In order for anyone else then to arrive at a time for a new job, it is unnecessary to go out physically and time the job, all that one requires is the job method. The work study man can then sit down with the job method and a book of standard times and construct a time for the job without actually seeing it in operation. In the chemical works all work measurement of fork-lift truck activities was done by using standard data. The data had been built up some years before and the elements in operating a fork-lift had been broken down into a time for running forward per yard, the time taken to move the truck and insert the fork into a pallet, and the time taken to lift the pallet up a number of feet, etc. All the activities of fork-lift work existed as standard data. To construct a particular time all that had to be done was to measure the distance that the fork-lift truck would have to cover in yards and simulate the motion pattern that would have to be followed, and the time could then be constructed from the standard data. It is, of course, totally unprofitable to produce standard data for activities or elements of jobs that might change substantially.

Activity sampling   This is an attempt to get over the costliness of the time study by a completely different approach. Instead of observing a job in detail from start to finish, the observer spends time finding out from a group of workers the activities that are involved in their jobs. If we were considering warehousemen, the activities could be filling bags, loading and unloading lorries, recording stock sheets, issuing goods to people in the factory, and so on.

Having established the main activities, the observer would walk through the warehouse at irregular intervals noting down which of the activities the worker is working on at that instant. This sampling of activities is continued until the observer feels that it has gone on long enough to ensure that a representative sample of the activities is achieved. He then counts up the frequency with which each activity has been recorded and expresses that as a percentage of the total number of observations. It is possible, too, to get a statistical sampling error on the figures and, therefore, quote that the percentage of time occupied by this activity is, say, 25 per cent of the working week plus or minus 3 per cent. The main problem in using activity sampling, of course, is in determining when a representative sample has been arrived at. It nevertheless offers a quick and cheap way of covering many activities and many operators, and has been used to produce standard data. Indeed, many of the clerical work measurement standard data in existence today were developed using the activity sampling technique.

Synthetic measurement   The basic motion patterns of a human body appear to be performed at a very constant speed. The time taken for one individual to grasp an object is very similar to the time taken by any other individual to grasp the same object. Work measurement experts found that by filming the motion pattern, using high speed photography, it was possible to calculate these time values. From this, data have been produced that represent the time taken for the basic motion patterns of the body. By reducing the activity down to a set of motion patterns and applying the data, it is possible to calculate a very accurate time for that job.

Two main systems were developed, one was used extensively in ICI called PMTS (Pre-determined Motion Timed Systems) and one developed by the

114

Maynard consultants called MTM (Motion Time Measurement). Since the activity is broken down into basic human motion, it takes a long time to calculate the time for a job. This form of work measurement is only really suitable for very highly repetitive jobs, such as are usually found on assembly lines.

Some organizations, using a combination of all three forms of measurement, have built up a set of manning data for their organization. The main activities of a plant or warehouse are measured and are related to the throughput of the plant or the amount of goods held for dispatch or issued from the warehouse. To arrive at the manning levels for any particular output then becomes quite easy. The output levels are specified and, by looking through the standard data, are used to calculate the manning levels required. The problem here is that the standard data have to be built up into very big blocks and these contain many assumptions about the pattern of production. If the standard pattern is departed from in any way then the manning level arrived at could be quite inaccurate. Hence the problem mentioned at the beginning of this section that, although the objectives might be well specified in terms of the total output required, it is often equally necessary to know the main assumptions as to how the objectives should be reached, before an accurate assessment of manpower levels can be obtained.

To sum up, assessing future manning levels using work measurement techniques is a very worthwhile exercise for repetitive jobs which have a high degree of manual content, and where the job methods do not change frequently. Additionally, to link the measurement to the future business level there needs to be a strong relationship between the levels of production and the activity of the group of manpower to be estimated. For instance, the work of the personnel function will be more related to the number of sites and the number of employees. So although we might be able to measure the work of the personnel function accurately it would still be difficult to forecast it using prospective levels of business.

STATISTICAL ANALYSIS

If it is not possible to measure directly the work content of a job it may be possible to estimate the manpower from some other parameter.

Perhaps there is a direct relationship between the number of tons produced and the manpower levels required. The organization finds it impossible to measure this relationship, but by looking back over a number of years, it finds that when the average output levels were x, the number of man-hours it used over the period was y. In another period it found that the output level was a and the number of man-hours used was b. Using statistics in this way it is possible to build a relationship (Fig. 4.4), a statistical relationship, not a measured one, between output levels and manpower. If, therefore, one can specify the output

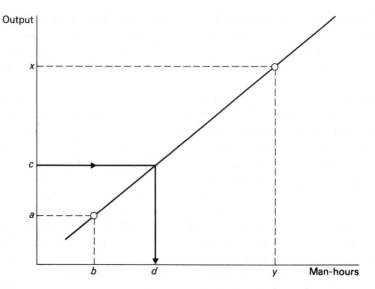

Fig. 4.4. Using regression techniques to estimate manpower/business relationships

levels, i.e., *c*, the manning implications *d* can be assessed. In this case we are using the statistical techniques of correlation and regression to help in the estimation of manpower requirements.

The manpower planner, however, should beware of spurious correlations, where a good statistical relationship between two factors appears to exist but it is a nonsense relationship. It is possible to correlate the number of lunatics committed to mental asylums between the two world wars in the United Kingdom with the number of BBC radio licences issued to the general public. Calculating the statistical correlation between the two gives an extremely high rate of correlation and it would lead you to the view that the broadcasting of BBC programmes was increasing the amount of madness in the population. While a few people might argue that there was a causal relationship between the two, the general view was that the statistical correlation of such a high level is only caused because we have two time series which were both increasing at the same time. Anyone who is using regression must have a good reason for believing that the two time series being measured are causally related to each other.

The statistical analysis of time series can also be used to estimate manpower requirements, rather than simply calculating correlation and regression coefficients. If we look at the next series of graphs, we can see that they depict the way that the manpower of an organization is changing. Figure 4.5 shows that the percentage of skilled craftsmen in the labour force was steadily increasing between 1964 and 1971. In estimating craftsmen levels for the

116

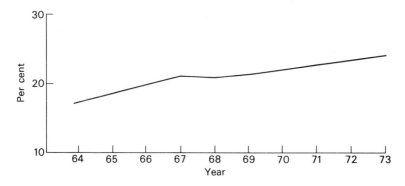

Fig. 4.5. Changing manpower proportions – 1. Skilled engineering workers

future, this trend can be extrapolated to suggest that in three years' time the percentage of skilled craftsmen will be 25 per cent.

The graph (Fig. 4.6) depicting the changes in the proportion of the workforce that are semi-skilled is an interesting one. As can be seen, only a very small proportion are semi-skilled and the level seemed to be decreasing rapidly until about 1967, at which point the relationship changed. From 1968 onwards, the percentage of semi-skilled craftsmen increases quite sharply. This is the result of a productivity deal which negotiated transfer of the less skilled craftsmen's work to the semi-skilled employees. This graph shows all too clearly one of the

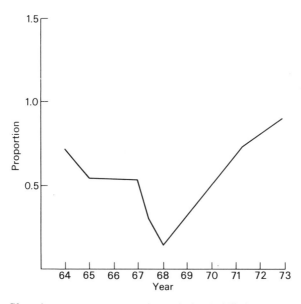

Fig. 4.6. Changing manpower proportions – 2. Semi-skilled engineering workers

117

problems of estimating using time series. We are never sure when a major change in a relationship is going to occur.

Of the two remaining graphs, Fig. 4.7 shows the changes in the percentage of unskilled engineering workers in the organization. The fall that can be seen in the early part of the graph is the result of determined effort by management to reduce the number of unskilled engineers and labourers by increasing the mechanical handling aids given to the engineering labourers to help them in

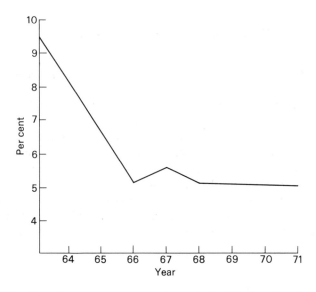

Fig. 4.7. Changing manpower proportions – 3. Unskilled engineering workers

their work. Eventually, the trade union became very concerned that the traditional ratio of one mate for every two craftsmen was being eroded and objected. The resulting negotiation about the level of mates to be used ended with re-establishing a fixed ratio of labourers to craftsmen as can be seen from the flattening out of the graph after 1968.

The final graph, Fig. 4.8, shows that the percentage of process workers in the organization was also increasing. That seemed a little surprising as this was a period when plants were becoming much more automated and the number of process workers was declining. In fact, the number was decreasing, but another group in the organization was declining even faster. The unskilled workers in non-engineering functions, the plant cleaners, etc., were being automated out of existence during this period. Instead of having teams of men to brush and sweep the plant, small ride-on, power-operated sweepers were purchased. Instead of men filling bags by hand in the warehouse, a completely automated line that took the product in hoppers at one end and produced bags in crates, fully sealed at the other, was installed.

118

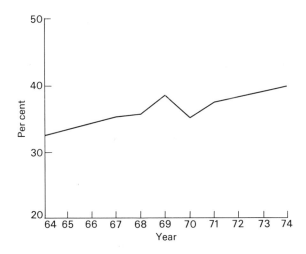

Fig. 4.8. Changing manpower proportions – 4. Process workers

Statistical time series like these examples, can be very useful in looking at the change in the composition of the labour force and, therefore, when estimating manpower resources needed to meet the business objectives, the changing composition should also be reflected, as well as the total manpower required.

Other people have tried more sophisticated statistical methods to relate manpower and output levels. Among these are input/output analysis, and the Box/Jenkins method of analysis

No matter what form of statistical analysis is used, it must be borne in mind that they all depend on one basic assumption, and that is that the pattern that has been calculated statistically from past data will still be appropriate in the future. This is not always the case and when such changes occur the statistical estimates can be quite wrong. Secondly, a statistical estimation needs a long historical base of data. If an organization's manpower is frequently changing by reorganization there will be problems getting sufficient data to calculate reliable statistical measures.

ESTIMATION

The Army has a saying 'if it moves salute it, if it doesn't move, whitewash it'. Manpower planners could have a slogan 'if you can't measure it, use statistical analysis and if you can't analyse it statistically, have a good guess'. No matter how much we might disguise it by suitable chosen words, estimation, like guesswork, is subjective assessment. One manpower planning department has an excellent title, for their estimates, 'Professionally Estimated Yardsticks'. Joking apart, the idea of 'professionally estimated' is a useful one in that it represents that the estimation tends to be more accurate when done by somebody who has professional knowledge of the jobs since there will be greater understanding of the difficulties and context that surrounds them. Attempts have been made to improve estimation using the techniques of analytical estimation, comparative estimation, and estimation from norms outlined below.

Analytical estimating   This is a technique which is used mainly by organizations operating incentive bonus schemes, to measure the work of craftsmen. In general, the craftsmen's trade unions have not allowed the use of the stopwatch in measuring craftsmen's jobs. They have agreed to the system of analytical estimating by which somebody who has been a craftsman in the past breaks down the job to be estimated into its component parts, and subjectively assesses how long it will take to perform that element of the activity. The hope is that by breaking the job down into small parts, the errors in estimation would tend to cancel each other out and that by estimating on a small part, greater accuracy is likely. The process is still quite time consuming and costly from the point of view of manpower, since highly skilled people are used as estimators and the job is broken down into quite fine detail.

Comparative estimating   Unlike analytical estimating, whereby each job that the craftsman does is separately analysed and each element is estimated, comparative estimating only does this for a certain number of jobs which have been selected to act as benchmarks. These jobs are estimated in detail using analytical estimating techniques. All other jobs to be estimated are compared with the benchmarked jobs and a time is given based on the relationship of the job under review to benchmarks either side of it.

   Take, for example, a workshop making wooden furniture. We might take a simple shelf as one of the lowest benchmarks and accurately calculate how long it would take a fully trained craftsman to produce a simple shelf of a specified length, width, and thickness. We would progress upwards in complexity and establish the making of a wooden stool as the next benchmark. This could be followed by a chair with a straight backrest and no arms, through bowbacked chairs to tables and on to sideboards and cupboards. In each case, the time taken for the fully trained craftsman to make the piece would be estimated. When we have a coffee table to produce, which is not one of the benchmarks, we try to assess in our minds the task of making that coffee table compared, say, with our benchmarks of a draw-leafed table at one end and perhaps a dining chair at the other. If the dining chair were estimated at 15 hours of work and the draw-leafed table at 35 hours of work, we might decide that the coffee table's production is nearer to the chair than the table and estimate 22 hours' work for the coffee table. Obviously, comparative estimating is much cheaper but there is a further loss of accuracy.

120

Estimating using norms   At its simplest level, estimating is the production of norms, or standard guesses. These are estimates of practice which gradually build up over the years and are codified into a body of norms or standards. The manning of the Health Service has traditionally been based on norms that have been established over the years.

The experienced finger in the air is not the last resort that it should be for many organizations, but the main tool of analysis for forecasting the demand for manpower.

Work measurement, statistical analysis, or estimation, all of them have their uses in attempting to assess manpower requirements and all of them leave much to be desired and, therefore, the degree of precision by which manpower resources can be assessed will be limited.

Building manpower levels into corporate plans

The organization has to take broad decisions about its future direction. In other words it has to plan its corporate future. Manpower is a very important element of corporate decision making and cannot be left out of the reckoning. In assessing the corporate future, the organization will wish to know what the business projection will require in the way of manpower over the period of the

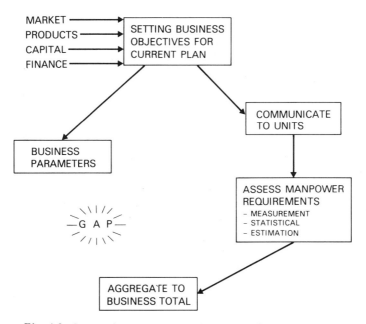

Fig. 4.9. Integrating manpower and corporate plans – the process

forecast. The manpower planner, whether he is at the corporate headquarters of the organization or at one of its divisional centres or on one of its units, will have to attempt to forecast future manpower levels on this broad basis (see Fig. 4.9).

The model around which the problems of assessing manpower requirement at the organizational level will be discussed is an organization in one basic business, manufacturing a number of products, selling in the United Kingdom and Europe, and manufacturing over one or two sites in the United Kingdom. The process by which an organization derives an estimate of the future numbers to be employed, will be followed and critically examined in detail, but it is represented diagrammatically in Fig. 4.9.

THE BUSINESS FORECAST

Circumstances occasionally occur in which the only sensible way to start the process of forecasting the organization's corporate strategy is to forecast the manpower levels to be expected first, and then to calculate what level of business can be achieved. For this case to be real, the company is likely to be making a product which no one else produces, which requires very specialized manpower, and which cannot easily be trained. A much more likely situation is that the company will need to calculate, as best it can, the level of business that it anticipates before it begins to assess the resources, manpower included, that are needed to sustain that level of business.

Many organizations have attempted to improve the process by which the corporate planning forecast is made in an attempt to improve its accuracy. Bringing together people from different functions into a common group whose responsibility it is continuously to monitor and forecast the changes in the business, is looked upon favourably by any organization. Such groups will comprise a senior executive as chairman, together with managers representing production, research and development, marketing, finance, and possibly construction activities in the organization. Each of these will have specialist knowledge of an aspect that will govern the future business and it is from a discussion between these people, all in-putting their specialist knowledge, that a better view of the corporate future is obtained. It is interesting to observe that there is often no personnel or manpower input into these discussions.

Let us eavesdrop on a typical meeting of such a group as it starts the process of producing the organization's corporate plan for the current year. This organization's business year begins on January 1 and it has become practice for the process of corporate planning to start as soon as the managers return from their summer vacation.

The business of the first meeting is to consider a paper produced by the marketing department forecasting the product sales in the different markets this year and for the next three years. The marketing manager leads off and has not got beyond an opening statement, saying that the anticipated sales of wellington boots are anticipated to reach 150 000 pairs, when there is an exasperated snort followed by a derisory laugh from the manufacturing manager who says that it is impossible as the total plant capacity, if everything went well and over 90 per cent occupation of the plant was achieved, is only 125 000 pairs. So the marketing manager had better go away and revise his forecast to take account of what the manufacturing department can produce.

The marketing manager is rescued from his discomfiture by the interjection of the construction engineer, 'Don't forget' he says 'the new micro-processor control on the injection moulding machine is going to improve the quality to such an extent that the yield will increase substantially and we won't be all that far from 150 000 pairs if all goes well'.

At this point in the discussion there is a mild statement from the research and development senior chemist that perhaps marketing should not be encouraging the sale of the current model of wellington boot. The present complaint from customers of excessive foot odour after wearing them for half an hour has been cured, but there will have to be a design change and the new product has just finished its trials, there has been a significant improvement in the odour and it is the opinion of the chemists that production could start by 1 January. Should they not be beginning to campaign in the market stressing the advantages of the new boot. The accountant, who has been silent so far, now interposes his opinion. He remarks that the cost of the raw materials of the current wellington boot has been rising rather rapidly, what with the rise in the oil price pushing up the cost of the plastic composition that is used. In addition, increased competition has been holding down sales prices and he has calculated that only a 2 per cent return is being made on the capital investment. He would like to see the resources moved into the new line of producing sou'westers for garden gnomes.

The group agreed that all these bits of information really required them to go away and reassess the position and to return and meet again in one week's time. Parody, yes. Over-exaggeration, yes, but underneath is the truth that the decisions about the future of an organization do involve similar circular discussions. Each of the functions and activities has to put in its knowledge which has to be considered in the light of each of the other functions' perspectives. It seems to take an age for the plan for the future to be founded. In fact, in many organizations what really happens is that this circular discussion continues on and on until there is really no time left for any more discussion because time has run out, the plan has to be with the chairman in two weeks. The plan that is produced is not an agreed objective but the latest position reached in the discussions. As such, it is a compromise and already the seeds of future disagreement have been built into it. Each function or activity will view how the objective fits in its perspective. Nevertheless, at this point, having set out what is believed to be a corporate view of the future it must be communicated through the organization down to the units of manufacturing, research and development, etc., for the manager of those units to begin to assess the resources that are needed to fulfil and meet the objectives.

Before we follow this process further and consider in detail how manpower resources can be assessed against a level of objectives in a corporate plan, it is appropriate to consider what role the manpower planner can have. He should consider at this point the magnitude of the relationship between an error in the business forecast and its corresponding impact on manpower numbers. An organization can be highly geared, in other words, a small change in business levels might generate a large change in manpower. Conversely, there could be very low gearing and a very large change in business levels can be achieved by a very small increase in manpower levels. Having been badly wrong earlier in assessing the manpower numbers required, as an exercise it was decided to look back at the accuracy of the market forecasts. Some very interesting points emerged from comparing the forecasts made for product sales for each of the target years one, two, three years ahead with what was actually achieved. Fortunately the company had an excellent set of historical records and it was possible to look back over a 20-year period to do this.

First of all, all the prices were converted back to a common base, removing the inflationary element from them. Then it was possible to see that in about two-thirds of all the forecasts, the error was within plus or minus £4 million. The average sales turnover was about £96 million over that period and so the forecast error was plus or minus 5 per cent in two-thirds of the years. There were larger errors in other years but, nevertheless, plus or minus 5 per cent was felt to be an extremely good level of accuracy.

Next an attempt was made to assess the manpower content of the error. Over that same period manpower costs as a percentage of total sales revenue were about 25 per cent. It could be said, therefore, that the error of the sales forecast in terms of manpower was plus or minus £1 million, i.e., one-quarter of the £4 million error. Divide that figure by the average wage and salary over that period and we get an estimate of the sales forecast error in terms of numbers of people. Doing this revealed that the error could be equivalent to plus or minus 960 people. Whereas a plus or minus 5 per cent error in forecasting the market might seem to be accurate, when translated back into manpower terms it reveals the impossible task of moving the organization's manpower up or down by 960 people in a year.

Obviously this is a very crude statistic and cannot be used for forecasting purposes, but it does get across the idea that manpower must be considered on a longer time base than one year in this organization given its relationship between wages costs and sales revenue. In other organizations the problem will not be as acute but in some it will be much more acute.

One interesting facet of this investigation was that it revealed the possibility of forecasting the direction of the error. The organization's business moved

124

with the trade cycles over a period of four to five years. If a forecast was made in a good year at the top of a boom, it tended to be highly optimistic. Conversely, when forecasts were made at the bottom of a depression, in almost every case they were pessimistic. It seems that the salesmen, in forecasting the future, were heavily influenced by the state of the current situation (see Fig. 4.10).

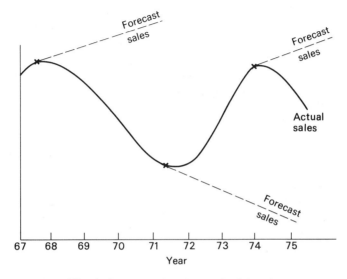

Fig. 4.10. Forecasting in a cyclical situation

ESTIMATING MANPOWER LEVELS AT THE UNIT

A set of objectives defining the organization's business plan for the next few years has been produced and has been communicated down to the unit so that the resources required to meet the objectives can be assessed.

The first problem that has to be faced is the difficulty that organizations have in communicating the objectives to the units well enough for them to be able to assess the resources required. Usually it is not these statements of objectives themselves that cause the problems; they can be quite clear, i.e., 50 tons per week of product x, 200 tons per week of product y, and so on. What are often not spelt out are the main constraints likely to affect managers when they try to achieve the objectives. 'Yes, but I need to know what my feedstock is going to be' said the works manager on looking at his objectives. 'A change in the feedstock has important impact on manpower levels, the commercial department is not yet in a position to tell me what my mix of feedstock is likely to be.'

Let us assume that the expertise needed to fill out the statement of objectives into workable plans is available. The techniques available to management are those already studied; work measurement, statistical analyses and estimation.

125

Our conclusion was that they are useful techniques but with limitations and much must be left to a manager's subjective judgement.

AGGREGATING TO AN ORGANIZATION TOTAL

The last task that remains is to take the individual unit estimates of the manpower required to meet the corporate plan and add them together to get the total manpower likely to be required by the organization to meet the objectives specified in the timescale of the corporate plan. There is little of complexity in this task unless the organization failed to specify the categories by which the units reported manpower needs, then the danger exists that different units will classify manpower in different ways. This will make it difficult to integrate the unit plans together to form a sensible picture of the total manpower required.

THE EFFECTIVENESS OF THE BOTTOM-UP PROCESS

What has been described is the traditional bottom-up forecast of manpower requirements. Over the years, people who practise this approach have found that it tends to overestimate the number of people required. It is worth considering why this is so. It is usually the result of a number of reasons among which the most important are the following.

The integration problem As with all bottom-up forecasting systems, the fact that the forecast is made at the unit level by different people means that forecasts are not integrated. To illustrate the point, let us consider the case of two plants on the same site. The managers of these plants have been asked to assess the manpower requirements for the current plan, defined in terms of output per week. The manager of plant A decides that the forecast increase in output will entail a much heavier workload for the fork-lift truck that brings the raw materials to the plant and takes away the finished product. Currently, he employs one fork-lift truck driver per shift who is fully occupied at the current level of output. At the new level of output, the workload will be increased 50 per cent. Since it is impossible to employ half a man, the manager, in forecasting the resources required to meet the objectives, increases his fork-lift truck manning by one.

In plant B, however, a slightly different situation appertains. Although an increase in output is forecast, the additional workload involved in taking away the raw materials and bringing out the finished products, does not amount to any increase in manpower. Currently plant B has two fork-lift truck drivers per shift, one of whom is under-occupied. The manager of plant B sets a requirement for two fork-lift truck drivers in his submission.

It can be seen that if the two plants are considered together, then the

126

additional capacity on plant B could be used to cope with the increased workload on plant A. This is especially the case if the two plants are close together geographically. Simple, says the head of the unit, integrate the work pattern and use the extra man. The problem is that most of the time has been used to produce the corporate plan and little time is left to consider such issues as whether the units are under pressure to meet the planning timetable. Many cases like this occur and when added together they substantially increase manning levels above those which are necessary. A typical case is that of the work study man who is given half a day to look at the plans produced by the production department for his works to see if he can integrate the plans together a little more and save additional manpower. Little more than a cursory glance can be given in half a day and no substantial savings can be agreed.

Productivity growth This is often the result of many small changes in working practices. We have seen, in looking at the effectiveness of work measurement, that there is a built-in incentive to change methods over time, to make jobs easier. Managers, when forecasting their manpower requirements, all too often simply take the level of productivity that exists currently and use that to estimate the manpower over the forecast. Productivity changes, as have been stated, can be considerable over a three-year period and it would be better if the manager, in forecasting future numbers, took into account the trend in

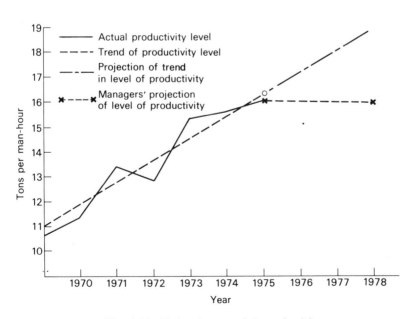

Fig. 4.11. Estimating growth in productivity

productivity and made an attempt to allow for the fact that the forecast in three years' time is much more likely to be showing a higher level of productivity than currently. This, too, will result in an overestimate of the manning being made. Figure 4.11 illustrates what happens.

A chemical company installed some new equipment. When the teething troubles had been resolved, it measured the productivity and found that a level of 1 ton per operator per shift was achieved. A productivity improvement team, consisting of a development engineer, a manufacturing manager, the technical specialist on the process, and a work study engineer, was set up to improve the productivity of the unit. The members worked as a team for a year and made many changes. At the end of the year, productivity was measured again and to their surprise they found that it had increased by 50 per cent to 1.5 tons per operator per shift. There was much head scratching as to what were the main causes of this large increase. They found that they could not attribute it to any one cause, but that they had done many things during the course of the year, each of which had had a little effect.

The engineer had measured the capacity of the vessels, and although they were within the specified design tolerances, in actual fact they were slightly bigger than the average. This slight extra capacity had no effect on the processing time but it enabled the batch size to be increased fractionally. Over the year the fractions added up to an increase in the production level with no change in the manpower.

The main point of re-equipping had been to re-equip the plant with a much bigger sized vessel in which the chemical reaction took place. It was the opinion of the process experts that the increased size would permit a much more efficient physical reaction, and instead of only permitting a 40 per cent mixture to be charged to the vessel, it would be possible to increase the amount, strengthening the mixture and substantially increasing the yield, with no change in the cycle time.

It is an ill wind that blows nobody good, says a proverb, and one evening this was proved to be true. The chemical process took place under vacuum conditions, and just before the shift changed over the vacuum pump failed. The maintenance operator, in hurrying to replace the pump before the end of his shift, fitted the wrong sized pump. It was much more powerful and reduced the vacuum in the chamber very much more quickly. Previously, the opinion was that too quick a reduction of the pressure would cause a loss of quality in the product. On investigation, this was found not to be true. Forthwith, all the remaining units were fitted with the bigger pump and a reduction in the cycle time took place.

The quality of the product had to be high and had to be kept constantly high since, when it was used, minute variations in quality would show very easily. Blending together different batches enabled the company to keep the quality level high and consistent. The blending process was quite time consuming. It involved every batch being segregated in its own container and stored away in the storage bay until the results of the chemical analysis were known. A team of operators would then collect together four batches which together would be within the blend specification when the chemical analyses of the four batches were known. Each of these blends was located, taken to the blender, emptied, and the contents stirred for four hours. The work study engineer in the team was investigating the number of containers required to store the batches and in simulating two weeks' operation of the plant in order to attempt to get the number of containers required, noticed that out of 2000 batches, every batch was not only within the batch quality specification, but also came within the blend specification. The quality control in the plant over the years had been improved to such an extent that the blending process was no longer necessary. It was stopped forthwith.

It is very easy to forget changes of this nature and so underestimate the level of productivity increase. In turn, this leads to an overestimate of manpower requirements.

Technological change   The impact of changes in technology on manpower numbers has until recently been rather slow. Most technological change has required substantial amounts of capital expenditure and, therefore, the timescale in which a new piece of technology can be implemented is necessarily slow. It has been possible, therefore, to anticipate the manpower consequences of technological change and build them in to the forecast. Nevertheless, some changes in technology can have such deep impact on manpower that no matter how slowly they come about they are difficult to deal with. The steel industry, over the years, has suffered particularly from massive changes in technology.

Take a simple example, the traditional way of making steel in the early 1960s was the open-hearth furnace. Three hundred tons of iron were heated for some 48 hours to produce steel. At about that time, or a little earlier, a new process, in which oxygen was blown at high pressure into the iron, reduced the time taken to make 300 tons of iron into steel from 48 hours to 40 minutes, with little change in manpower levels.

The jumbo jet has similarly had an impact on the productivity of airlines. Whereas, in the 1960s, the 707 carrying about 200 passengers was the most efficient way to fly people, the coming of the wide-bodied jet has increased the number that can be carried with the same number of flight crew to about 400. It can be said, however, that it has had a detrimental effect on the productivity of the airport staff. Instead of 1000 passengers arriving in five batches, now two jumbos landing can produce nearly 1000 passengers. This bunching of passengers makes it much more difficult to schedule baggage, customs clearance, and deal with immigration, with consequent increases required in the number of such staff in the airports. Today, technological change has taken a form in which it can be implemented quickly. A word processor, a mini-computer, or an on-line process controller can be installed in a very short space of time with substantial savings in manpower. Now, well within the three years of the traditional corporate planning forecast, such technological changes can come about and be implemented. If such a change takes place then a serious over-estimate in manpower will occur.

Annual budgets   Most managers suffer at the time of the annual budget review. Budget systems that have been in operation for a number of years have become a bit of a guessing game. The manager, in considering his forecast, believes that in previous years whenever he has asked quite genuinely for an increase in resources, his request has been treated in a cavalier fashion and his forecast reduced without justification. He, therefore, begins to overestimate his requirements to anticipate the cut. The manager above him who is responsible for overseeing his budget, notices this overestimate in the manpower numbers and begins to cut the numbers more sharply. The cycle carries on in this way until the 'he thinks that I think that he thinks' situation becomes quite ridiculous. Since most organizations will combine together their annual budget review and their estimates for the corporate plan, when manpower is forecast in this way it becomes heavily subject to this pressure, and consequent over-estimates of manpower numbers occur.

Overheads' functions   There has been a tendency, in describing the process so far, to use the example of the production unit. Even here, where objectives are a little easier to define, there is a serious overestimate of the manpower forecast. When we turn to the overheads departments, such as personnel, finance, management services, we can see that the problem becomes much more acute. How do we specify the objectives of a personnel function from year to year as part of a corporate planning process? All too often, the overheads' departments are left out of consideration and are not referred to directly in the corporate plan. To make matters worse, there is a strong pressure on the overheads' departments from the direct departments, continually to improve their service and give better value for money to the line department. These two pressures result in the manpower forecast from overheads' departments being subject to the ratchet effect. There is a tendency either to stay at the current level or steadily to increase.

It is a commonly held view that when computers were brought into the accounts functions in the late 1950s and early 1960s, that they failed to have the impact on manpower numbers that was anticipated. The general expectation was that the numbers employed in the accounting function would be decimated. Observation shows that this was not the case and too many people have, therefore, said that computers failed to improve productivity on being applied to accounts work. The reality is quite different. A substantial improvement in productivity took place and the large number of book-keepers and ledger

130

clerks that were employed in an organization completely disappeared, but instead of the finance departments reducing their numbers, the opportunity was taken to set up departments dealing with management information or to improve the standard costing system or to rewrite the costing procedures of the organization and the spare manpower was retrained and absorbed.

An organization, in the heyday of its expansionary period, recruited between 80 and 100 graduates every year from universities. Four personnel officers were employed in going round the universities and selecting graduates. A team of secretaries looked after the administrative records of all the applicants and the whole of the management of the personnel function was involved at some stage, because when the shortlisted candidates were brought to the division for final assessment, the senior personnel people were required to entertain them at the senior staff club during the evening. When that organization turned into recession and did not recruit any graduates for two years, the numbers in the personnel function did not change. Instead, those who had recruited the graduates were now used to help the organization to reduce its numbers. One of the personnel officers ran a job shop, a room in which every periodical that advertised jobs was displayed and kept up to date, he liaised with the Department of Employment to ensure that all jobs that might be suitable for the division's people who were surplus to requirements were notified. Another of the personnel officers spent most of his time going round the country seeing the organization's customers in an attempt to place the scientific people surplus to requirements in jobs. It was only some three years later, when the contraction rate had reduced, that the personnel function began to reduce its numbers. This ratchet effect seems to operate in most of the overheads' departments and again leads to an increase in manpower numbers in the forecast.

Current pressures   The final problem that has been noted with the bottom-up forecast is the tendency for the forecast to be strongly affected by the current business situation. An individual manager, on receiving his objectives, disbelieves the planners and their forecasts and unofficially re-forecasts the business situation to match what he believes. In assessing his manpower requirements, therefore, he uses this re-forecast. In this case the error in the manpower forecast can be in either direction.

In most of the problems that have been dealt with, 'the natural error' to coin a phrase in the forecast, is one which will give an overestimate of manpower numbers. Bottom-up forecasts almost invariably do this.

THE TOP-DOWN FORECAST

Manpower planners who had experienced the tendency of the bottom-up forecast to increase manpower numbers began to look at other ways of producing manpower forecasts. The idea of a top-down or a forecasting system based on business parameters began to be tested. The approach that was followed consisted of attempting to find some stable relationship between manpower and the business. Since manpower is one of the main parameters of a business, and although it can be allowed to vary in the short term, there are medium- and long-term constraints on the limit of the variation. Many different business parameters and manpower ratios have been used to do this, e.g.:

– Return of capital (trading profits/capital employed).
– Profit margin (trading profits/sales).
– Sales/capital employed.
– Profits/gross value added.
– Gross value added/capital employed.
– Gross value added/employees.
– Capital employed/employees.
– Gross value added/payroll costs (and payroll costs/gross value added).

It is stressed that the organization must find the particular measures of business performance and manpower performance suited to the situation. There is little to be gained in looking at manpower costs as a proportion of total costs in industries that are capital intensive when manpower costs are down to less than 1 per cent of total costs.

The method consists of finding some stable relationship between manpower and the business. The relationship does not need to be static as long as it is changing in a predictable way.

In this example the organization found that wages and salaries as a percentage of total sales seemed to be a good indicator of manpower performance (see Fig. 4.12).

It can be seen from Fig. 4.12 that wages and salaries changed from around 26 per cent in 1953 to about 20 per cent in 1969. The change was not a smooth one; there were fluctuations around the trend line. These increases and decreases obviously affect the business cycle. In this organization, manpower levels cannot be changed quickly as the business situation changes. In running a chemical plant, when output increases, it is rarely necessary to increase manpower by the same amount. Often it is sufficient simply to increase the throughput of the plant, leaving the production manpower unchanged but with a slight increase in manpower responsible for bringing in raw materials and removing the finished products. When the country is booming and sales rise, manpower levels do not need to rise so much; therefore, manpower costs as a percentage of total sales revenue fall.

The converse is true when the organization goes from expansion into contraction, and the recession follows the boom. Manpower levels cannot be cut back as quickly as the recession progresses and, therefore, manpower costs as a percentage of total sales costs begin to increase. Nevertheless, the fact that

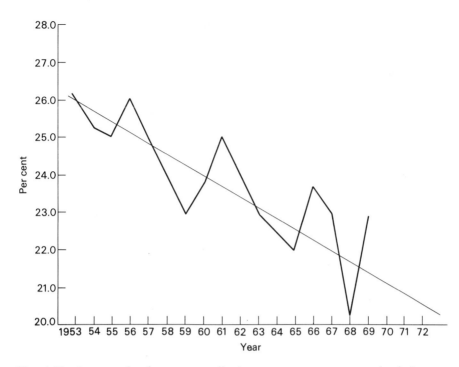

Fig. 4.12. An example of a manpower/business parameter – wages and salaries as a percentage of total sales revenue

there is a clear trend, means that it could be used in a top-down forecast of manpower levels.

Starting with a market forecast of sales and calculating the sales revenue gives the starting figure. We can project forwards the trend in the wages and salaries as a percentage of total sales and see that by 1972 it should be around 20 per cent. If the marketing people are forecasting £100 million of total sales, then 20 per cent of that can be attributed to manpower costs, i.e., £20 million. Dividing that £20 million by the average wage and salary will give us the average number of people who could be employed during that year and still maintain the proper relationship between business and manpower. Using ratios to weight the wages and salaries it is possible to break that manpower forecast down a little into the numbers of the different types of manpower required. This approach to manpower forecasting was quite popular in the 1960s and one or two organizations have used it extensively in trying to control manpower as well as forecasting future levels.

Problems in using the approach The main difficulty in using this approach to get a detailed forecast of manpower numbers is the assumption that the future will follow the past relationships and, therefore, the analyst has the problems of extrapolation to contend with. Statistical measures have never been very good at predicting change points in relationships.

Secondly, parameters of this type are very badly affected by high rates of inflation recently experienced. Even in this example, it was only possible to see the underlying trend by reducing both the business parameter and the manpower measure down to constant prices, i.e., taking out the inflation element in them over that period of time. This was relatively easy because the inflation rate was fairly constant and low. In the conditions of the last few years it would be very difficult to do this.

Finally, and most tellingly, forecasts arrived at in this way have a very theoretical and impractical air. Can you imagine the problems of attempting to convince a hard-headed production manager that he cannot have another process operator because the ratios of wages and salaries to total sales have moved by 0.5 per cent against the organization over the last year. Since it is derived without anyone having any part of it, there is no commitment whatsoever to such a forecast.

One of its main uses, however, is that it offers a very good yardstick by which to judge the bottom-up forecast. In this particular case, both forecasts were done. The manpower planner sent the questionnaire along to all the managers at the time of production of the corporate plan to get the manpower forecasts. On receiving this, he added it up and calculated the manpower costs involved. He then calculated the percentage that these manpower costs would be of the total sales that the organization's market managers were forecasting and found that the managers were forecasting a wages and salaries to total sales ratio of some 27 per cent, a figure, when compared with Fig. 4.12, that was outside the organization experience for the last 17 years.

Summary

This 'gap' that develops between the bottom-up forecast and the top-down forecast is of fundamental importance to the organization in determining manpower strategy. The topic will now be left until Chapter 9 which deals with manpower strategy. It can be seen that the manpower planner at the organization level has an extremely difficult task in attempting to forecast the overall level that the organization is likely to employ in the future. This reinforces even further the need for a monitoring approach to manpower planning.

5.

Key influences on manpower planning – analysing wastage

The importance of wastage

Reviewing the attitudes of managers to wastage from the organization is a little like watching a film on the life of Doctor Jekyll and Mr Hyde. In the 1960s, when organizations were expanding rapidly, a high level of wastage was a subject for considerable management concern. If two or three of a company's graduate trainees, recruited very expensively on the university milkround, left within a few weeks of each other, the events were exhaustively investigated to find out if morale within the organization had deteriorated. If this rate of outflow continued, the investigation might turn into a witch hunt for scapegoats or for policies that could be changed to stop the flow. The term, wastage, which is almost unique to this country, was coined in the 1960s and emphasizes the attitude of the personnel profession to this type of loss. The experiences of a young graduate in the Wellington Chemical Company serve to illustrate this most aptly.

From the early 1960s the company was expanding its production capacity. The speed of sanctioning new expansions in production capacity was increasing so rapidly that whereas in the early part of the 1960s one plant was finished, commissioned, and running satisfactorily before another one was sanctioned, by the end of the 1960s new additions to capacity were being sanctioned on a yearly basis. To staff this rapidly increasing capacity, the organization needed a large number of university-trained scientists. Experienced production managers, scientists themselves, were drafted into the personnel function to add credibility and aura to the normal graduate recruiters as they visited the universities, to attempt to get the very best of the science graduates. The candidates chosen for short-listing were invited to the organization's senior staff residential club where they were assessed and in a convivial atmosphere could see how they might be treated as the future managers of the company. The ones who were selected and accepted were carefully inducted into the organization and thoroughly trained.

STEMMING THE FLOOD

At the height of the production boom, just when these people were badly needed, the company noticed it was beginning to lose one or two, although the numbers were not enough to cause great concern. The trickle turned into a stream, the stream into a flood, and soon the percentage of graduates lost within their first year had risen above 25 per cent and was approaching 50 per cent.

At this point, the company decided that it must do something; its first reaction was to examine the way it treated graduates during their first year, since it believed that poor morale was causing disenchantment.

One day, to his surprise, our young graduate found a letter from his works manager inviting him to a luncheon in the private dining room with the deputy chairman of the organization. His surprise was increased when he found out via the works bush telegraph that all other managers and professional staff on the works who were graduates had received a similar invitation.

The appointed day came, a very pleasant lunch was had by all and the deputy chairman rose to speak. He addressed the problem of wastage. He and his colleagues felt that the processes of communication must have broken down. All those graduates that had left could not have been aware of the tremendous opportunities that were open to them within the company. The purpose of this address after lunch was to set that to rights, by letting the graduates know just how important they were in the organization's future, and how much that future was being jeopardized by the high rates of loss. His parting shot was to encourage everyone in the room to speak if he was dissatisfied and thinking of leaving. 'Tell your manager', he exhorted. 'If there is a misapprehension, it can be removed; if there is a source of dissatisfaction, perhaps it can be alleviated; if we are unaware of the problem, it is impossible to help.'

This was music to our graduate's ear. He was waiting to hear the results of an interview he had had the previous week for another job. It was not that he was disappointed or dissatisfied with his progress within the company, it was just that there seemed to be so many good jobs going, and although his chances of promotion were very good in the organization, since it was expanding so rapidly, the pull of the good jobs being advertised had induced him to apply: he had been interviewed and was waiting for the results. He told his manager, and soon he was sent for by his works manager, who gave him an honest assessment of his promotional opportunities if he stayed.

PROBLEMS OF RETRENCHMENT

Contrast the lengths that that company went to to try and minimize wastage of its key staff with that of a company in today's conditions. The chief executive is a deeply worried man. Although his organization is basically efficient, it has suffered badly in the recession. Its sales and profit margins have been squeezed successively by high rates of inflation in costs – particularly wages and salary costs – by the rapid escalation in the strength of the pound, and now when inflation rates have reduced and the pound declined in value, the depth of the recession has reduced the market for the commercial services that he supplies and for the third year in succession he is having to retrench.

To add to his problems, retrenchment is getting even more difficult. He has cut back stockholding, instituted severe economy measures, and banned recruitment unless he personally authorizes it. These measures have enabled the organization to reduce costs sufficiently to survive for the last two years.

Now he is faced with the need to reduce costs again. Stocks and short-term costs cannot be cut any further. He has decided that the only way that costs can be further reduced is to cut manpower levels.

The implementation of this policy is the source of his misgivings. In the previous year, he had only just managed to balance his books by getting an unexpected order, since his manpower levels were rather higher than usual. The problem was that the level of wastage seemed to be reducing rapidly. Whereas in the past the level fluctuated between 10 and 15 per cent from year to year, over the last two years it had fallen from 10 per cent to 8 per cent and in the last three months of the second year, if the figures were to be believed, it was down to 4 per cent. At this rate, using wastage to run down manpower levels, he would not get to the target levels he needed to achieve in order to cut his costs sufficiently.

Should he take a long- or a short-term view? The long term indicated the need to reduce manpower levels generally in order to improve productivity and to make him competitive. In this case he could increase the rate of outflow by bringing in policies of compensated early retirement and compensated redundancy, but he would probably have to borrow money from the bank to afford to do that. Taking the short-term view, he need only reduce the manpower levels in so far as the wastage would take them down. Damn the current low level of wastage!

These two situations with the level of wastage are at opposite ends of the spectrum, and yet equally bad for the organization. In each case the achievement of the organization's manpower objectives was being obstructed by the pattern of wastage. The high rate of loss in the first situation was militating against the company's need to build up experienced staff to match its expansion and in the second case the reduction in costs could not be achieved because the rate of wastage was too low to allow the manpower levels to be run down quickly enough.

The two examples show the importance of wastage in achieving an organization's objectives. Taking manpower decisions about recruitment and promotion policies requires information on the rate at which people are leaving the organization or are likely to leave within the planning period. Wastage, however, is even more important than one of the four key influences on manpower decisions. To some extent it can be held to be the driving force in the achievement of manpower policies and, therefore, its study demands even greater attention.

In Fig. 5.1 we have a box which represents a group of people – it may be accountants, it may be secretaries, it may be systems analysts. The arrows into and out of the box represent the flows into and out. Suppose we are planning to increase the number of systems analysts employed in the organization. Perhaps we have set target numbers to be achieved in three years' time and we have

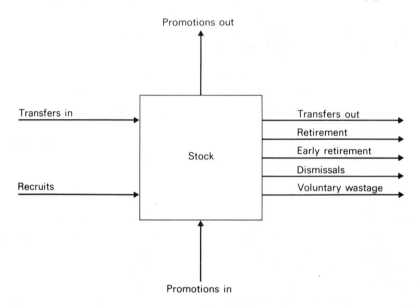

Fig. 5.1. The importance of the wastage flow

decided to do this by recruiting people from outside the organization. How do we decide how many recruits are required? We have to quantify all the flows into and out of the box. Some of the flows we determine as a matter of policy; some are not under our control and have to be estimated. In this case what options are open to us? One option is to transfer people from other departments within the organization, possibly departments that might be declining, or there could be the option of promoting surplus computer programmers, from the level below.

Before we can decide between the inflow options there are a number of flows out that have to be evaluated. How many systems analysts need to be promoted to the management level in the function? Possibly (but highly unlikely as systems analysts tend to be young), one or two may be on the point of

138

retirement or deciding to take early retirement. We could decide to transfer some people from this group to other functions, perhaps to strengthen the analytical ability within those functions. We will certainly have to make an estimate of the numbers of voluntary leavers during the period in which we are trying to build up the targets.

To a greater or lesser extent, the organization has control over most of the flows described here. It can decide how many people to recruit, although there will be a labour market constraint. It can decide how many people to promote into the systems analyst group from the computer programmers group, because it sets the criteria for promotion. It can decide how many people it is willing to transfer from one function in the organization to another. To a greater or lesser extent all the inflows are under the control of the organization.

If we look at the outflows, the same case applies. Who else controls the number of promotions from systems analysts into management but the organization? Again the decision to transfer people to other parts of the organization is one that it takes as a matter of policy. It does not actually control the number of people that are about to retire, because that is a function of rules that have been specified, but it is the organization that specifies the rules and can change them from time to time and, therefore, also can be said to be governing the rate of outflow by means of early retirement and retirement.

The one flow that it cannot control is the rate at which people decide to leave the organization and join other organizations. It cannot control voluntary wastage. It must, therefore, if it is to achieve the targets that it has set itself, be able to predict the rate at which people will leave the organization voluntarily with a degree of accuracy.

Having recognized its importance, we must also admit that in the majority of companies voluntary wastage is one of the least understood of all the manpower flows. For a number of years, in most organizations, the level of voluntary wastage was held to be totally unpredictable, despite being the object of study for many years, but the results of those studies had been contradictory and very disappointing. The studies had tried to find relationships between the rate of voluntary turnover and factors like distance of travel to work, occupation, sex, the degree of satisfaction of the workforce within the organization, etc. Sometimes there seemed to be good correlations between the rate of turnover and other factors. At other times, exactly the same factors in apparently similar situations were examined and found to give contradictory results or showed no correlation whatsoever.

DOMINANT FACTOR

The key to the mystery of the two scenarios which opened this chapter lies in the fact that one factor has such a strong influence over the rate of voluntary wastage that unless this factor is allowed for at the outset, any attempts to measure the influence of other factors will be subject to this misleading situation. Work in the Coal Board at the turn of the twentieth century indeed isolated this factor, the length of service of an employee, but the work had gone largely unnoticed, until the early 1960s when Professor Bartholomew of the University of Kent, along with Andrew Forbes of the Institute of Manpower Studies, were researching statistical theory. In this research they came across the fact that there was an extremely strong and predictable relationship between the length of service of an employee and the risk of leaving. Figure 5.2 shows the shape of this relationship.

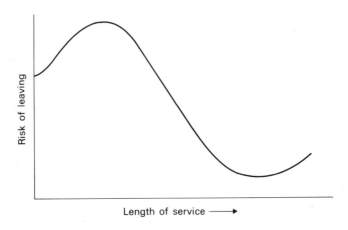

Fig. 5.2. The relationship between length of service and rate of leaving

At the point when an employee joins the organization, the risk of leaving is extremely high. In general the risk will rise immediately after joining the organization and reach a peak when it will begin to fall away rapidly to a low plateau until, as length of service begins to increase again, there is a little increase in the rate of wastage at longer lengths of service.

The shape of this curve was the reason why the earlier researchers had difficulty in finding sensible relationships between factors such as travel to work and the rate of voluntary wastage.

Suppose that one researcher had chanced upon a circumstance in which an organization had just recruited a lot of people who had to travel a long distance to their work. The situation could be an organization that was expanding rapidly in an area in which most other organizations were expanding. The search for labour in competition with other organizations could mop up the available labour within the local area, and the organization would have to recruit from further afield. This organization, then, would have a lot of short-service employees who lived a long way from the works, and a lot of long-

140

service employees who lived near to the works. Any study of the voluntary severance over the next year or so, would show a high number of people leaving who lived a long way away from the works. The conclusion might be drawn that there was a relationship between the distance a worker has to travel and the chance of leaving.

A second researcher, in a different organization at a different time, might attempt to repeat the work that the first researcher had done and show a similar relationship between the distance of travel and the rate of voluntary wastage. In his case, however, he has by chance chosen an organization that has been stable for quite a few years. It has got over its peak when it expanded and when it, too, was forced to recruit people from a long way from its works. Although a lot of these people had left, it still has, in the upper bands of the length of service curve, a considerable proportion of employees who have a long distance to travel to work. Its latest recruits, the people with the shorter length of service, have tended to come from the local area since, as it is not recruiting many people, the local area is able to satisfy the demand. Following our assertion that length of service and rate of voluntary wastage are very closely linked together, the chances are that leavers over the next year or so would be the people who have just been recruited, who have the shorter length of service. This researcher would conclude that the people who were leaving were those who lived near to the works and the people who were staying were the people who lived a long way away.

Correcting the statistics before the analysis for the length of service distribution would have allowed the researchers to compare the wastage rates of those who have, say, 10 years' service and live eight miles away from the works with those who have 10 years' service and who live only two miles away from the works. In this case we have isolated the length of service factor and any variation will largely be due to the fact that people live a different distance away from work. If this is done it is possible to show that there is indeed a relationship between the distance that people have to travel to their work and the rate of voluntary severance.

When this phenomenon is explained at length to personnel managers, there is often an expression of enlightenment. 'So that's why, when we attempt to expand the organization, we appear to get problems with our rates of turnover.'

A CASE HISTORY

This personnel manager's organization had just come through a rather difficult time. The works was long-established and had maintained the same size for over 10 years. Its length of service profile showed a fairly flat distribution with more people with over 10 years' service than with less than 10 years' service. A decision had been taken to expand capacity in response to a major increase in the market for the organization's products. The works manager was extremely enlightened and had for a number of years felt that the way that the general workers were recruited, trained, and inducted to the plant was quite inefficient. Current policy recruited operators from the labour market with little in the way of formal qualifications into the labour pool on the plant doing cleaning jobs until vacancies arose in the production ranks. At this point the worker would be moved into the production ranks on the lowest rung of the ladder, with no preliminary training. He would then be taught the job by an experienced operator, who would tend to emphasize the routines to be followed and not the implications of reading the instruments and interpreting their meaning.

Recruitment and training of operators   The works manager decided that this was an appropriate opportunity to end all that by purchasing a plant simulator. On this simulator the conditions of operation could be set up and be manipulated by an instructor. Now there was the opportunity to train new process operators under simulated plant conditions.

The selection of recruits was improved. Previously all that what was needed was men who were physically fit and could read and write. Psychometric tests were used as well as aptitude tests designed to find out whether they had the ability to visualize what was happening within a complex plant from looking at collections of dials. A higher level of intelligence generally was sought, and whereas in the past people with reasonable levels of intelligence were not selected as process operators, because it was felt that they would not stay in the jobs, an attempt was now made to change this.

Each operator received six weeks' training on the plant simulator, and the general opinion on the works was that the change was an exceptional success. The works manager was pleased and the production manager was looking forward to the day when the new units were commissioned and the operators brought on to the plant.

The day duly arrived and the hopes of the works manager appeared to be borne out. The men settled themselves into plant operation very much more quickly than other recruits seemed to do. With a new batch of recruits going on to the plant, some sort of plant-operating problem was usually encountered within the first few days, according to the older and more experienced operators. Such incidents were much reduced and this was attributed to the fact that the new operators who came on to the plant were well versed in the rudiments of plant operation. One and all sat back, basking in the success of the idea.

About two months later, at the works council meeting (a consultative body chaired by the works manager with representatives of management and men on it), the works manager, who was an extremely volatile individual, was thumping the table with his fist and saying 'What's the matter with the morale of this works. The level of natural wastage has increased rapidly. They are leaving in droves. Not only that, but many of these leavers are precisely the people we have spent so much money training on the new plant simulators. Was it worth the money? Should I not have listened to the traditionalists in the works who were arguing that it never was worth training operators because we always did lose a rather large number of them.'

Wastage investigations Three separate investigations were commissioned into this high rate of wastage, to try to find out the causes. The stakes were high; if no satisfactory reason could be found then it would appear that training the operators in this way, getting a higher quality operator, had been a complete failure and the policy would probably have to be reversed. Perhaps the new operators who had been recruited tended to live further away than previous new recruits? Could it be that the people with the higher levels of intelligence really did find the plant-operating jobs far too simple and boring? The results of the investigation were of course inconclusive because no one was taking into account length of service. Some time later, when this relationship with length of service was understood more fully, one of the investigators concerned decided to have a look again at the evidence. He found indeed that when there was a correction made for the length of service of the operators, the people who had been trained in the new way, the recruits who were of a higher quality, were tending to stay longer than the normal type of recruit to the works.

We can clearly see how easily the right policy decision can be overcome in these circumstances. Any organization that starts to expand should expect an increase in the number of people leaving. The percentage of people at the lower levels of service in an organization that is expanding is continually increasing. The percentage of people with the highest chance of leaving increases and, therefore, the number of leavers will increase.

The converse of this can easily be seen. To many organizations' distinct discomfiture, an organization that goes into recession and wishes to reduce staff finds that rates of wastage fall off very quickly indeed. In the 1975–76 recession a number of company chairmen, in declaring to their employees how the organization was prepared to meet the hard time, said 'We have to reduce staff but we will run the organization down by natural wastage.' The chairmen had been looking at their figures before making such statements, showing that the rate of wastage was 18 per cent per annum.

Of course such an organization had stopped all recruitment to allow the numbers to run down, and very soon the organization began to notice a decrease in the number of leavers. The 18 per cent very quickly became 15 per cent and the 15 per cent became 12 per cent and the chairman was soon sweating as to whether he would have to revoke his promise of no enforced redundancy and increase the rate of outflow to get the organization to the targets he envisaged. An organization that stops recruitment immediately reduces the number of people in the part of the curve with short service,

representing those with the highest risk of leaving. It is not surprising, therefore, that there is a sudden and increasing fall in the numbers of leavers.

SHORT-SERVICE EFFECT

This effect of short service and how strongly it is linked to the risk of leaving, is
such a strong effect that it even shows on the most generalized of analyses. In
the example shown in Fig. 5.3, recruitment and wastage levels are plotted each
quarter for a number of years. The group of people concerned include the

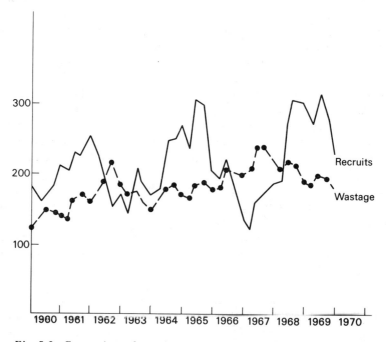

Fig. 5.3. Comparison of recruitment and wastage trends in an organization

secretaries and clerks of the organization, right up to the senior managers. The
different groups that are covered will have different lengths-of-service/risk-of-
leaving relationships and one would normally expect the effect to be less
noticeable when combining the groups together since some of the occupational
groups' wastage rates will cancel each other out in their effect.

We can see that the number of recruits per quarter is strongly cyclical over a
four- to five-year period following the economic cycle. At the same time the
wastage figures go up and down as well, but they lag behind recruits. If we
follow the recruitment from the beginning of the graph, it rises and shortly

afterwards wastage also rises. The recruitment levels eventually reach a peak and begin to fall as the organization hits a recession. The wastage figures carry on rising for two or three quarters as we would expect since, even in the worse case, recruits are highly unlikely to leave on the exact day that they start, and then begin to fall. The recruitment levels fall further and wastages follow until the bottom of the cycle is reached when recruitment levels begin to rise again. The wastage levels again lag behind recruitment levels before starting to increase, and so the cycle goes on.

The keen-eyed observer will notice that between the high peak of recruitment and the subsequent wastage peak in the early years of this time series is a much shorter lag than in the later one. This simply reflects that the new recruits to the organization in the first peak were of a type who left more quickly than those recruited in the second peak.

Summarizing, we can say that the relationship between length of service, wastage, and the risk of leaving falls into three distinct periods.

First of all there is the 'induction crisis', named by the Tavistock Institute in their Glacier Metal Study, a high rate of wastage immediately after recruits have been taken into the organization. The height of this peak and how long it lasts varies from occupation to occupation, from organization to organization, from geographical location to geographical location, and so on, but there will be a high peak of wastage shortly after the recruits enter the organization. There follows a low plateau in which wastage is fairly constant and at a low level. The exact length of service at which this plateau begins again will vary, as also will the length of time for which this low plateau is sustained.

Finally, the rate of voluntary wastage begins to increase again towards the end of the length of service distribution. It is becoming difficult to separate this last phenomenon from the increasing use that individuals are making of early retirement within organizations. In the past, when early retirement schemes were not formal, people who were not too well or who were tired in their jobs often took early retirement but it was classed as voluntary wastage. In today's conditions, when early retirement is much more common and is used by organizations as a means of reducing manpower levels, such leaving is likely to be classified as early retirement and not recorded as voluntary wastage. Some difficulty might be experienced, therefore, in isolating this phenomenon.

Types of outflow

Although this chapter has started by heavily emphasizing the part that voluntary wastage plays in assessing the outflow from organizations, it is not the only outflow that must be studied by the manpower planner. In other circumstances, other outflows may usurp the importance that is normally accorded to natural wastage. The outflow from the organization should be looked at under four broad categories, namely, retirement, premature retirement, redundancy, and involuntary wastage.

RETIREMENT

Most organizations have rules which specify in terms of age or length of service, or a combination of both, when an individual retires from the organization. Often the State's minimum pensionable ages are used for the rule, although in many organizations the age limit for retirement is lower. Because many individuals leave before the age of retirement, through natural wastage, death, ill-health, or early retirement, the number of people who survive to the age of retirement is quite small and this outflow is often overlooked in its impact on manpower policies. In general, the older employees are concentrated towards the top of the organization and, therefore, the impact of retirement on promotion rates can be considerable. The retirement of a general manager of a bank will, if he is replaced, create a chain of promotions since few banks recruit managers direct from the labour market. When the natural rate of wastage is low in the career structure, retirement plays an influential part in career management, since it is the only way of providing vacancies that will lead to promotions.

Those planning careers should pay close attention to the age or length of service structure of the organization, since it is relatively easy to predict the numbers retiring by comparing the retirement rules with the age or length of service structure. It is interesting to note that many organizations currently have a considerable number of employees reaching retirement. This bulge can be attributed to the influence of the Second World War. Immediately after the war many organizations expanded their manpower to get back to a peacetime footing. The recruits were mainly younger people returning from the army. Thirty-year-olds recruited then are now due to retire from many organizations. The career structure that expanded immediately after the war and recruited large numbers of younger people, will have been experiencing for the last two or three years, and for the next two or three years will continue to experience, a high rate of retirement, bringing in its wake increased promotion chances for those within the structure and a need for the organization to ensure that it has the requisite number of people ready to replace those leaving.

PREMATURE RETIREMENT

Until about 1970 early retirement from the organization was much reduced. In the main it consisted of people who were not too well physically but who were not poorly enough for them to be considered under the failure of health schemes that the companies operated, and one or two companies dealt very generously with employees who wished to go a little before their time and

146

enhanced their retirement provisions accordingly. Although the level may be low, nevertheless, it can be extremely significant. One organization created a management development plan for potential managers to ensure that it could replace managers who left. The scheme was well thought out and began to operate. After two or three years there was concern that the scheme was not fulfilling its function. On a number of occasions managers had retired or left and there had been no one obviously ready to replace them.

In setting the number of people to be developed over the next 10 years, the manpower planner made the assumption that anyone who was within 10 years of retirement age would reach that retirement age and retire normally. In actual fact, the organization found that this was far from the case. The personnel records showed that over the last 10 years only half the people who were within 10 years of retirement age, actually reached retirement age; the others died or had failure of health and retired early. So, even when companies' early retirement plans were not as generous as they are today, there was a significant level of early retirement to be expected.

In today's conditions a greater degree of confusion exists. One of the earliest ploys that a company uses to attempt to reduce its manpower levels when it is in deep trouble, is to enhance significantly its pension terms and offer all and sundry in the organization the option of premature early retirement. Undoubtedly, some of the managers who accept this option would have gone of their own accord and, therefore, we can expect the voluntary wastage from the organization to be reduced. Undoubtedly, too, some of the managers would not have gone under normal circumstances; however, there is often associated with early retirement schemes a degree of subtle pressure, even if it is only making the terms so attractive that it is hard to refuse them.

In trying to assess future levels of early retirement, the manpower planner should accept that early retirement is unlikely to happen before the age of 50, since this is the earliest legal age at which pensions can be granted, and the rate will diminish the nearer one gets to normal retirement age. A yearly analysis of the early retirement distribution, comparing it with the number of managers of the same ages or lengths of service in the stock from whom these people have retired, will enable rates of early retirement to be deduced. Since, however, companies and organizations use early retirement to get them out of trouble, we might expect that during a recession the number of early retirements would be higher than when the organization was booming. This type of bias should be looked for in the figures and if statistics are available, five years' past data should be looked at in an attempt to assess the possible trend.

REDUNDANCY

The third type of controlled wastage is redundancy. The chance of accurately forecasting the number of redundancies is low. Redundancy, that is forced redundancy, is the last resort of organizations. Since the legislation governing redundancy is complex, most organizations find that they have to take these decisions considerably in advance of when they implement them. The manpower planner in an organization should, if he has good links with the corporate planning function, get an early warning of when redundancy is likely to happen.

Before declaring forced redundancy, organizations often call for volunteers. The provisions of the redundancy scheme are available to employees who wish to have their own particular situation calculated. The employee then decides whether to accept the terms. The line between voluntary redundancy and voluntary wastage is difficult to draw and the phenomenon has been observed that when the grapevine within a company gets wind of the possible announcement of redundancy packages, the level of voluntary wastage falls right off, until the terms of the package are known.

INVOLUNTARY WASTAGE

This category covers death, ill-health, retirement, and dismissals over which both the employee and the employer have little or no control. In particular, where death or ill-health is concerned, it is truly involuntary. Rates of death and ill-health are stable and the manpower planner should analyse as many of the previous years' records as possible to establish the rates and relate them to length of service or to age.

Dismissals complete the trio of involuntary wastage flows. At least they are involuntary as far as the employee is concerned. There was a case recently of a senior manager in an organization who went into partnership hiring out canal boats. He took his annual holidays but did not return to work. Eventually the organization was forced to dismiss him, since he neither answered letters nor returned to work. Was this a dismissal or was it a peculiar form of voluntary wastage? There appears to be a relationship between dismissals and lengths of service. The shorter the length of service, the greater the risk of dismissal.

Important factors in the analysis of voluntary wastage

The serious study of voluntary wastage in the organization with its objective of using predicted levels of total wastage to quantify many manpower decisions, forms the basis of the organization's attempt to plan its manpower. To minimize errors in prediction we must understand the part that the following factors play in voluntary wastage.

LENGTH OF SERVICE

The importance of this factor has been dealt with at length at the beginning of this chapter, and little needs to be added at this point. Suffice it to say that it is the first analysis that the manpower planner should do, because until the analysis is organized on the basis of length of service, the other important factors that undoubtedly affect it cannot even be observed.

AGE

This, too, is an important factor in the analysis of wastage. In the majority of cases the prime determinant of rates of retirement and early retirement is age, and there is also an impact on voluntary wastage. An analysis by Andrew Forbes at the Institute of Manpower Studies has shown that if different age groups, having the same length of service, are analysed, the younger age group will tend to have the higher rates of voluntary wastage.

The analyst must be extremely careful, however, for when there appears to be a close relationship between the person's age and the risk of leaving, perhaps showing that young people have very much higher rates than older people, all that may be being measured is the relationship that already exists between length of service and voluntary wastage. Suppose, for example, that an organization recruits all its people between the ages of 16 and 18. In that case a 40-year-old employee will have between 22 and 24 years' service and so the age distribution will be almost identical to the length of service distribution; therefore, all we may be measuring is the fact that there is a relationship between length of service and the rate of leaving.

Nevertheless, there is an independent age effect and if the organization recruits over a wide age band, this may have some significance in forecasting and predicting levels of outflow from the organization.

OCCUPATION

Studies of occupations have demonstrated very different patterns of wastage, although they all have in common the fact that at lower lengths of service the wastage rates are higher. In some occupations the risk of leaving at the beginning is extremely high; it rises to an even higher point within weeks or months of joining and falls off to a moderate but stable level again within a few months. Other occupations have low levels of risk with the initial high risk being little higher than the lower rates found at higher levels of service.

The reasons for differences between occupational groups are not easy to explain. In some cases the difference is due to the fact that the labour market for that particular occupational group is either booming or in decline. At the moment, wastage rates of computer programmers and systems analysts are

149

much higher than other groups, simply because the new technology of the micro-chip demands people with those sorts of skills. If it were possible to find the information and measure it, the chances are that the wastage rates of the metallurgists in the United Kingdom would be quite low. There has been such a reduction in the number of jobs within the steel industry that the labour market for people with metallurgical skills is probably extremely limited for the present.

SEX

The difference in wastage patterns of men and women is often overestimated. Again, there may be other important factors which appear to show that women have much higher rates of leaving than men. Let us exclude for the moment the obvious reason for women leaving work, that is, to start their families. Because of their late historical entry into employment women have tended to be concentrated in those jobs where it has been difficult to use men. The jobs are often monotonous and boring and little attempt is made to make them interesting. Is it not natural in such circumstances that the wastage rates of people in those jobs will be high? If we were to put men into such jobs we might find that they had equally high rates of wastage. Unless the leaving rates for men and women are corrected for length of service and for the occupational grouping, then there is a possibility of asserting differences which do not exist.

Maternity legislation, by protecting their jobs, has tended to reduce the levels of natural wastage among women in the age bands 20 to 30 years. On the other hand, there is good evidence to suggest that when women return from having families to the labour market and into employment, they have lower rates of wastage than men of the same age.

THE FIRST JOB EFFECT

There is evidence to support the suggestion that people in their first job experience higher wastage rates than people in the same job with similar length of service and similar ages.

The best explanation that has been put forward suggests that unsatisfied expectations are the key to the higher rate of loss. When people join an organization they have expectations from the job. Their expectations may include career prospects, monetary rewards, and job interest. Wastage occurs when these expectations are not satisfied, and the time that it takes for an individual to decide whether his expectations are being met will vary according to the job. A process worker who is expecting a basic salary plus four hours' overtime a week, will find out within a matter of weeks whether that expectation is likely to be realized. The manager of a company may have joined expecting to be responsible for his own unit within two or three years. It will take him longer to judge whether those expectations will be realized and he is unlikely to leave quite so quickly.

Graduates and school leavers, groups who have never had jobs before and who are encouraged by the education system to aspire and fulfil themselves, will enter their first job with very high expectations. Some will quickly realize that their expectations were extraordinarily high and will gradually adapt to the reality of the organization. Others will feel bitterly disappointed and leave. Another factor can now be added to the explanation of the high rate of graduate wastage experienced by the Wellington Chemical Company in our opening example. As well as recruiting large numbers of young people with short service, it is recruiting graduates who have never had a job before.

LOSSES AFTER TRAINING

Organizations with jobs needing long initial training periods not only find high rates of wastage during the initial part of the training period but also find that at the end of the training period, when people have qualified, there are very high losses. On leaving university, graduates often choose the organizations that will give the best training and not the ones that they wish to join eventually. The same thing is true of apprentices. The person who wishes to set up his own commercial business might decide that a bank or an insurance company will provide the best basic training for his chosen career.

For some people, therefore, their first job is a means to train, and when the training period is over they will leave. Others become dissatisfied with the organization as the training progresses and stay with the organization purely to complete their training. The Wellington Chemical Company is an organization with a good reputation for its basic training and a number of those who joined may have been looking for training rather than for a career, thus accounting for its high rate of loss for graduates.

THE EXTERNAL ENVIRONMENT

Evidence has been increasing of late that there is a strong relationship between the rates of voluntary wastage and the level of economic activity. It is a commonly held view that levels of wastage are related to morale within the organization: if morale falls for any reason, the level of wastage will rise. Before we follow that assertion further, let us ask ourselves what it is that triggers an employee's decision to leave.

In the vast majority of cases it is the fact that there is another job on offer. Very few people leave their organization to join the unemployment queue; almost all of the voluntary leavers go to take another job. Even in the free-wheeling, easy-riding times of the 1960s this was still the most common trigger for people to change jobs. If, therefore, the number of job vacancies in the country falls as the economy goes into recession, the triggers are much reduced. We should expect the opposite when the economy is booming and the number of job vacancies is high; there would be an increased flow from organization to organization. When the economy is in recession the number of jobs dries up and we find, too, that the level of natural wastage dries up very rapidly.

Recent work by David McGill and Andrew Forbes at the Institute of Manpower Studies has extended the work done in the Coal Board on the relationship between the levels of wastage and the local level of unemployment and relative pay. These relationships can be observed in the initial analysis of a major bank's data. The analysis shows that it is possible to predict wastage rates from unemployment levels or relative pay.

Many other factors have been suggested as having an influence on the rate of voluntary wastage. For example, travel to work, the further an individual lives from his workplace the more likely he is to leave. We can add to the list siting/geographical location, the morale of the organization, promotion opportunities, the number of jobs an individual has had. All these factors are likely to have some influence on the rate of voluntary wastage. It will only be possible, however, to quantify the relationships when the main factors such as age, length of service, and occupation have been taken into account.

In choosing any manpower group for analysis or to predict the levels of wastage to be expected, we must not only do our first analysis by length of service or by age and then consider and break down the groups into occupational groups, sex groups, etc., but we should remember too that in each of these subsets, levels of natural wastage are going to be affected by what is happening in the world outside our own organizations. The impact of the economic situation can clearly be demonstrated in one of IMS's case studies. Before that demonstration can be made, however, we must consider how wastage is measured.

The measurement of wastage

The 'BIM labour turnover index' is the measure that the majority of organizations use to assess their labour turnover. It is a simple measure to calculate, the number of leavers during the previous period divided by the average number of people in the group throughout the period multiplied by 100. It is simple to calculate, easy to understand but completely useless, except where the population of the group is only changing very slowly.

The XYZ company has two plants on the same site. The plants make products from a similar set of raw materials. Plant A is the company's first plant, built some 15 years ago, and plant B has recently been completed. The processes involved in the manufacture of the products are similar and the same types of employees are used to manufacture the products. The labour turnover has been related to length of service for the two plants and the analysis shows that the pattern of wastage is the same. Figure 5.4 shows that for employees with less than five years' service, the chance of leaving is 25 per cent and employees who have more than five years' service have a diminished rate of leaving at only 5 per cent.

Plant A was built some 15 years ago; of its 200 employees, 150 have more than five years' service and only 50 have less than five years' service. Since plant B was only recently built, its length of service structure is much shorter. Of its 200 employees, 150 of them have less than five years' service and only 50 have more than five years' service. Figure 5.4 sets out the length of service distributions and the wastage rates.

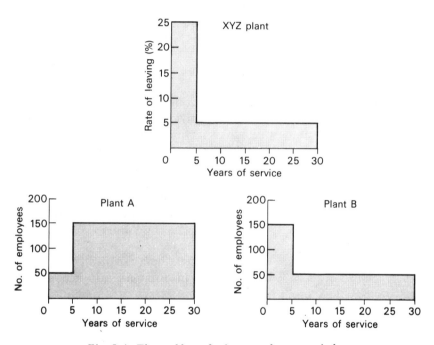

Fig. 5.4. The problem of using a crude wastage index

Let us apply the risk of leaving curve that we have found applies to both these plants, and use it to predict the number of leavers that we can expect over the next year. The rate of leaving for people with less than five years' service is 25 per cent. Plant B has 150 people with less than five years' service and, therefore, we can expect some 38 people to leave out of that group from that plant. The rate of leaving for those with greater than five years' service is 5 per cent and in Plant B we have 50 people who have more than five years' service and so we can expect approximately three people with more than five years' service to leave. Adding the 38 leavers with less than five years' service to the 3 leavers with more than five years' service gives 41 leavers out of our stock of 200, which is a 20 per cent rate using the BIM labour turnover index.

Repeating the same calculations for Plant A with its much longer length of service structure, we find that around 12 will leave with less than five years' service and 8 with over five years' service, a total of 20 in all. Calculating the 'BIM turnover index' by dividing the 20 leavers by 200 stock will give us 10 per cent labour turnover index. One plant has 20 per cent labour turnover, the other has 10 per cent labour turnover and yet the wastage behaviour of the two plants is identical. All that the BIM labour turnover index is showing is that there is a difference in the length of service structure of these two plants. Presented with figures like these the site manager might be tempted to judge the plant managers' employee relationships as being of different standards.

WASTAGE RATES

Any analysis of wastage must start by adjusting the whole of the data for length of service. Indeed, what we must do is to divide the data into length of service groups and for each of those length of service groups, in fact, a 'BIM labour turnover index' is calculated. For the zero to one year's length of service group, the number of leavers with less than one year's service is divided by the average number of people over the period with less than one year's service, to establish a wastage rate for this zero to one year's length of service band. This calculation is repeated across all the bands, and wastage rates by length of service result. This is the only sensible way to analyse wastage if we wish to avoid inaccurate, misleading results.

The simplicity that is so strongly attractive about the BIM labour turnover index has now been lost. The calculations involved in measuring wastage are now tedious, but the problems of comparing wastage rates for different groups of people, or comparing how wastage rates are changing for the same group of people through time, are even more complex. Now we are trying to compare one distribution with another. Most people who are studying statistics for the first time will probably admit that one of the most difficult things to grasp is the idea of sampling error. Whenever we produce a result in the form of a distribution, there will be a statistical error attached to it, and although we might measure other groups, keeping all the conditions absolutely the same, the chances of getting exactly the same result are remote. So it is if we compare two sets of wastage behaviour together.

In this example we calculate the wastage rates by length of service for a group of people for one year. As can be seen from the plotted frequency distribution, Fig. 5.5, the relationship between low length of service and high wastage holds,

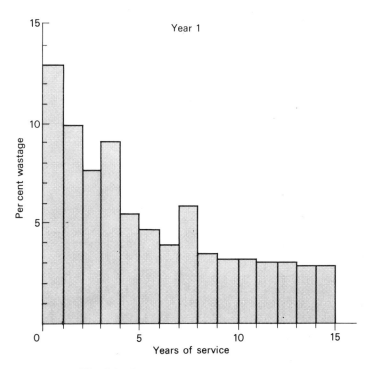

Fig. 5.5. Comparing wastage rates – year 1

but noise in the figures introduces two irregularities in the regular reduction of the wastage rates from the high point to the low point.

We then compute wastage rates by length of service for the previous year and plot these as a frequency distribution as in Fig. 5.6. It, too, follows the same general pattern, that wastage rates reduce as length of service increases but again with irregularities.

The object of analysing the two years was to compare the two, but unless we superimpose them it is actually quite difficult; it means reading the height of each bar against each chart and is a laborious and slow process. If we decide to superimpose one graph on the other, we can see that our problem is not really solved because the noise in the system causes the two lines to cross over each other and it is difficult to compare the two curves to see where the wastage behaviour is different (see Fig. 5.7).

THE SURVIVOR FUNCTION

The solution is to convert the wastage rates by length of service into a survivor function in order to be able to compare the two curves together visually and

155

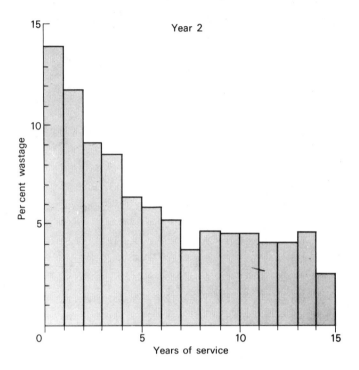

Fig. 5.6. Comparing wastage rates – year 2

easily. The survivor function shows the opposite to that of the wastage rate distribution: it shows how the survival of employees in the organization decreases as length of service or age increases. The survivor function is a cumulative decay function and as such the curve is either horizontal or declining. At no point can we have more people surviving than we had in the previous period. This is a good presentational device which greatly facilitates the comparison of different sets of wastage behaviour, whether this be between groups or over different points in time, as in our previous example. In Fig. 5.8 the previous examples have been converted into survivor functions. There is little to choose between the two sets of rates, which begin to divide at seven years' service. Year 2 has the lower survival pattern.

The cohort method This method follows the survival of a group of people who are recruited at roughly the same time. It is extremely simple to calculate – at the end of each year the number of people from the cohort who survive is expressed as a percentage of the total number of people who were recruited at the beginning when the cohort was formed. The simplicity of calculation and the ease of understanding recommend the cohort method for use in measuring

156

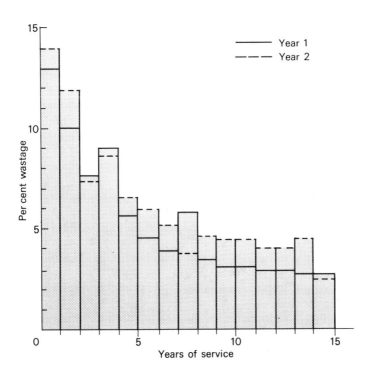

Fig. 5.7. Comparing wastage rates – year 2 superimposed on year 1

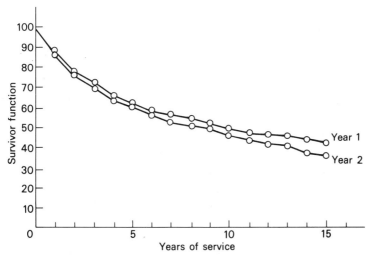

Fig. 5.8. Comparing wastage patterns using the survivor function

157

the survival patterns of groups of people whose total life in the organization is likely to be short, or where the percentage surviving falls to a very low level within a short space of time. It is an excellent measure for process workers on a chemical plant where, after two years, only 15 per cent of the cohort could be expected to remain. Successive cohort analyses of the year's recruits will quickly establish a pattern of the way that the wastage behaviour is changing.

In Fig. 5.9 a series of cohort survivor functions shows that: (1) the final percentage of people who remain in the job is constant at around 10 per cent;

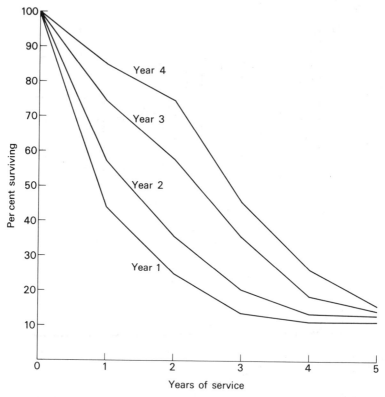

Fig. 5.9. Using cohort survivor functions to compare patterns from year to year

(2) there has been a steady increase in the percentage of people surviving for one and two years; and (3) there has been a marked reduction in the percentage surviving in the third, fourth, and fifth years. From analyses like this we can attempt to find causal relationships with the organization's policies. The cohorts in Fig. 5.10 show that not only has there been a substantial increase in the percentage surviving to the first year, but this is also reflected in a higher percentage surviving to the fifth year. Could this be the result of improving induction training?

158

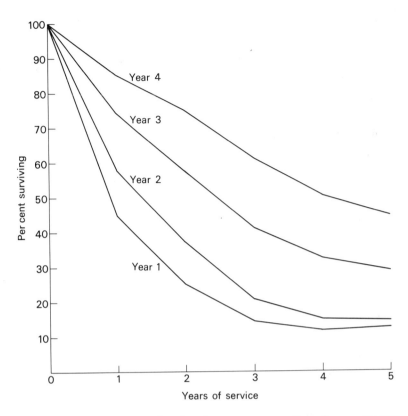

Fig. 5.10. Using cohort survivor functions to compare patterns from year to year

The census method Consider the problems of attempting to calculate the survivor function by the cohort method for accountants, where after eight years' service around 50 per cent of them survive. It will take a long time and many observations for a similar set of survivor functions to be built up using this method of analysis. The census method attempts to get over these problems by taking a snapshot of the different cohorts at a point in time and then combining them to give an estimate of survival across the age or length of service distribution. Look at the survival of people with less than one year's service in the organization and then look at the people with between one year and two years' length of service and from the knowledge of these two groups we can construct the survivor function of the whole of the length of service range from zero to two years. Let us follow the calculation through in detail. In Fig. 5.11 we have the number of people who left the organization during the last year, with between zero and less than five years' service.

First we calculate the wastage rates for each length of service, using the

159

Length of service at beginning of year (years)	0–1	1–2	2–3	3–4	4–5
No at beginning of year	10	35	22	14	8
No of leavers during the year	2	5	3	1	0
Wastage rate	0.20	0.143	0.136	0.072	0
Survival rate	0.80	0.857	0.864	0.928	1.0
Survivor function	0.80	0.686	0.593	0.550	0.550

Fig. 5.11. Table showing calculation of survivor functions using the census method I

stocks of people from which the leavers came. We collect the number of people in the organization with less than five years' service at the beginning of the period, as shown in Fig. 5.11.

In the 0–1 length of service class in Fig. 5.11 we had 10 people at the beginning of the year and during the year 2 of those 10 people left. In the 1–2 years' service class we had 35 people at the beginning of the year of whom 5 left; in the 2–3 years' service class there were 22 people at the beginning of the year and 3 left; in the 3–4 class there were 14 in the stock at the beginning of the year and 1 left; and in the 4–5 years' service class we had 8 people at the beginning of the year and none of them left, and so on.

First calculate the survival rate in each of the service classes. This is very simply done; the number of people who survived from those people in stock at

Length of service at beginning of year (years)	5–6	6–7	7–8	8–9	9–10	Total
No at beginning of year	15	23	11	7	12	68
No of leavers during the year	1	0	1	0	0	2
Survival rate	0.933	0.10	0.91	1.0	1.0	0.971
Survivor function	0.512	0.512	0.466	0.466	0.466	0.475

Fig. 5.12. Table showing calculation of survivor functions using the census method II

the beginning of the year is expressed as a percentage of the stock at the beginning of the year, and so, in the 0–1 service class we had 8 people surviving from the number we started with, 10, and, therefore, the survival rate is 0.8. The survival rates calculated for the remainder of the classes are 0.857, 0.864, 0.928 and, of course, in the fourth- and fifth-year class we had 100 per cent survival since no one left.

The census method of calculating the survivor function depends on the assumption that people in their second year of service will have experienced the same pattern of survival in their first year as do the people who are now in their first year. The validity of this assumption will be discussed later in the chapter. It means, however, that to calculate the survival rate of people from the date of joining the organization to the end of their second year, we take their chance of survival in the first year (in this case 0.8) and their chance of survival in their second year (0.857) and multiply them together to give us a survivor function of 0.686 at the end of the second year.

In the same way we make the assumption that people in their second to third year of service will have followed the same pattern as the people in the 0–1 and 1–2 year classes; therefore, to arrive at the chance of a person surviving to the end of the third year, we multiply the three individual survival rates together, so we can take the 0.686 as a survivor function at the end of the first year multiplied by the survival rate 0.864 during the second and third year and this will give us a survivor function of 0.593 at the beginning of the fourth year.

Transition survivor function In attempting to calculate the survivor function for the next few years in the length of service distribution we hit a problem. Between the beginning of the fifth year of service and the beginning of the tenth year of service there are only two leavers, the first of them leaving between five and six years' service and the second with seven to eight years' service. How do we deal with the service classes with no leavers? The best way to deal with this problem is to group together the data and calculate the survival rate over the whole of the 5- to 10-year length of service band. We add the stocks up and find that they come to 68; we have two leavers so the survival rate is 0.971. This survival rate is an annual rate calculated on one year's leavers' figures. Anyone who is in the 5–10 years' service band will be exposed to this annual rate for each year that he is in the band. So the chance of a person surviving to the end of the sixth year is the chance of surviving to the beginning of the sixth year (0.550) multiplied by the survival rate for the sixth year. If that person survives another year, then he will again be exposed to the same survival rate of 0.971. To calculate the survivor function value at the end of the tenth year we have to multiply the survivor function value at the beginning of the period of 0.550 by $0.971 \times 0.971 \times 0.971 \times 0.971 \times 0.971$ and this will give us the survivor function of 0.475 at the beginning of the tenth year.

The correct term for the survivor function that we have calculated is the 'transition survivor function'. By using the stocks at the beginning of the year and the leavers from those stocks during the year, we have in fact excluded from the calculation anyone who leaves and is recruited during the same year. An alternative calculation, called the 'central rates survivor function', is used when it is necessary to take into account leavers from recruits during the year.

Central rates survivor function   The central rates survivor function uses average stocks in its calculations instead of stocks at the beginning of the year. It is immaterial whether the average stocks are calculated by taking the beginning of the year level and the end of the year level, adding and dividing by two, or whether each individual monthly stock level is added together and the final result divided by 12. Instead of only leavers from the stocks at the beginning of the year being used in the calculation, we now put in all leavers during the year from this group. The remainder of the calculation is identical to that of the transition rate survivor function.

The advantage of the transition rate survivor function is that by using stocks at the beginning of the year, it makes a comparison between different wastage patterns and survival patterns easier. The central rates calculation is mainly used when we wish to project the impact of wastage on future stock levels forward in time. For anyone who wishes to explore the method of doing the calculations further, there is comprehensive literature on the subject referred to in the guide to further reading on page 307.

Using the survivor function

Essentially, the survivor function is no more than a presentational device. Its advantage is the visual impact it brings to the comparison of survival and wastage patterns over time or between different groups. It tells us little more than the wastage rates by length of service and, because it is a cumulative curve, it is harder to interpret the behaviour at any point on the survivor function since it has to be translated back into what is happening within the particular length of service band.

In interpreting the function, we must first of all remember that it is a cumulative curve so that the survivor function can never increase; it can only have the same proportion surviving or a decrease in that proportion. If, in our data, we have the unusual case of everyone leaving from the stocks at the beginning of the year in a particular group, then the survival rate for that group will be zero; multiplying the survivor function up to that point in the length of service distribution by zero will make the survival function come to zero, even though there may be significant wastage taking place after this point. Where the survival rate for any group is very, very small, it is worth combining that particular length of service group with the groups on either side of it to even out

162

the pattern and stop the survivor function becoming zero, before the whole of the length of service distribution has been taken into account.

Where the survival function is falling rapidly, it indicates low survival and high wastage. Where the survival rate is parallel to the length of service axis, it indicates that survival is high and wastage is low. A useful concept that has been developed in interpreting the survivor function is to describe the curve in terms of the number of years of service that are completed at different percentages of survival. For instance, when we are comparing the survivor function of a group of people over a time, we find that in one year the curve shows that five years would be completed before 50 per cent of the people left, whereas the analysis for the next year shows that 2.5 years only are completed before half the people have gone. There has been a significant drop in the survival of those with less than four years' experience. We could use a range of similar percentages, i.e., the point at which 75 per cent remain, the point at which 25 per cent remain and we can also measure what percentage survive to retirement. These are useful shorthand ways of describing the survival or leaving from a survivor function.

AN EXAMPLE

This example is drawn from a problem of the 1970s. The objective of the project was to provide management with better information about levels of recruitment for different circumstances. There were two groups of managers in the organization, ex-graduates recruited directly from university and those who had joined with a technical background around the age of 18 and had been promoted to management level after experience in the organization. These groups had different levels of wastage. The level of wastage from the graduate managers was much higher than it was from the non-graduate managers.

The organization had taken the trouble, even though this had to be done manually, to extract losses of managers over the five previous years from its records and the stock levels at the beginning of each of those years.

Age-based picture Although this chapter has invariably calculated the survivor function using length of service to measure time in the organization, it was stated at the beginning that where the organization recruits within a very narrow age band, then age and length of service are very similar. If that is the case there is an advantage in calculating the survivor function by age, because most organization retirement rules are age based and, therefore, a survivor function by age presents a complete picture. Using the census method on the data for 1972, the transition survivor function in Fig. 5.13 was calculated for non-graduate managers within the organization.

The curve is a rather flat one, indicating a high rate of survival of these people during that year: 75 per cent of employees can be expected to reach age 35 and

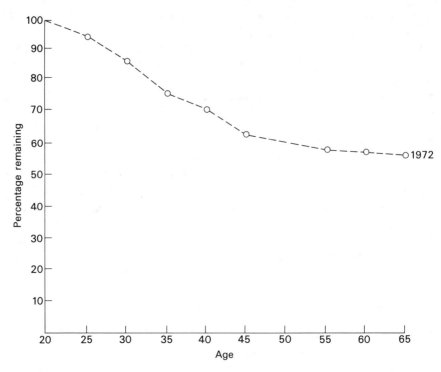

Fig. 5.13. Using survivor functions – 1. The 1972 non-graduate managers' pattern

at the retirement age of 65, 56 per cent of people still survive. The curve shows its steepest drop between the ages of 25 and 35, where the percentage falls from about 95 per cent down to 75 per cent. The best way of describing it in words is to say that if we had 100 non-graduate managers and they experienced the 1972 pattern of survival for the rest of their working lives, then 56 of them would remain at age 65.

The analysis was repeated using the 1973 stocks and leavers. In Fig. 5.14 the 1972 survivor function is depicted along with the 1973 survivor function.

The visual impact of survivor functions Comparing survivor functions in this way, it becomes immediately clear that in all but two age bands these curves are remarkably parallel. The points at which the curves diverge indicate differences in behaviour but where the curves are parallel, behaviour is identical. There appears to have been a change in the survival pattern between the ages of 25 and 30, and between the ages of 55 and 65. In each case the 1973 pattern shows a more rapid fall in survival. Instead of 86 per cent of people remaining at age 30 as in the 1972 curve, the 1973 data indicate that only about 75 per cent would survive. Also at the upper end of the age distribution there is a significant

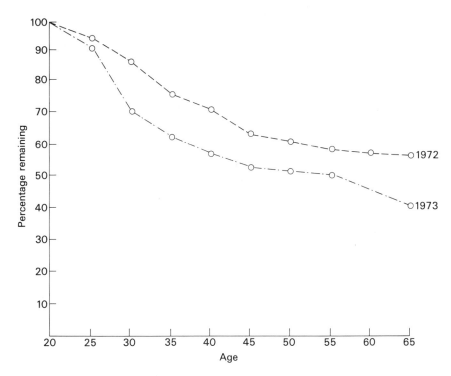

Fig. 5.14. Using survivor functions – 2. The 1973 non-graduate managers' pattern

change in behaviour. In the 1972 curve, the percentage survival only changed from 59 to 56 per cent over the period and yet the 1973 data show a survivor function dropping from around 50 per cent down to 40 per cent over that 10 years' age range. The change in behaviour of those over the age of 55 was easy to explain. The management had been concerned for some time that rates of promotion in this group of people were rather lower than it would have preferred. To ease this blockage, a decision had been taken to introduce an early retirement policy and allow those who wished to retire early to do so. It was much more difficult to find an explanation for the change in behaviour of the 25- to 30-year-olds. Why had the rate of survival diminished? No one was very clear.

The analysis was continued by looking at the 1974 survival pattern to see if that gave a clue as to why there was a change in behaviour in the 1973 situation for the 25- to 30-year-olds. If the change in the pattern from 1972 to 1973 was significant, then the change from 1973 to 1974 was dramatic. Instead of 75 per cent surviving to the age of 35 as in the 1972 analysis, only 35 per cent would have survived to 35 if they had experienced the 1974 pattern of survival for the rest of their working lives. Indeed, by retirement age, only 14 per cent could

165

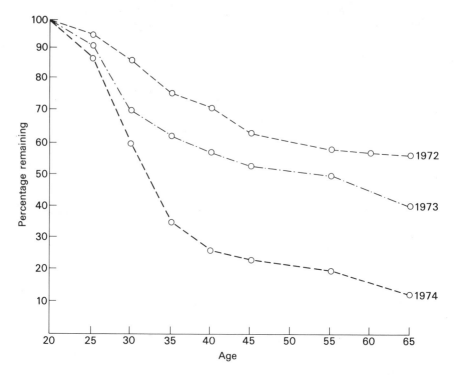

Fig. 5.15. Using survivor functions – 3. The 1974 non-graduate managers' pattern

still be expected in the organization. Looking at Fig. 5.15 we can see that the major change has occurred between the ages of 25 and 35, but from that point the 1974 curve is remarkably parallel with the 1973 curve.

The pattern is developing. From a low survival pattern in 1972 we find a deteriorating rate of survival of those in the age group 25 to 30 and then 30 to 35. Examining the economic situation in the country in those years reveals that between 1972 and 1974 there was an expansion in the job market. The most mobile people in any organization are the younger ones without family commitments, and as the job market begins to open up, it is the younger ones who respond to it first. We see, therefore, in 1973 that it was the 25- to 30-year-olds who initiated the lower survival pattern. This was continued in 1974 not only with an even lower survival of the 25- to 30-year-olds, but also the 30- to 35-year-olds responded to the job market with a big drop in their survival rate. In passing, we note that the early retirement policy of 1973 is still having an impact in 1974 and the pattern of survival between ages 55 and 65 shows the same significant reduction in survival as 1973.

The suspicion that the change in the survivor function might be due to the economic environment was confirmed when we analysed the survival pattern for 1975. By 1975 the effects of the first oil crisis were being felt on company profitability and the job market had collapsed. The survivor function for 1975's non-graduate managers was almost identical to that of 1973 and the mobility of the 25- to 35-year-old people reduced considerably (Fig. 5.16).

The survivor function, with its ability to display changes of this kind visually, shows the movement from year to year in the behaviour of this organization's managers. Equally graphically, survivor functions can show the difference between two groups of people. In this case study, the second group of managers were those who had been recruited direct from university as graduate entrants. The same sort of analysis showed the difference between the behavioural pattern of the two groups. Figure 5.16 also shows the survivor function for 1972 for graduate managers. In this case 75 per cent of them have gone by age 30 and 50 per cent of them by age 37 and only 18 per cent would survive through to retirement age. If we compare this with the survival pattern for the non-graduate managers for 1972, where over 56 per cent were surviving through to retirement, we must conclude that there is a completely different pattern between these two groups.

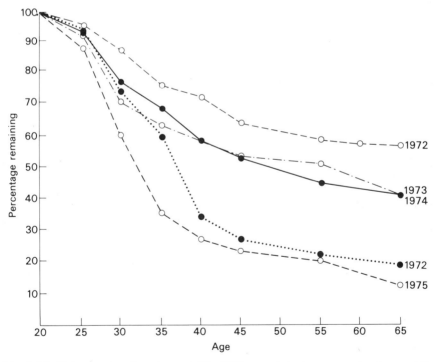

Fig. 5.16. Using survivor functions – 4. The 1975 non-graduate managers' pattern and the 1972 graduate managers' pattern that is shown by the dotted curve

This link with the level of economic activity is of fundamental importance in manpower planning. When an organization wishes to contract, its ability to do so is seriously hindered as we have seen, because those most likely to leave are the ones with the shortest service, and since it will probably stop recruiting in order to run down its organization very quickly, the number of people leaving will reduce. If, at the same time, the general level of economic activity in the country is declining then there will be fewer job vacancies on the labour market and wastage rates will fall further among the most mobile group, the 20- to 35-year-olds. An interesting observation from the previous data is that the levels of wastage in each of the years seem to vary very little after about the age of 40. All the curves seem to be parallel to each other and are hardly influenced by the economic situation.

Using wastage data

Primarily we have analysed wastage data to help us assess the outflow from the organization. Companies which are expanding need to allow for the additional wastage that will come from the additional recruits because in the expanding organization there are more people with short service. Furthermore, if this expansion is part of a generally expanding economy the rates of wastage by length of service will increase, creating the need for more recruits.

To make the calculations is a simple enough task of applying the wastage rates by length of service to the stocks of people and calculating the numbers that will leave. We can then add in the number of recruits needed to replace those people and to reach the new target for the expanded organization. To do this, of course, we need to use the central rates method of calculating the wastage rates, since there will be wastage from the recruits during their first year. Unfortunately, although the calculations are easy, they can be quite tedious, especially if the wastage rates are changing rapidly across the length of service distribution. A simple model, such as the Institute of Manpower Studies' WASP (Wastage Analysis Statistical Package), is most useful. It has a projection module built into it which will perform the calculations quickly and easily and output tables showing the number of recruits that will be needed to meet the targets specified.

It is not enough, however, to do one calculation and use that for determining policies. If we are in the fortunate position of the last case study, in which several years' historical data are available, we can use the wastage rates for the years which displayed the highest and lowest levels of wastage. We can calculate the number of recruits that will be required in each of those situations and see how much they vary. If we are not in that fortunate position, and have no historical data, we must estimate to the best of our ability what we believe might be the possible divergences from the data that we have for the previous

168

year. If we knew that that year was at the bottom of the economic cycle then we could assume that wastage rates would probably increase for the next two years. Judgement of how much they will increase will be arbitrary but nevertheless it will be better than using only the latest year's data which relate to the wastage patterns to be found at the bottom of a recession.

In arriving at wastage rates, the WASP package calculates the statistical error and prints this out as well as its estimate of the wastage rates by length of service or by age. A simple way of allowing for some variability is to add that sampling error on to the wastage rates, and use that as a top estimate and then deduct the sampling error from the wastage rates and use that as a bottom estimate of the likely wastage pattern.

The organization that is contracting should be making extensive use of the data it has on wastage. Since there are legislative constraints on dismissing people from the organization and since it is costly to make people redundant, as much forewarning as possible is needed of problem areas. One very useful statistic to calculate is how fast a group of people would run down if they were allowed to waste away with no replacement. Again, if the organization is not only contracting but in recession, some attempt should be made to adjust the wastage rates for the impact of the recession.

Summary

An organization that is searching for a place to begin its manpower planning would be well advised to begin by studying its wastage patterns. In all probability, data about the length of service or age of leavers may not be easily and readily available and steps will have to be taken to collect those data. However, even very few data are immediately useful and begin to throw light on the organization's manpower policies and, in particular, to pick out areas in which the organization might have immediate difficulty.

6.

Defining replacement policies and the need for labour market information

So far, in describing the influences on the manpower system, we have quantified the changing requirement for jobs in the future by examining the relationship between manpower and the business and analysed losses from the system, in particular voluntary wastage. We now turn our attention to the third key influence on the system, replacement policies.

The replacement policies of an organization are the rules and assumptions governing the flow of individuals into the manpower system and between the job groups within the system. It is through the operation of these flows that our perceived needs for future jobs are filled, whether increases or decreases on current numbers are met, and our need to replace losses through retirement and wastage is satisfied.

Three types of flow make up replacement policies. First, recruitment brings individuals into the manpower system from outside the organization. Secondly, promotion moves individuals from one box in the manpower system to boxes at higher levels (the converse of this is demotion where the reverse occurs). Finally, transfers involve lateral moves within the manpower system and across the organization between manpower systems. In order to describe and quantify our policies relating to any of these types of flows we must consider four key issues.

Push/pull flows

The distinction between push and pull flows has been made earlier, but to reiterate: a push flow occurs when individuals are moved into a box in the manpower system, whether by recruitment, transfer or promotion, irrespective of whether there is a vacancy in the box waiting to be filled. Most commonly it occurs where there is a need to maintain stable levels of recruitment in order to justify the continuation of training systems, or where individuals automatically receive promotion at the end of a training or induction programme as a reward for satisfactory performance and as an incentive to perform as well in the future. In contrast, a pull flow reflects the situation where individuals are moved into a box within the system when there is a clearly defined vacancy waiting to be filled, as a result of either a loss occurring requiring replacement, or an increase in the overall job numbers making up a box. Pull flows are the most usual type of flow other than at the entry points into the system.

Whether a push or a pull flow is operating at any point in the system is going to have a significant impact on the overall movement of people within that structure. The effects of push flows are completely predictable since the number of people being moved is specified and so target numbers may be exceeded or under-achieved without any control being possible. The effect is most marked where the 'push' flow into a box is opposed by the 'pull' flow out. Unless the flow in by chance equates the flow out there is a real risk of significant, and possibly unwanted, changes in the size and composition of the job group in question, and this could have implications for relative career prospects, work loading, and motivation.

The mixing of flows

The routes or flows by which vacancies are filled need to be defined. Whether we choose to recruit, transfer, or promote, singly or in combination, will not only constrain the movement of people along the other flows, but also, by implication, will affect the characteristics and behaviour of the population within the manpower group where the vacancies lie. A recruitment flow, for example, other than at the lowest level within the manpower system, will have a serious impact on promotion possibilities lower down in the system, at the same time as introducing individuals into the system whose propensity to leave, for example, may be different from that of those individuals who might have arrived in these positions by promotion.

There are three definitions of the way that flows into any one box should be mixed. The first uses the historical mix of flows to see, for any job group, whether we have traditionally filled vacancies by recruiting people, by promotion or by transfer, or by some combination of these three things. However, looking at what has happened in the past may not be a good basis on which to define our policies in the future. In many cases the problems we are suffering from, for example the quality of our workforce, may be the result of adhering to an inappropriate set of replacement policies.

To overcome this, a second way defines our replacement policies in terms of some ideal mix. So, for example, we have an ideal preference for promotion in order to 'grow our own timber'. This is the common preference of many

171

established large organizations, who normally recruit individuals on leaving school or university, and mould them into their organizational culture with a view to a long-term career. Other organizations, in contrast, will see as their ideal a pattern of filling vacancies by recruitment in order to bring new blood into the organization. This is most common in areas of creative work where there is a need for a continuous flow of individuals with new ideas and experiences, and in organizations which, often as a result of a period of expansion, have exhausted the potential of promoting people from within.

A common ideal flow mix tempers recruitment and promotion with a desire for an increased amount of lateral transfer movement in order to encourage broader experience in employees generally. This again is often to be seen in organizations which traditionally have had a manpower system based on a number of specialist functions with only very little cross-mobility possible, other than at the very lowest levels.

While it is an important exercise to consider the ideal flow mix that one would like into any part of the manpower system, we must always be conscious that, in practice, ideals are never achieved, and so the third way of defining the mix uses neither the historical nor ideal solutions but a pragmatic mixture. While we might wish to increase the amount of fresh blood coming in by increased recruitment, we might also expect that, if insufficient satisfactory recruits are available, we will still continue to fill jobs by promotion. Alternatively, a 'growing our own promotion' policy might need to be supplemented by accepting the need for recruitment or lateral transfer when insufficient promotees of suitable capability or potential can be identified.

Quantifying replacement flows

Whether or not we choose to define flow mix policy in terms of the historical situation, our ideal position, or what we see as being acceptable in a pragmatic sense, there are a number of ways we can actually quantify our recruitment. In the case of push flows we will normally specify our requirement either in terms of a simple number moving along the flow during a fixed period, or the rate expressing the required flow as a proportion of the stock from which that flow originates. For example, if the required promotion rate from Box A to Box B is 10 per cent, and we start with a stock of 100 people in Box A, we would expect 10 per cent of 100 (or 10 people) to move during the period in question.

Where we are dealing with a pull flow the option specifying our requirement as a simple number no longer applies, as the flow will be exclusively determined by the number of vacancies to be filled in the entry box and the rules as to how they should be spread between the various permitted flows. The simplest way in these circumstances to quantify our requirements or assumptions is in terms of simple proportions. So, for example, if we have two flows supplying Box X then we might specify that 60 per cent of any vacancies will be filled via flow 1, and the remaining 40 per cent via flow 2, with the result that if we have 20 vacancies to fill, 12 will come from flow 1, and 8 from flow 2.

The limitation with specifying our flow mix rules in terms of simple proportions is that it takes no account of the size of the box or source from which the flow comes. One consequence of this is that applying the specified flow rules may result in a required flow to fill the given proportion of vacancies which exceeds the size of the source stock or, if not exceeding it, would unreasonably reduce it. A different sort of problem arises where we are concerned with ensuring equality of promotion or transfer chance along two competing flows, particularly where the source stock is considerably different in size. Without taking account of the source stocks in our calculations there is no way we can ensure that any given set of simple proportions will give us the necessary relative flow chance.

To overcome the problems of using simple proportions, the alternative way of quantifying our flow rules is to use the idea of flow rates. The use of rates merely implies that the mixing of flows is determined in relation to the relative size of the source stock. So, for example, if we have two groups of staff competing for promotion to a managerial post where one group of 50 people has received some form of technical qualifications, while the second group of 100 is made up of people who have not, then relative weights of four to one in favour of the technically qualified group mean that staff in this latter group must be given four times as much chance as those in the non-technical group of being promoted. In practice, the result is that if there are 12 vacancies to be filled at the management level, then 8 will need to come from the technically qualified group, giving a promotion rate of 8 over 50, or 16 per cent. The remaining 4 will come from the larger non-technically qualified group with the promotion rate of 4 over 100, or 4 per cent, i.e., the technically qualified group has been given four times the promotion chance.

Weighting of flows becomes particularly important when we are looking at equality or balance of promotional opportunity, e.g., between male and female candidates. In this circumstance to specify simply a 50 per cent male, 50 per cent female, promotion rule would only have the desired effect if there were equal members of males and females in the stocks from which the promotions were being made. In practice we usually want to adjust to reflect any imbalances in the stock so that by using a one-to-one weighting rule the results of promotion rates are equal. As an example, if we had 50 men and 100 women competing for nine vacancies, and an equal promotion chance assumption, then, applying one-to-one weighting of the male/female flows would require us to promote three men and six females, i.e., a 6 per cent promotion rate for each group.

On occasion, vacancies into a particular box within a manpower system will need to be filled by a mixture of both push and pull flows. In this circumstance, the resultant movements will be very much governed by the order of priority in which the flows occur. If the push flow is given priority, e.g., we wish to maintain a steady rate of graduate recruitment into the organization each year, then the proportions or weights applying to the pull flows involved will be determined on the vacancies remaining after the push flow has been taken account of, e.g., if there are 100 vacancies, and we make a priority assumption of 20 recruits each year, the number of promotions that will take place from lower levels along any selected flow will be determined in relation to the 80 remaining vacancies and not to the original 100. In contrast, where the pull flow or flows have priority over the push flow, it is feasible that the total inflow could exceed the number of vacancies estimated, e.g., if we assume that in order to fill 100 vacancies, 90 per cent will be filled by our pull flow, and that independently our push flow will bring 20 individuals into the system, then the total effect will be actually to increase the size of the entry box by 10.

The arithmetic procedure for transforming promotion rates into promotion weights or vice versa is very simple.

Replacement characteristics

Having determined whether individual replacement flows operate on a push or pull basis, and the rules for determining the contribution of competing flows in the entry of staff into any box within the manpower system, it now becomes important to be able to define the characteristics of those being moved. What we require is to be able to describe the features of those who are being moved along any flow, whether recruitment, transfer or promotion, in such a way that we can determine the effect that this will have on the future dynamics of the manpower system, and, as a consequence, on other decisions and issues we need to look at.

In this context the age and/or length of service profile of the individuals moving along a particular flow is of considerable interest to us since it will give us a basis for assessing the implications that these movements will have on future losses from the system, and changes in the overall experience profile.

In contrast, the examination of detailed selection criteria, for example that all successful candidates have to have blue eyes, will be of less interest to us unless our primary concern is with the distribution of blue eyes through the organization over time. Where distinctive selection criteria are used to define groups with different levels of wastage patterns, promotion opportunities, or other differences in manpower behaviour, it is important that we recognize those distinctions in the way we draw our manpower system. If, for example, we select a mix of O-level and A-level recruits, and we observe these to have different patterns of subsequent behaviour, then it is important to separate these two sorts of entrants into distinct flows into the manpower system. We must then describe the characteristics of those moving along the two flows in terms of age or length of service in order to facilitate a quantitative estimation of the differences that will occur in wastage or promotional movements, which in turn will affect experience levels within the organization. The need to reflect different selection characteristics in terms of difference streams or flows within the manpower system becomes particularly important where the relative mix of those defined by these selection criteria is likely to change significantly in the course of time.

In practice then, when we are talking about describing the replacement characteristics of individuals moving along any recruitment, promotion or transfer flow, we are essentially referring to the age or service profile of that group. As in defining the rules for mixing flows, we can also define different sets of rules to describe the age profile. The simplest is merely to define a set of proportions by age. You might, for example, reflect the need to bring more mature recruits into the manpower system by specifying that, of all recruitments along a particular flow line, only 5 per cent will be individuals under the age of 20, 10 per cent will be aged 20 to 25, 20 per cent aged 25 to 30, 35 per cent aged 30 to 35, 15 per cent aged 35 to 40, 10 per cent aged 40 to 45, and the remaining 5 per cent over 45. This simple way of describing an age profile will satisfy most of our requirements and give us some basis for assessing the impact of age-specific wastage rates or the effect of subsequent age/experience specific promotion rules. Where they can create difficulties is in the area of transfer or promotion where the effect of applying a particular age profile in these terms may be to draw an unreasonable number of people in a particular age band from the source stock, e.g., if we had 100 vacancies and our age proportions indicated that 30 per cent of the people moving to fill the vacancies will be aged 30 to 35, i.e., 30 people, then we will have problems when the numbers aged 30 to 35 in the source stock only total 25. Again, as a substitute for simple proportions we can describe our age profile in the form of weights, that is, we might say that individuals aged 30 to 35 have four times as much chance of being promoted as somebody aged 20 to 25.

Whether we specify our age profile in terms of proportions or weights, we again have the choice of basing it on the historical situation by analysing movements that have taken place in past periods, or, alternatively, we can assume a profile which we see as meeting our future requirements in terms of the suitability and experience of people for recruitment and promotion. If we try and use historical information, difficulties may arise if the amount of internal mobility in the system is low, and, therefore, particularly in looking at promotions, we have little data to go on. In these circumstances, and where we were concerned with looking at movements from one level to another within the organization, then it may be possible to deduce the underlying age profile pattern by looking at the career progression diagram for that particular set of promotional movements.

In summary, therefore, we have identified the need to describe the age profile characteristics of those moving along the various flows within our manpower system, in order to assess properly the resultant implications for the system itself. Because we will very often assume age or length of service, i.e., time duration specific wastage rules, it becomes important to assess the impact of applying these rules to see how the underlying age profiles of the stocks within the manpower system themselves change over time. Apart from the natural process of individual ageing, the main impact on the age profile of any particular stock will be the net effect of movement out and the subsequent replacement by recruitment, transfer, or promotion. It is, therefore, important that we know something about the age characteristics of those entering or moving within the system.

Availability constraints

The last dimension we need to examine in specifying our replacement policies is whether any constraints exist on flows of people through the manpower system. It is as important to assess this as it is to note whether a flow is push or pull generated, or the way it mixes with other flows, or the characteristics of those being moved, since the value of any decision based on the parameters will be lost if, in the event, insufficient people are available to move along a particular flow when the rules say they ought to.

There are a number of different kinds of constraint which need to be looked for. First and most obvious is the recruitment constraint, whereby insufficient people of the right sort in terms of skills, or qualifications, or whatever other attributes are important, are available in the external labour market to be recruited. It would seem obvious that we should assess whether sufficient people are likely to be available, and yet, all too often, recruitment decisions are reached on the assumption of an unlimited supply of suitable people, and are only thrown into question when insufficient can be found. Recruitment constraints highlight the importance of taking serious account of the structure and behaviour of the external labour market in undertaking our manpower planning work in relation to the internal manpower system. We shall pick this up again later in the chapter, when we examine more specifically the importance of labour market information.

A second form of constraint is that affecting the availability of people suitable for promotion. We tend to assume that any individual, within a box within our manpower system from which promotion flow is generated, is available to be promoted and, therefore, base our calculations on that fact. In practice it may well be that only a proportion of those are actually suitable for promotion. For example, employees who have recently entered a particular level in the system will not have sufficient experience to make them suitable for progression for some time, and even those who have sufficient tenure in their current level may lack the basic skills, attributes, and potential for promotion to a higher level and have effectively 'topped-out' in a career development sense. Whatever the reason, we need to be aware, possibly by examination of the historical picture, as to how significant a constraint there is to promotability, and if it is of some magnitude, take it into account in our replacement policy function. In practice, we can often achieve this by making adjustments to our age profile rules regarding that particular promotion plan; perhaps this is most easily achieved when we use an age weight rule since we can adjust the promotion chance of any age group to reflect assumptions of tenure and experience which we would ideally like to see in any of our promotees.

A different sort of constraint relating to internal mobility within the manpower system is that where the stumbling block is actual geographical movement. This may be as much associated with lateral transfer as with promotion. Normally, this constraint will be taken into account in the drawing of the manpower system.

Organizational constraints of various sorts may also be a problem. If, for example, we require all our entrants to go through a training and induction programme, then clearly the capacity of our training scheme will be a determinant of the number of people we can recruit. The same would apply if we require all our trainees to go through some external training school. A different type of organizational constraint is an accommodation one. It is no good assuming unlimited scope for entry or geographic mobility if there is literally not the space to accommodate more than a handful of people.

Taking account of the labour market

The discussion regarding recruitment constraints in the last section mentioned the importance of taking account of the external labour market in our manpower planning work. No organization operates in total isolation from the external conditions around it. The labour market affects in many different ways the operation of the manpower system, and as a result creates opportunities and constraints for manpower planning and decision making.

If nothing else, the external labour market is important because it provides the basic source of all manpower for the organization. Any employing organization must know whether it can meet its current and future recruitment requirements without problems. How much competition is there for various sorts of manpower, for example school leavers or graduates? Will trained craftsmen or technicians be available in sufficient numbers? Or will the organization be forced to train its own? Will it face genuine skill shortages, or are individuals available if offered the right employment package? Are there difficulties in recruiting traditional sorts of skilled or qualified manpower? Are

177

there alternative sources of labour available, e.g., part-time workers, females, higher level recruits?

We have also already seen that the external labour market is a major factor in determining the level of labour wastage from the organization. This has two aspects to it: the qualitative, and the quantitative. On the qualitative side, we know that the relative job conditions within an organization, when compared with other organizations outside, will often be a major factor in determining employees' decisions to leave. We are thinking here of relative pay, whether locations of other organizations are more favourable to the individual as far as travelling is concerned than those of the firm in question, the relative attractiveness of the jobs on offer, of security, and prospects. However, the motivation to seek better terms of employment is not the only thing; what also matters is the quantitative impact of the external labour market, in terms of the actual level of availability of alternative jobs. No matter how motivated an individual is to leave an organization, through awareness of how much better the conditions are in other firms, if these firms have no recruitment opportunities available, then the individual is very unlikely to resign his position. Similar factors will apply where an organization is trying to increase losses through, for example, enforced redundancy. In this case the availability of alternative jobs and relative pay and conditions will act as a major determinant of how easily a redundancy programme can be implemented and the amount of compensation likely to be needed. In a buoyant labour market, with many job vacancies, redundancy programmes are easier to negotiate and cost less.

The external labour market is, thirdly, a major influence on employment policies and practices. This may be through the way it affects social attitudes to work, e.g., willingness to be mobile; employment legislation; government intervention policies; national/international trends in working practices, e.g., shorter working weeks, holidays, harmonization, single status, worksharing, part-time work, and trends towards service sector employment; developments in technology and work organization, e.g., the growth and implementation of micro-processors, robot assembly, and the automated office.

In summary, the external labour market affects the organization in so many ways that it is essential to see it as an integral part of the manpower system, as important as any internal stock or flow.

LOOKING AT THE LABOUR MARKET

Until recently labour market analysis has been the preserve of the specialist, more concerned with the theories of economics than the practicalities of successfully managing an organization. As a result, the manpower planner trying to take a very pragmatic look at the local labour market surrounding his particular organization faces a number of problems: there is no established approach relevant to the needs of employing organizations for examining their labour market, or even helping them identify the basic questions they ought to be asking; while there is a mountain of labour market data available, it is extremely disorganized and patchy and in the past there have been no clear guides as to how to search through it in a selective way; many of the data have also suffered from being at the wrong level of detail, being often at a broad national or sector level unsuitable for the use of the individual organization; and many data are out of date with, for example, the main source of household and workforce data – the census – being up to 10 years out of date at any one time.

Overall then, the manpower planner faces the problem of having to commit a tremendous amount of resource to examining the external labour market with the prospect of very little return for his investment. More recently, however, and in recognition of the importance of external labour market information to the employer in determining manpower policies, attention has been directed towards rectifying this situation, and a practical approach to labour market analysis is now emerging. The key steps in this area are as follows:

– Monitor and be aware of the overall labour market scene and future trends.
– Identify employee groups which require a closer examination of their particular labour market.
– Define the boundaries of the market for these groups, e.g., local, national, international.
– Collect and analyse the relevant information on the characteristics of the labour market so defined and the flow of people into and out of it.

Let us look at each of these stages in a little more detail.

Structure of the labour market   All employing organizations are affected to a greater or lesser extent over time by broad long-term changes in the structure of the labour market. A sensible step in analysing the labour market relevant to the organization is to gain some awareness of these overall labour market features. The sorts of things that we are thinking of here are as follows:

1. **Demographic trends and changes in the structure of the working population**   Knowledge of the age structure of the current population and the pattern of birth gives us a very good basis for estimating how many people of working age should be available at points in the future.
2. **Flows from the education system**   Clearly, if we wish to know something about broad skills and qualifications of those who will be available for employment in the community as a whole, we need to be aware of the pattern of outflows from the education system at both school and further education level.
3. **Participation rates**   These are important because they give us an indication of what proportion of those of any given age can be expected to offer

themselves for work. While this tends to remain fairly constant and remains high for males of working age in past years it has increased quite dramatically for females, particularly married females, indicating a much higher willingness of this section of the population to put themselves forward for employment.

4. **Area of employment**   Knowledge is also useful of general changes in the main sources of available employment. This has shown the most noticeable trend in recent years towards the service industries away from manufacturing.

5. **Hours of work**   There is a steady underlying trend over time towards shorter working hours and longer holiday entitlement. This could affect all organizations in terms of a requirement for higher levels of employment by way of compensation unless there is a commensurate change in productivity levels.

6. **Changing working patterns**   In addition to the general trend towards shorter working hours there are also changing patterns of demand for part-time employment. This is particularly associated with periods of high demand for employment of female staff seeking work to fit in with family commitments. It can have major implications for the structuring and organization of working routines in order to fit part-time jobs into what had previously been full-time working situations.

In many ways, information covering the above areas is the most readily accessible since it tends to form the substance of official returns and statistics. Major sources of information are the census, Office of Population and Census Surveys reports, the Department of Employment's *Employment Gazette*. A wealth of information is available on educational flows and this has been most effectively summarized in the annual Institute of Manpower Studies' compilation of educational statistics.

Examining particular employee groups   While looking at and monitoring broad labour market information and trends will give us an overview of the direction in the structure and behaviour of the working population as a whole, the real need of the manpower planner in an organization is to assess the specific labour market conditions affecting the particular groups of individuals it employs. Clearly in an organization of any size this would be an onerous task, to map out the labour market characteristics for every employee group, and, therefore, it is sensible to concentrate on those groups where the labour market dimension is most significant. The sorts of factors which can be used to identify such groups are the following:

1. **Size**   A job category covering a relatively large number of employees may well imply a proportionately large recruitment need and, therefore, de-

mand special consideration as to whether that recruitment need will be met in the future.

2. **A significant increase in recruitment requirement** This might be the case where, for example, there is growth taking place, or, alternatively, an increased level of wastage is being experienced.

3. **Key skill groups** The labour market for job groups involving individuals with exceptional skills needs to be monitored very closely as the organization could be at considerable risk if there is even a small change in the numbers of such individuals available for employment.

4. **Shortage groups** Job groups where there has traditionally been scarcity or shortage clearly need to have their labour markets monitored.

5. **Establishing a new location** Where an organization is setting up in a new location, or relocating its existing activities, careful attention must be paid to the availability of suitable staff at the new site and of other characteristics of the local labour market.

6. **Reliance on external training** Changes in the amount of training opportunity available, whether increased or decreased, could have a significant impact on the availability of staff to the organization.

7. **Transferable skills** The retention of employees with skills of interest and attraction to other employers is clearly susceptible to the changing availability of external job opportunities and, therefore, demands careful monitoring of this facet of the external labour market.

Having identified the key manpower groups requiring a closer examination and monitoring of the associated labour markets, there is a need to define the boundaries or catchment area of the labour market involved. Traditionally, the higher the skill or professional content of the job, the geographically broader the boundaries of the associated labour market. So taking categories of an employee in the Health Service as an example, staff such as porters, cleaners, and catering people would typically be recruited in the local vicinity of the hospital in which they work and if they left for another job, would seek it in another hospital or firm in the near vicinity. Nursing staff, on the other hand, would typically be recruited on a broader geographical basis, often being recruited through national advertisements and seeking jobs throughout the country. Doctors in contrast not only operate within a national, but also an international, labour market in that posts are often filled by employees from overseas and doctors will also seek appointments in other countries as well as in the United Kingdom.

Boundaries of labour markets for employee groups The sorts of information which can help to determine for any particular job group the boundaries of its catchment area include:

(a) the home location and travel to work patterns of existing employees;

(b) home locations relative to work of recent recruits and of applicants for jobs;
(c) the estimation of individuals leaving the organization to take up other appointments;
(d) local patterns of housing and transportation.

Collection of information   Having defined the boundaries of any particular labour market, what sorts of information need to be collected in order to make a proper analysis of it? In practice a labour market is a dynamic structure akin to the internal manpower system in that it has both stock and flow features. We need, therefore, to collect information which will not only give us an indication of the numbers and characteristics of those within the external labour market, but also of the factors which will cause these structural features to change over time. Information might therefore include:

(a) the size and characteristics in terms of age, sex, qualifications, etc., of the local workforce;
(b) levels and types of unemployment and vacancies;
(c) patterns of movement into and out of the labour market and between firms within it, i.e., labour turnover;
(d) entries into the labour market from the educational system;
(e) the alternative employment opportunities and future changes to these;
(f) relative pay and working conditions.

Unfortunately, there are no clear-cut sources for these kinds of information. Local job centres can sometimes supply a wide variety of information on the characteristics of the local working population, trends in unemployment, and indications of developing shortages or surpluses. However, this is very much on a discretionary basis, and the amount of assistance will vary from area to area. Other sources for information include careers offices, which can supplement information on the future availability of school leavers and the relative demand for their services as well as the operation of work experience/youth opportunity programmes in the area. The local authority can also be a very useful source of information on residential, transportation, and industrial development trends which may affect the availability of suitable manpower and the demand for it from competing employers; the local authority structure plan can be a very valuable source of information in this area. Other information may be available from trade associations, chambers of commerce, employers' federations, and local trade union offices. However, there are no overall standards as to what is available and from whom and, therefore, the collection of information usually relies on the knowledge and goodwill of local officials and on cross-checking what is often anecdotal information from one agency against that from another.

What can we do with the information when collected? Well, first, we can examine the current and the future estimated availability and demand for the occupation and skill groups we may be interested in to ascertain whether there are likely to be any obvious shortages in either number or quality of individuals available for recruitment. Secondly, we can use the information as a basis for comparison to give us an indication of whether the characteristic of our own workforce is in line with that of the labour market as a whole; if not it may be indicative of significant differences in pay, job conditions, or employment policy, which can be investigated. Thirdly, we can ascertain whether there are any impending changes in the labour market, particularly in terms of the availability of increased amounts of alternative employment which might put pressure on our being able to retain the staff we want.

Summary

Many of the long-term manpower problems of an organization cannot be solved or alleviated without reference to its replacement policy. For example, an organization changing its technology will find itself having to consider how it recruits, trains, and develops the employees it needs for the new technology. It will also have to consider how it can utilize existing employees who only have skills appropriate to the outdated technology. Quantifying the options dealt with in this chapter is difficult but very rewarding.

In many cases the outcome of such considerations is to focus attention on the sources from which we replace employees – the labour market. At this point organizations faced with shortages give up and throw money at the problem, increasing starting salaries to attract recruits. Their pessimism is often based on hearsay: casual conversations with other organizations which are also experiencing difficulty in recruiting.

Obtaining a quantitative assessment of the shortage is regarded as too difficult an exercise and the results too subjective but it is a practical proposition to quantify the supply of particular types of labour in localities and those organizations that have conducted such studies have found them beneficial.

7.

Looking into the future: the use of manpower models

In following through our approach to manpower problems and issues we began by stressing the importance of describing any manpower group in a way which reflects the key elements of its structure and the main routes by which individuals move into, through, and out of it. This definition of the manpower system, in terms of its component stocks and flows, provides our basic framework for understanding how manpower behaves in the organization and the implications this has for policy and decision making.

Influences on the manpower system

We then looked at the problems of analysing and quantifying the three main kinds of factor influencing the behaviour of the system:

1. **Our future manpower requirements** How many and what sorts of people do we currently have within the boxes of our manpower system? What changes do we see occurring in the nature and scope of our organization's activities or the technology we use which might require us to increase or decrease our numbers or change the balance of skills? How much manpower can we afford?
2. **The pattern of future losses** How many people will be reaching their normal retirement age? Do we have or might we be instituting any early retirement or severance policies? What factors can be most strongly associated with the loss of voluntary wastage out of the different parts of our manpower system and can this help us assess how losses might change over time?
3. **Our replacement policies** When a recruitment, promotion, or transfer occurs, is it always because there is a vacant job to be filled, or sometimes do we move people for the sake of moving them, e.g., to reward performance? Do we prefer to 'grow our own' or 'buy in' from outside? How much

experience do we demand in our promotees and how much maturity in our recruits? Is there a limit on the number of people suitable for promotion at any point in time? Can the external labour market adequately supply all our needs for new entrants?

At this point let us return to our basic objective: helping managers to respond in a more informed way to questions such as:

- How many apprentice trainees do we require in the future?
- What would be the impact of introducing graduate recruitment?
- How can we meet our estimated need for experienced senior management into the next decade?
- Can we make the desired reduction in our workforce without creating more problems for ourselves in the future?
- What are the consequences of a large retirement bulge in the age profile of our technical staff and what are the options available for dealing with it?
- What would happen if we maintained current promotion prospects into the future?
- What are the implications of actively introducing equal opportunity employment?

These questions, typical of those facing every employing organization, require us to look at the behaviour of our manpower systems in a dynamic way so that we can examine how they are likely to respond over time to the key influences on them and then assess the impact of any new policy option which might be pursued. This process by which we turn the handle on a manpower system to move it into the future is that of 'modelling the manpower system'.

Manpower modelling is undoubtedly one of the most rewarding areas of manpower planning work but at the same time it is one which is still viewed with a good deal of scepticism and apprehension. Much of the problem is a reflection of the way manpower planning developed during the 1960s and the early 1970s as a highly mathematical-technique-based activity, to the extent that 'manpower planning' and the use of mathematical 'manpower models' became synonomous. The presumption was that by making manpower planning techniques and in particular manpower models more and more complex, striving to reflect every small detail of the real situation, that they would more accurately represent the present and as a consequence better predict the future and the manpower policies which should be followed. The resulting techniques were invariably expensive to build and run, required vast quantities of historical information as their input, produced vast reams of paper as their output, were so complex as to be unintelligible to all but a very few specialist 'model builders' and, with a very few exceptions, failures as useful aids to manpower management. Where the 'model builders' had gone wrong was first to presume that a striving for increasingly accurate forecasts of the future was anything more than a search for spurious precision given the change and uncertainty surrounding even the most apparently stable organizations. By building more and more complexity into their tools, they had also engendered a mystique which forced those involved in using the outputs from the models either blindly to accept what they said or, more sensibly, reject it out of hand on the basis that they could not judge its value without appreciating how its results were arrived at.

It is only recently that our perception of how we should look at and use manpower models has matured. Manpower models are simply a means of translating the logic and rules underlying the operation of a manpower system and in particular the flow of individuals into, through, and out of it into a set of simple mathematical relationships. For any given assumptions about future job numbers, loss rates, and replacement policies these relationships can then be used to calculate the outcome for the manpower system over time. To understand and use manpower models does not depend on a degree in 'difficult sums'; they do not necessarily require large amounts of historical data; they can provide powerful insights at a practical level into the behaviour and effective management of an organization's manpower resources.

Manpower modelling: the basic steps

The essential simplicity yet power of manpower modelling is best conveyed by an example.

Let us assume for a moment that we have received an urgent summons from the Generalissima of the little known republic of San Lavoro. She is very worried about the state of her army, famed for the number of battles it fights with neighbouring countries. Unfortunately, it has lost most of these in recent times and although the Generalissima's immediate reaction was to shoot one in ten of the soldiers that had survived, she now reflects that this might not be the full answer. We are asked to investigate the problem.

Following our usual approach to looking at manpower problems, the first sensible thing for us to do is to define the underlying manpower system of the army. This does not prove too difficult to do and is shown in Fig. 7.1. As we can see, there are only two significant groups of employees, Generals and Privates, and an obvious thought is that their lack of success on the battlefield may result from there being more than twice as many of the former (102) as the latter (50). We also note that retirement and wastage occur out of both levels and that the established replacement policies mean that vacancies at General level will be filled only by promotion from Privates who in turn will be replaced only by raw recruits from outside.

On seeing the manpower system, the Generalissima determines that the fighting ability of her army might be improved by reducing the number of Generals, who plan the battles at a safe distance, and increasing the number of

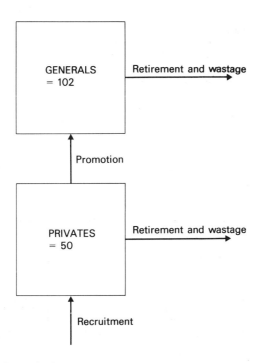

Fig. 7.1. The San Lavoro Armed Forces – 1. Manpower system

Privates who actually go and fight them. After giving the matter some careful consideration she concludes that, as a start, over the next year the General level can be safely reduced by six, from 102 to 96, without fear of a *coup d'état* by those made redundant. At the same time she believes that the Private level should be increased from 50 to 58 soldiers. What she needs to know is what the implications of achieving these changes will be, particularly in terms of the effect on promotions and recruitment.

QUANTIFYING THE KEY FACTORS

Our next step in meeting the Generalissima's requirements is to express in quantitative terms our assumptions about the key factors influencing the behaviour of the manpower system over the year in question. We have set out these assumptions or operating rules in Fig. 7.2:

1. **Future number of jobs** Defining the future manpower requirements of the army has been simplified by the Generalissima setting the numerical targets she wishes to achieve over the next year: namely a contraction of the Generals from 102 to 96; an increase of Privates from 50 to 58.

187

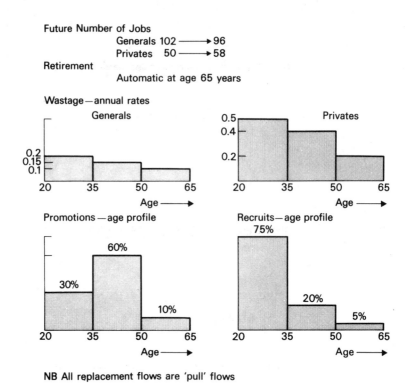

Future Number of Jobs
Generals 102 ——→ 96
Privates   50 ——→ 58

Retirement

Automatic at age 65 years

Wastage—annual rates

Fig. 7.2. The San Lavoro Armed Forces – 2. Operating rules and policies

2. Losses As in many organizations, the current retirement policy of the republic's army is to release its Generals and Privates on a pension if they manage to survive to the age of 65; there are no immediate plans to change this policy. All the remaining members of the army are considered to be at risk of other forms of wastage, which usually take the form of a military funeral. A small exercise has recently been undertaken to examine past patterns of wastage and the results of this are shown in the form of two sets of age-specific wastage rates, one for Generals and one for Privates. Visual analysis clearly highlights two important features of the wastage behaviour of the army:

(a) The rates for Generals are clearly lower than those of the Privates reflecting the High Command strategy of leadership from behind. In fact, the highest rate for Generals, 20 per cent of those aged from 20 to 34, represents the lowest rate for Privates.

(b) Both groups show the classic association between propensity to leave and duration of time within the organization, as measured by age. The historical analysis has suggested that this relationship can best be

188

reflected by presenting raw data in terms of three broad age bands, 20–34 years of age, 35–49, and 50–65. In the case of the Generals, annual wastage rates decreased from 20 per cent for the youngest group to half this amount, 10 per cent, for those aged 50 or more. In contrast, half of the youngest Privates are expected to be lost to the army each year. The analysis, however, suggests that with some experience in the field, Privates learn something of the art of survival and as a result the annual wastage rate for those aged 35–49 is a little bit less at 40 per cent. Those who reached the age of 50 in this particular army have clearly learnt how to keep their heads down and the rate of loss for them falls to only 20 per cent being lost in each year.

3. **Replacement policies** The first point which emerges in discussing the policies underlying recruitment and promotion is that up to now movements occurred only when a vacancy had been created which had to be filled, e.g., a promotion would only take place from Private to General if a vacancy arose at the higher level. Replacement policies are, therefore, assumed to be 'pull' driven as opposed to a 'push' policy where recruitment and promotions would occur at a given specified number or rate per year, regardless of whether jobs in the box of the manpower system being entered had become vacant.

4. **Promotion policies** In the filling of General posts a further assumption based on current practice is that all vacancies will be filled by promotion from the Private level. By examination of the records on historical movements and an analysis of the career progression diagram for this system, we have concluded that the requirement for some experience in the Generals means that we would expect about 60 per cent of Privates being promoted to be in the 35–49 age range. We also expect about 30 per cent of promotions to go to high flyers in the youngest age category of Privates or at least to those in this group who can afford big enough bribes. It is unlikely that more than 10 per cent of promotees would come from veteran soldiers of 50 or more.

5. **Recruitment** In the past the filling of vacancies at Private level has been exclusively by recruitment, with the concentration on finding muscle-power rather than brains and experience; this way the army kept its payroll down and anyway why waste money when so many Privates are 'lost' in their initial period of service? Translated into a recruitment profile, we assume that if past policies continue, approximately 75 per cent of new recruits would be in the youngest age category, with only about 20 per cent from the middle age group and a token 5 per cent of older soldiers aged 50 years or more; this latter entry represents the army's policy of social responsibility in recruiting Privates made redundant by neighbouring countries' armies.

We are advised that there are no constraints on the availability of recruits or the suitability of privates for promotion.

Having set our assumptions about the factors we believe will influence the San Lavoro Army's manpower system let us now model the system to see how it is likely to behave over time.

The Generalissima has asked us to look at the effect of reducing the number of Generals and increasing the number of Privates and, in particular, the impact on recruitment and promotions over the next year. If we take recruitment into Private for a start, we have assumed this to be a 'pull' flow and the numbers required are, therefore, going to reflect the number of vacancies which occur during the year in the Private level. Some vacancies may occur at this level because of the need to replace individuals leaving during the year through retirement or wastage and others as a result of the extra posts created by the Generalissima's expansion policy at this level. Vacancies, however, will also arise through the need to replace Privates promoted to fill vacancies which arise at General level during the year. As a consequence, therefore, to be able to say something about the impact of the Generalissima's plans on recruitment means we must first ascertain the impact they will have on promotions between Private and General.

In turn, promotions between the two levels are also assumed to be a 'pull' flow and they will arise only when vacancies occur at General level, because of the need to replace retirees and other leavers at the higher grade; in practice the requirement to reduce the number of Generals means that we will not require to replace everyone who leaves. The implication for our analysis is that if we are to learn something about the resultant promotion flow, we must first look at and estimate the level of outflow from this higher level.

Logical sequence   In essence then, the logical sequence of steps we need to go through to model the behaviour of the system over the period of a year must start by looking at the flows out of the top of the system and follow through the ripple effect this has all the way down to the point where we recruit outsiders into the Private level; the details are set out in Fig. 7.3. Putting this into practice we first analyse what is likely to happen at General level (the calculations are shown in Fig. 7.4).

1. **Estimate retirements**   As retirement is an age-based rule, it is clearly necessary that we know something about the age profile of the Generals in service at the start of the year in order to make an estimate of the numbers likely to retire. The age profile is shown in Fig. 7.4. Of the 102 Generals at the start of the year, 10 are in the youngest age band, 60 in the middle (as one might expect from the age profile for promotions to General), and 32 are aged 50 or more. As we do not have information available on the numbers in service by individual ages, we estimate the annual level of

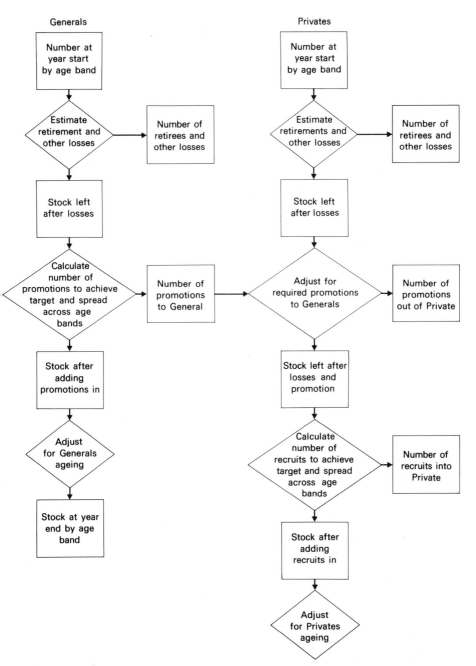

Fig. 7.3. The San Lavoro Armed Forces – 3. Flowchart of the basic modelling steps

191

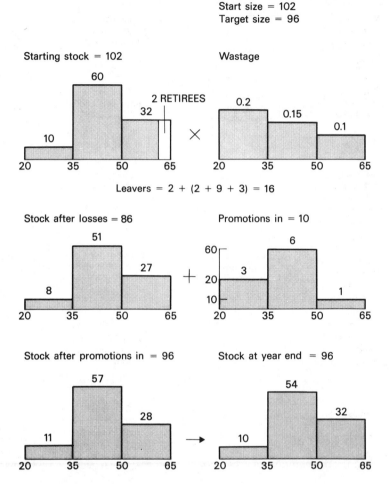

Start size = 102
Target size = 96

Starting stock = 102

60

2 RETIREES

32

10

20   35   50   65

Wastage

0.2

0.15

0.1

20   35   50   65

×

Leavers = 2 + (2 + 9 + 3) = 16

Stock after losses = 86

51

27

8

20   35   50   65

Promotions in = 10

60

6

20

3

10

1

20   35   50   65

+

Stock after promotions in = 96

57

28

11

20   35   50   65

Stock at year end = 96

54

32

10

20   35   50   65

→

Fig. 7.4. The San Lavoro Armed Forces – 4. Calculations year 1 for the Generals

retirements by assuming that the numbers in the oldest age band are equally spread and, therefore, 1/15 (there is a range of 15 years from 50 to 64 inclusive) or approximately two Generals will be coming up to retiring age each year.

2. **Estimate other losses** Our researches suggest that those within a year of retirement invariably make it; by this stage they are expert at keeping out of trouble and well away from any fighting. Setting aside the two anticipated retirees then we assume all the other Generals are at risk of wastage, for one reason or another. In order to estimate how many this is likely to be we apply the annual wastage rates, assumed as part of our operating rules to

192

the number remaining. Of the Generals aged 20–34 we assume 20 per cent (or 0.2) would be lost each year and as we start with 10 individuals in this age band, we would estimate a loss of 2, i.e., 10 × 0.2. Similarly, we expect to lose 15 per cent (or 0.15) of the 60 Generals in the middle age band (i.e., 9). Of those over 50 we expect to lose 10 per cent (or 0.1) which, when we exclude the two Generals coming up for retirement, leads us to estimate a loss for the year of 30 × 0.1 or 3 individuals. Therefore, we expect our losses excluding retirement to be 14 Generals and with retirement a loss over the year of 16 individuals.

3. **Estimate vacancies**   Taking our expected retirements and other losses away from the appropriate parts of the initial age profile, we are left, assuming for the moment no replacement has taken place, with 86 Generals at the end of the year of whom 8 are in the youngest age group, with 51 in the middle and 27 in the oldest. We know that we do not want to replace all these leavers since we require to reduce numbers at this level to 96, a target rundown of 6 over the year. As a result, against the total estimate of 16 losses, we only require to replace 10 of these individuals to make the numbers up to our end of year target, i.e., we have 10 vacancies.

4. **Estimate promotions**   As the replacement policies assume that all vacancies at General level will be filled by promotion of Privates, we now need to promote 10 individuals from the lower grade. We want the majority of these, some 60 per cent (or 0.6), to have some degree of experience and maturity and, therefore, in terms of our assumed promotion age profile we would expect 6 (= 10 × 0.6) individuals to come within the middle age range. Similarly, we would expect 30 per cent, or 3 of the 10, to fall within the 20–34 year age band and only 1 (10 per cent) in the oldest.

5. **Adjust for promotions in**   Correcting the overall age profile of the Generals to reflect the age profile of those promoted in, gives us the 96 individuals the Generalissima requires spread in terms of the age bands as 11, 57, and 28.

6. **Adjust for the ageing process**   The final step we must make to complete our initial modelling exercise on the Generals is to reflect the natural process of ageing in the population. Specifically, we can expect some individuals to move automatically from one of our broad age bands to another each year and by implication assume different behaviour patterns, for example, a reduced likelihood of leaving. It is, therefore, important that we adjust the age profile of the Generals after promotions in have been taken into account to reflect these changes. In this particular case, and by again assuming that individuals are evenly spread by age within each of the age bands, we would expect one General to reach the age of 35 by the end of the year and, therefore, need to be shown in the middle rather than the youngest age band. Similarly, four individuals can expect to be moved from the middle age band to the oldest; the net effect in the 35–49 age band is a reduction of three. This still gives us an end year position at the General level of 96

individuals but the age profile is now 10, 54, 32. We have now completed the analysis for the Generals.

We can now carry out an identical analysis for the Private level as shown in Fig. 7.5.

Looking first at the initial age profile we see that the majority of the 50 Privates are in the youngest age category reflecting the recruitment age profile and the high level of loss from this group. Using the same basis for estimating the likely number of retirements as for the Generals indicates that none of the five Privates in the oldest age band can be expected to retire during the year. It is assumed, therefore, that all Privates are at risk of wastage and we can estimate the numbers affected by using our assumed annual wastage rates. This leads us to expect that 50 per cent of the 30 Privates in the youngest age band (i.e., 15) will leave during the year, 40 per cent of the 15 in the middle age band (i.e., six), and just one or 20 per cent of the five in the 50+ age band. This leaves us, after wastage, with 28 Privates spread across the age bands 15, 9, and 4.

From our previous analysis of the Generals we know that movement out of the Privates will be caused not only by wastage but also by the need to promote upwards to fill vacancies at the higher level. Our analysis showed the need to promote 10 Privates with an age profile 3, 6, and 1. This implies that if no replacement takes place at the Private level, the effects of wastage and promotion out will be to reduce the number from 50 at the start of the year to a mere 18, of whom 12 will be in the youngest age band and 3 in each of the other two bands. In practice we do want to replace these losses and, in addition, fill eight new jobs which the Generalissima wishes to create. This means a vacancy requirement of 40 individuals who, by following the current replacement policies, will all be recruited from outside. Again, examination of the assumed age profile for recruits tells us that 75 per cent or 30 will be in the youngest age band, 20 per cent or 8 in the middle, and 5 per cent or just 2 in the oldest, under our policy of social responsibility. Adding in these recruits, having first adjusted for wastage and promotion out, gives us a Private complement of 58 people as targeted, with an age profile 42, 11, 5.

As the final step in modelling the Privates we must, as with the Generals, adjust for the ageing process. We estimate that two Privates will reach the age of 35 during the year and one Private will reach the age of 50. The number in the 20–34 age band, therefore, reduces from 42 to 40, the oldest band increases from 5 to 6 and in the middle age range we anticipate a net increase of 1 from 11 to 12. We have now concluded the analysis of the Privates.

Figure 7.6 summarizes the outcome of our exercise in modelling the behaviour of the army's manpower system. At the General level we have reduced from an initial complement of 102 to the required target of 96 and in the process anticipate that there will be 2 retirements, 14 other losses, 10 promotions in from Private level and expect the resulting age profile for Generals to show a

194

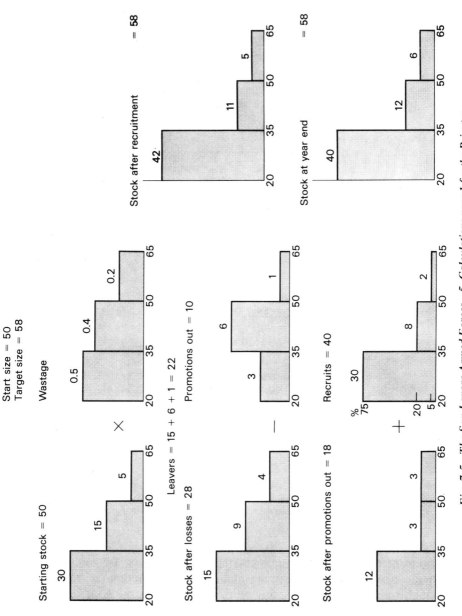

Fig. 7.5. The San Lavoro Armed Forces – 5. Calculations year 1 for the Privates

195

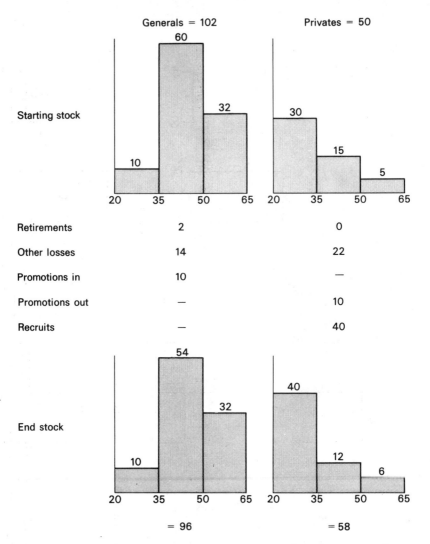

Generals = 102   Privates = 50

Starting stock

Retirements   2   0

Other losses   14   22

Promotions in   10   —

Promotions out   —   10

Recruits   —   40

End stock

= 96   = 58

Fig. 7.6. The San Lavoro Armed Forces – 6. Summary of year 1 manpower changes

significant reduction in the numbers aged 35–49 years. By contrast, at the Private level we have looked at the implications of expanding from 50 to 58 and though we are not expecting any retirement, we estimate 22 other losses, 10 promotions out to the General level (a 20 per cent promotion rate in relation to the 50 Privates at the start of the year) and the need to recruit a substantial 40 recruits (an 80 per cent recruitment rate for the year) to make up the required

196

numbers. At this level the change in the age profile mainly reflects the effect of the large number of young recruits into the Private ranks.

ASSESSING CHANGES IN POLICY

Let us now suppose that when we report back the results of our initial investigation to the Generalissima, she expresses great interest but has second thoughts about the target numbers set for the end of the year. Specifically, she does not believe she can get away with a reduction of six Generals in one year without needing to double the size of her bodyguard. 'For instance' she queries, 'if we just went for a reduction of three, how would that change the picture?'

Minor changes To answer her question is easy since all we require to do is repeat the simple calculations we have just been through but, on this occasion, our estimated vacancies at the General level over the year will have to be increased by three because the smaller targeted drop in numbers means more of those leaving will need to be replaced. We can then easily work through the implications of the resulting increase in promotion numbers as it affects vacancies at Private level and the consequent need for recruits.

In fact, having carried through our analysis once with one particular set of assumptions, we could repeat it any number of times with a whole variety of different assumptions; the simple logic and calculations remain the same even though the details of the rules and assumptions may change. Not only could we look at different end-year targets in the two levels, but also the effect of a different retirement age, increased or decreased wastage rates, and possible changes to replacement policies in terms of, for example, an older recruitment age profile.

Further, if we can carry through the analysis for one year we could do it for any number of years. If, for instance, the Generalissima asked us to examine the effect of continuing the same target changes in numbers for five years all it would mean would be that we should carry through our simple sequence of calculations five successive times, but each year starting from the age profile arrived at at the end of the previous year. The outcome on this basis for the second year is shown in Fig. 7.7. Readers are invited to follow through the calculations for themselves to see if they can reach the same results.

Changes that affect the manpower system So far we have done very well and avoided being cast into the republic's dungeons for an indefinite period. However, the Generalissima now presents us with a rather more complicated requirement. Having seen the results of the initial analysis, she wishes to retain the original rundown of the Generals to 96 and expansion of the Privates to 58, but is concerned that the need for some 40 recruits, which is likely to result, is much too high for the army to cope with: 'We won't have enough uniforms

197

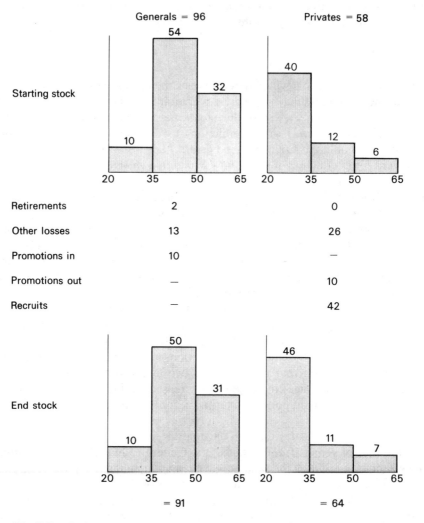

Fig. 7.7. *The San Lavoro Armed Forces – 7. Summary of year 2 manpower changes*

without bullet holes in them to go round.' How can we meet the required targets without needing so many recruits into the Private level?

To examine whether we can come up with an alternative policy which will meet this new constraint, let us first take another look at the basic manpower system for the army; it appears in Fig. 7.8, drawn to scale.

Examining the alternatives We wish to reduce the level of recruitment into the Privates and we know from the manpower system and the operating assump-

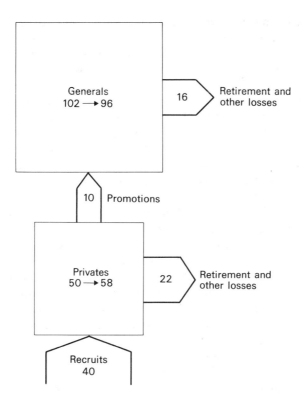

Fig. 7.8. The San Lavoro Armed Forces – 8. Year 1 manpower changes shown visually

tions we have made, that the size of this flow will depend on the number of Private vacancies which arise. To try and change the recruitment level, therefore, we need somehow to reduce the number of vacancies. What are the possibilities?

1. **Vacancies arising through the creation of new posts**   Since the Generalissima wants to stick to her expansion target at this lower level, no real opportunity exists to reduce the number of vacancies and hence the recruitment resulting from this policy.

2. **Vacancies resulting from promotions to General**   Clearly, there is potential scope for reducing the vacancies at Private level by allowing fewer promotions to the higher level. How might this be achieved? Two possibilities present themselves:

   (a) *Try and reduce the number of Generals leaving each year*   By putting the retirement age back, for example, we might reduce the overall losses during the year by two which would require two fewer promotions and hence two fewer recruitments at the lower level. Similarly, by

199

siting command headquarters even further away from the battlefields and by paying our Generals a bonus for not changing sides, we might attempt to reduce other losses and the resultant impact this has on movements into and through the system: as many of these losses are beyond the direct control of the organization, how much effect we would have is open to question and would probably have to be seen as a longer term possibility. However, just looking at the relative magnitude of the outflow from the Generals compared to the recruitment flow into the Privates (Fig. 7.8) immediately suggests that we would need dramatically to effect losses from the Generals in order to make any noticeable change in the unacceptably high recruitment figure.

(b) *Do not fill all the vacancies arising at General level by promotion of privates* The suggestion here is that the army could, for the first time ever, recruit some Generals from outside its own ranks. This is a radical new departure in thinking and, before we have the nerve to go and suggest it to the Generalissima, we need to investigate the consequences of doing it. In practice, all this means is working through the calculations of our model once more but this time taking account of the effect of a new flow into the General level. Before we start though, we will need to amend the manpower system (see Fig. 7.9) to extend our replacement policies to reflect this change.

Specifically we have to answer the following questions:

(i) Will this new recruitment flow be pull or push generated? Clearly, as their objective is to reduce the number of vacancy-driven promotions, we will wish this to operate in the pull mode.

(ii) How will we mix recruitment and promotion flows when vacancies occur? Since the army has never recruited Generals before, there is no historical information to guide us on this question. Our best practice, therefore, is to identify a range of mixing assumptions which reflect either the relative proportions we would desire ('I think it would be good for us to fill at least half our General jobs with those who have had experience of this work in other armies') or which we would accept ('if I can't find anyone suitable to promote I will buy in all I require from the outside market').

(iii) What will the age profile of recruits look like? Here again, we cannot base ourselves on the past and must make some form of guesstimate, e.g., that the age profile will correspond to that we would expect for promotees from Private level.

(iv) Are there any constraints on the availability of new recruits? Again, knowledge might be limited in this area and one might have to guess what a reasonable maximum limit might be.

With this additional information we can follow through the sequence of modelling calculations but, having established the level of vacancies at the

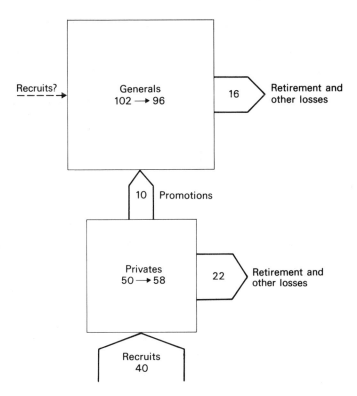

Fig. 7.9. The San Lavoro Armed Forces – 9. The recruit generals direct policy option

General level, we will only assign the specified proportion to promotions, the remainder to recruits, and this in turn will have consequences on the number of vacancies for Privates and hence the number of recruits we need to bring in at this level. The important thing is that having determined the new replacement policy encompassing the possibility of external recruitment into Generals, we must follow through using our modelling process to highlight for the Generalissima the resultant effect on the behaviour of the system and hence the viability of this policy option.

3. **Vacancies arising from the need to replace losses at Private level** As for the Generals, it is now worth considering the scope for reducing the currently high rates of loss among Privates. Given the current state of the army there are a whole variety of options we might recommend to the Generalissima. For example:

(a) *Sign peace treaties with neighbouring countries* In effect we would be changing the organization's objectives and if there are no more battles to fight we can expect a rapid decrease in the levels of wastage and our basic manning in the army would also be suitable for review.

201

(b) *Invest in some armoured bicycles and form a mounted unit*   By employing the increased technology of the armoured bicycle we should produce a more mobile and better protected army and see less unnecessary wastage among the foot soldiers. We can again examine the implications of such a policy, first by redefining our manpower system to introduce this extra dimension. There is more than one way we could approach the manning of the new unit and this will influence the way the manpower system is redrawn. The manpower system in Fig. 7.10a assumes, for example, that we directly recruit experienced bicycle personnel from elsewhere. In contrast, Fig. 7.10b shows a system where the mounted unit is manned by transfer of foot soldiers. Whatever system is decided on we must then follow through the sequence of steps in our modelling process to see how it is likely to behave over time and the implications for promotion and recruitment.

(c) *Introduce a training programme for new Privates*   Up to now the practice of the army has been to put all its new recruits directly into the front line of battle. The argument was that this policy of immersion training was the best way of giving individuals experience and would effectively deal with poor performers. Not surprisingly, a high percentage of these new arrivals never lived to fight another day. Against this background, the introduction of a training programme looks, at face value, a very plausible way of giving the average Private the necessary skills and experience to stay alive.

Assessing the implications   As the introduction of training seems to be a very promising idea let us look at how we would go about assessing the implications in quantitative terms of implementing such a policy. As always, our first step must be to consider how the introduction of this policy will change our basic manpower system. In essence we are talking about the creation of a new box at the bottom of the system into which a large component of our recruits will come and spend a period of time before appointment as front line Privates. As well as adding this extra box to our system, we must also identify the additional flows associated with it, namely: an entry flow into the training box; a flow out of training representing in-training losses and failure, e.g., sitting on one's own hand grenade; post-graduation losses to, for instance, other armies; a flow representing the appointment of graduates of the training school into the fighting force. How the revised manpower system might look is shown in Fig. 7.11.

As before, we will need to describe the rules governing movement along these flows. For example, in the case of the losses, age-related wastage rates will need to be specified, probably based on guesstimation or drawing from the experience of other armies. In defining the recruitment and appointment flows, the four questions relating to replacement policies identified earlier will need to

202

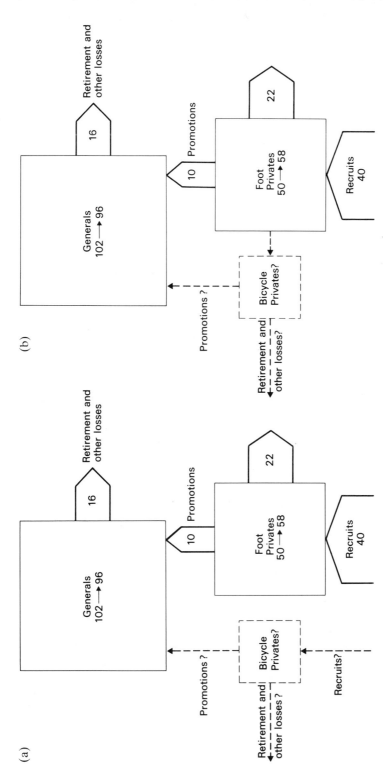

Fig. 7.10. The San Lavoro Armed Forces – 10. Adding a bicycle corps. (a) Direct recruitment. (b) Transfer from foot corps

203

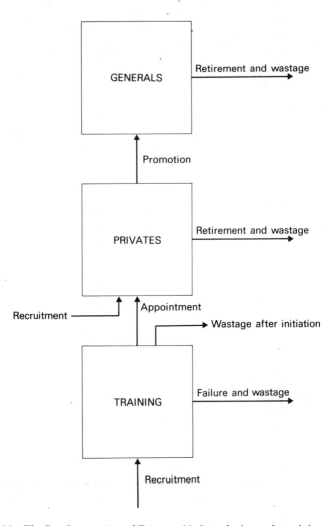

Fig. 7.11. The San Lavoro Armed Forces – 11. Introducing cadet training scheme

be answered. However, once this extra information has been put together we can still revert to our basic process of calculation which, despite the increased number of computations required, will allow us to see not only the impact of training on the direct recruitment of Privates, but also give us an indication of how many we need to bring in to training to ensure we have sufficient to appoint as the vacancies arise.

To give readers further practical experience in carrying through the manual calculations of the modelling process, an exercise, 'A "Major" crisis' is to be found at the end of this chapter. It follows through in more detail the impact of introducing a training programme to resolve the problems of high wastage and recruitment into the San Lavoro Army.

Up to this point all the problems posed to us by the Generalissima have required us to look at the consequences of meeting specified future manpower number targets. To help us do this our modelling process has exploited the basic relationship between the boxes and flows in any manpower system, namely that the change in numbers in any particular box over a period of time will be the net result of the movements into and out of that box. If, as for example in Fig. 7.12a, the sum of the flows out of the box – retirement, wastage, promotion, etc. – is greater than the sum of the flows into the box – recruitment, transfer in, promotion in, etc. – then we would expect the box to contract. Conversely, as in Fig. 7.12b, if the outflows are less in total than the movements in we would expect the box to expand.

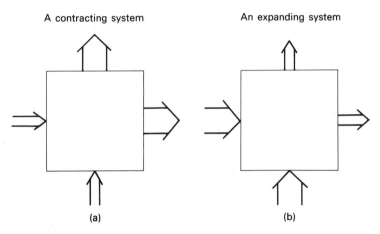

Fig. 7.12. The San Lavoro Armed Forces – 12. Two systems. (a) Growing. (b) Contracting

From quantity to quality – from pull to push Clearly, if, as the Generalissima has instructed, we set the change in numbers for the box as a target and the movements from the box are prescribed by our age-based retirement and wastage rules and by the need to 'pull' individuals out of the box to meet number targets at high levels, then the number of movements into the box must exactly equal the outflows plus (or minus in the case of a contraction) the required change in numbers; how we split these inflows between recruitment and promotion in will then depend on our replacement process.

Let us now suppose that the Generalissima poses a different sort of enquiry to us:

'Having carefully looked at the results of your investigations to date, I have concluded that many of our problems are a consequence of the rate at which we are forced to recruit and promote Privates; there is no time for proper experience to build up. I have, therefore, decided that in future what matters is quality, not quantity, and am going to limit the annual intake of new Privates to 20 each year (compared with the projected 40) and restrict the rate of promotion of Privates to Generals to 10 per cent per annum of those in the lower level at the start of each year (compared with the projected 20 per cent). I'm not after specific number targets but I clearly need to know how many Generals and Privates I'm going to end up with so that I can order the right number of boots!'

How do we approach this question? We are no longer starting by targeting manpower numbers, but we can still specify the requirement and model it in terms of the basic relationship between the boxes and flows in the manpower system. This time we are able to pre-define the movements into, as well as out of, each box in the manpower system. By implication the net balance between the total inflows and the total outflows for each box will determine whether the box expands, contracts, or stays the same size. Where our analysis will be different from before, however, is in the sequence with which we carry out the steps of the modelling process.

Since we are now 'pushing' soldiers through the system instead of 'pulling' them to fill vacancies, we can complete the analysis of movements for each box without first having to analyse vacancy requirements in higher levels. What we do need to know is what 'push' movements can be expected from boxes lower in the system. In essence then our analysis must start at the lowest point of the system and work to the top.

Following through the calculations for the army system (see Fig. 7.13), we first calculate the number of losses we can expect from the lowest box, the Privates, through applying the retirement and wastage rules previously specified. To those losses we may add the promotions out to the General level; the number of those movements is now determined by the Generalissima's requirement that it should equal 10 per cent of the number of Privates at the start of the year and no longer be based on vacancies arising. Having calculated all the movement out of the Private level we can complete the analysis for this group by adding in the 20 recruits specified by the Generalissima. (For simplicity we have assumed that new recruits do not leave during their year of entry.) The net result of the movement out of and into the Privates will give us the final size for this level and by applying the age rule as previously we can see how this is spread between the age bands in our age profile.

Working up to the General level we can follow through a similar, if simpler, analysis. Movements out of this level are restricted by the definition of the manpower system to retirements and other losses, which we can estimate using our established age-specific annual rates. Movements into the Generals will be limited to the promotions from Private under the Generalissima's 10 per cent rule. The net result of these in and out flows will again give us the final size

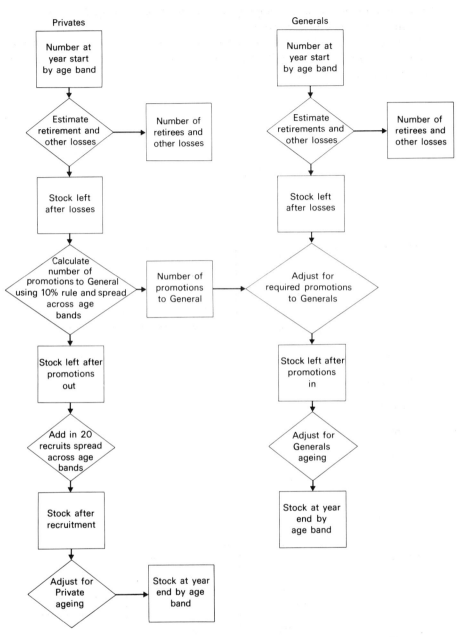

Fig. 7.13. The San Lavoro Armed Forces – 13. Flowchart of 'push' modelling steps

of the General level, and applying the ageing rule, will again allow us to determine the year-end age profile.

The results of this bottom-up analysis of the army manpower system are summarized in Fig. 7.14. Readers are again invited to work through the detail of the calculations to see if they reach the same conclusions.

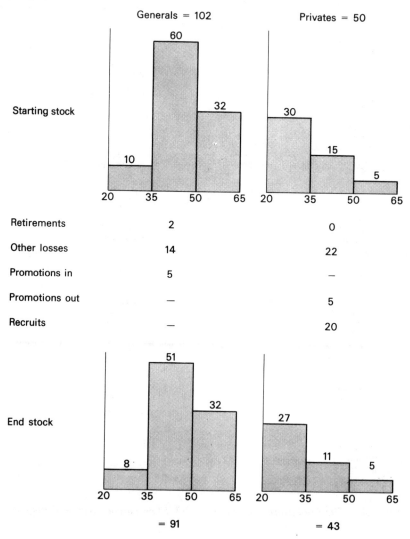

Fig. 7.14. The San Lavoro Armed Forces – 14. Year 1 summary assuming 'push' flows

Applying manpower modelling to the real world

The problems of San Lavoro's Generalissima and her army have provided a useful vehicle for introducing the principles and essential pragmatism of manpower modelling. In reality, we may have to look at the behaviour of manpower systems much more complicated than that of the army. However, though the increased burden of calculations that a complex system might bring may quickly lead us to the convenience of computerization, the essential purpose that a model fulfils and the logic of its operation will remain unchanged.

A CASE STUDY – MODELLING AS AN AID TO DECISION MAKING

As an illustration of how modelling has been used in a real decision-making situation consider the following case. It relates to the longer term examination of recruitment needs for a particular technically skilled group within a public sector organization; the manpower system is shown in Fig. 7.15. There are three basic grades with entry into the higher two grades on a 'promotion only' basis from the grade below and entry into the system as a whole only possible

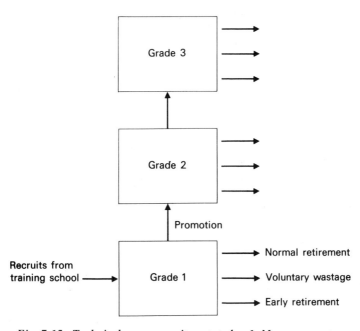

Fig. 7.15. Technical group recruitment study – 1. Manpower system

209

into the bottom level; recruits in fact have to go to a full-time training school for two years prior to entry into the system.

Every two years or so the organization engages in an exercise to determine its long-term recruitment requirements. What is unusual about its approach is that it is a participative venture with the active involvement of the employees' union representatives alongside the organization's management.

At the start of the exercise, each side is given details of the organization's future business review which indicates future types and levels of activity, likely changes in technology, etc. Against the background of this review, each side is asked to provide sets of operating assumptions for modelling the behaviour of the manpower system in question, with a particular emphasis on the implications of policy assumptions for recruitment requirements.

Different manpower assumptions of management and unions   On examining the results of this preliminary work, three important areas of difference emerged between the manpower assumptions of the management and those of the union as shown in Fig. 7.16.

Policy area	Management	Union
1. Change in number of posts	−ve	+ve
2. Take-up of early retirement option	Low	High
3. Promotion ages	Older	Younger

Fig. 7.16. Technical group recruitment study – 2. Differences in policy assumptions

1. **Future numbers of jobs**   The management argued that although the business review was predicting increased levels of activity, a massive investment in technology would mean that more could be achieved with fewer people. Management, therefore, made the assumption that it would be reasonable to contract the workforce over the period in question. In contrast, the union's position was that despite any introduction of new technology the organization would continue to demand the services of its highly skilled members and that it was only right to assume that manpower numbers should expand into the future in line with increased activity.
2. **Losses**   Although both management and union accepted that the normal retirement age would remain unchanged at 65, and that voluntary wastage was reasonably stable so that past patterns would be followed, they disagreed over the likely effect of an early retirement policy. Management had

recently had this policy forced on it by the union and because of the cost involved was anxious that it should attract the smallest number of near-retirement employees as possible. Management, therefore, predicted that the loss rates by this means would be small. The union position was again very different, seeing it in the members' interests to ensure that the policy was available and attractive to as many people as possible. The union, therefore, assumed a high level of early retirement losses.

3. **Replacement policies** The main area of difference between management and union on the question of replacement policies was with regard to the age profile of promotees. The management insisted that for individuals to be eligible for promotion they would need to have acquired significant experience at their current level. As a consequence it was argued that promotees out of any level would need to be relatively old and mature in comparison with the age profile of the population they were coming out of. In clear contrast, the union reiterated the desire of its members for rapid promotion prospects and saw this as being reflected in promotion profiles biased towards younger individuals.

Quantifying the effects With these three key points of difference between management and union identified, initial long-term projections of the manpower system were made for the two sets of assumptions using an identical sequence of calculations to that worked through in the Generals and Privates example. The main resultant outputs, the annual recruitment requirements

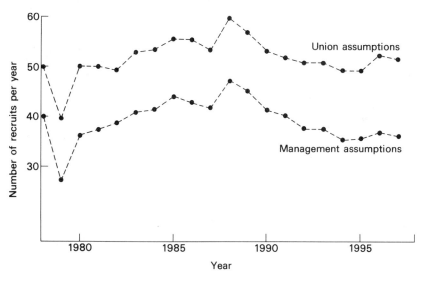

Fig. 7.17. Technical group recruitment study – 3. Initial runs of the model

into the system, are shown in graphical form in Fig. 7.17. As can be seen, the levels consequent upon the union's assumptions were considerably higher than those based on the management's assumptions: approximately 50 recruits per year in the case of the union and 35 recruits per year in the case of management.

On seeing this information, the managers who administered the exercise felt that the modelling exercise had achieved its purpose and they proposed to go into protracted negotiations with the union to try and gain acceptance for their policy assumptions and hence for the resultant small and less costly recruitment need. It was suggested, however, that as there were three points of variance between management and union there would be value in first looking more closely at the relative impact of these policy differences.

Rule of thumb tells us that for every 1 per cent per annum change in the number of jobs in a manpower system there is a consequent change of the order of 10 per cent per annum in the system's flows. For example, the introduction of a 5 per cent per annum growth rate in job numbers is likely to lead to a 50 per cent per annum increase in promotion and other flows. Conversely, the imposition of a 5 per cent decrease in numbers is likely to lead to a 50 per cent per annum reduction, or halving, of promotions, etc. It, therefore, seems likely that much of the difference between the results of the management-based projection and the union-based projection is attributable to the variation in their thinking regarding future manpower numbers. To test whether this indeed was the strong influencing factor, a third run of the model was carried out on the basis of the union's stated assumptions with the exception that their

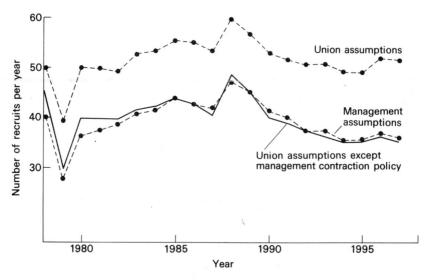

Fig. 7.18. Technical group recruitment study – 4. Identifying the major policy difference

assumption of a growth in numbers was replaced by the management's predicted contraction rate. The results of this run are shown on Fig. 7.18.

Rapprochement The results of this third run of the model are almost identical to those on the original management assumptions, i.e., the supposition that the growth factor is the most important influence on the behaviour of the system seems correct. This was an important piece of knowledge from the management point of view as, in discussing policies with the union, there was now no longer a need, as far as setting long-term recruitment levels was concerned, to take great issue regarding the different assumptions about early retirement policies or the age of promotees. What mattered was to try and hammer out agreement over a sensible trend in future manning levels.

Again, the exercise could have been concluded at this point. However, one further key item of information remained to be added into the decision-making process. Namely, that the output from the training school for new recruits was currently 30 individuals per year (see Fig. 7.19) and would, therefore, produce fewer entrants each year into the lowest level of the system than the runs of the model predicted were necessary to meet either the management's or union's assumptions! The moral was that no matter what set of assumptions and policies was finally settled on, unless something could be done to increase the size of the training establishment or significantly alter the recruitment strategy to bring in already experienced individuals, no way could future requirements be met.

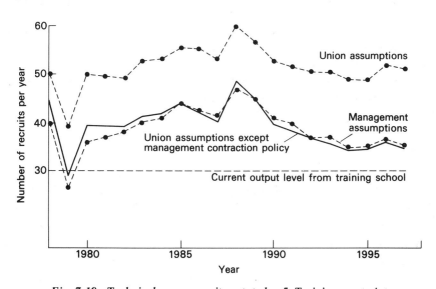

Fig. 7.19. Technical group recruitment study – 5. Training constraint

To summarize, the organization has set out to determine its future recruitment requirements in the face of uncertainty and differences of opinion about the future. Through modelling the manpower system in question the organization has been able not only to assess the implications for recruitment of different sets of manpower assumptions, but also to determine which of these variable factors was most influential on the situation. In the event the modelling process has highlighted that the most critical problem facing the organization was how to overcome the blockage presented by the size of the pre-entry training school, which represents a major constraint on the organization being able to achieve its anticipated future activity levels.

The practicalities of manpower modelling

In our brief foray into the world of manpower modelling the aim has been to highlight what a powerful but flexible aid to manpower management and decision making modelling can be. The manpower model lets us not only describe but also observe in a dynamic way the structure and behaviour of a manpower group and lets us view each box and flow not in isolation but in interaction with all the other elements in the system. The contribution of the model is not spuriously to forecast the future – changes and uncertainty put paid to that – but to let us see how combinations of assumptions about the system are likely to interplay with each other and their combined influence on its operation. It puts us in a much more informed position to identify policies which are robust to change or are at least capable of adaptation when the need arises.

As in our Generals and Privates example, there is considerable advantage, particularly at first, in carrying through the modelling calculations manually. However, the benefits of computerizing the computational chart are quickly seen. Using a computer model not only adds speed and accuracy, but also encourages the kind of flexible, interactive approach to analysing manpower problems and issues which we would wish to encourage.

COMPUTER POSSIBILITIES

The use of the computer also allows us to introduce some added dimensions of sophistication into our modelling. While there is a real danger in trying too hard to reproduce reality, extra features which can be helpful include the following:

1. **Complex systems**   By relieving the need for calculations to be carried out manually, computerization facilitates the modelling of much more complex manpower systems than Generals and Privates, with many interacting boxes and flows.

2. **Push/pull interactions**   As mentioned in Chapter 6, many real-life manpower systems include examples of both 'push' and 'pull' flow types. A typical example would be 'pushing' staff out of a training grade at the end of their instruction and promoting them to the first job grade, exit from this grade only being possible, however, if a vacancy arises at a higher level, e.g., a 'pull' flow. Computerization again helps make light work of the computational chart involved in simulating such a flow system.
3. **Fluid grading**   This facility allows a target to be set on the numbers employed not in one specific grade, but in a number of grades, usually at the same level in a manpower system or within a single stream of the system. Such a facility is particularly useful where the object of the modelling process is to highlight the impact on a manpower system of an equal opportunity policy (see Fig. 7.20) as the main point of interest is the

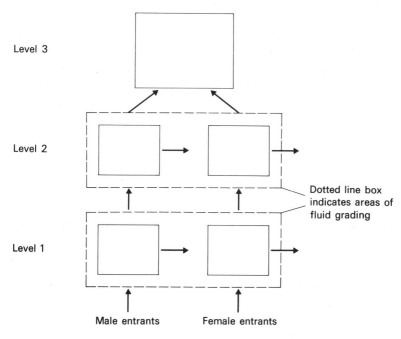

Fig. 7.20. An example of fluid grading

differential promotion flows between men and women. In such a situation we will want to recognize these separately within the manpower system. However, it is unlikely that we can specify in any sensible way targets on the number of men and women at a given level as opposed to a total target on the number employed at that level.
4. **Flow and age profile weighting**   As described in Chapter 6, weights are an alternative way of defining the promotion mix between two or more flows or

age bands, taking account of the numbers in the boxes or bands from which promotees are being drawn. Computer models easily handle the extra calculations required when using weights.

5. **Promotion spreading facilities** Having set an age profile to characterize the promotees from one box in the manpower system to another, problems can again arise if there are insufficient people in one age band to satisfy the required call upon it. Some computerized models have rules built into them which allow for the spreading of unsatisfied promotions from that age band. Sometimes these work by filling up to the required number of promotions from the next youngest age band, sometimes by spreading in either direction from the exhausted age band in relation to the relative contribution of these bands.

6. **Costing** While manpower models have traditionally used manpower numbers as their unit of measurement, it is frequently more important from a management point of view to look at manpower decisions in terms of their financial impact. Computer models are increasingly being developed to allow cost analysis to be carried out either at a simplistic level of applying an average cost per head to all staff in a particular manpower box or in a more refined manner by applying a more detailed costing structure taking account of such factors as age and experience. Costs can also be attributed to the movement of a typical individual along any particular recruitment, promotion, or leaver flow to give a total cost picture over time for any particular set of operating assumptions and policies.

OTHER TYPES OF MANPOWER MODEL

Whether or not we enlist the help of a computer to carry out our arithmetic for us, the steps we go through in modelling our manpower system remain the same. Manpower model builders sometimes describe the modelling approach we have used in this chapter as an aggregate, deterministic simulation:

– **Aggregate** because we model the behaviour of each manpower stock or box in our system as a whole and do not try to follow the movements of each individual.
– **Deterministic** because we assume no element of chance in the application of our operating assumption, i.e., if we set the annual wastage rate for a particular group to be 10 per cent we know the model will always estimate exactly 10 losses in every 100 employees.
– **Simulation** because we try to re-create in a simple mathematical form the sequence of events that occurs in real life as people move into, through, and out of manpower systems.

'Aggregate deterministic simulation' models are the most commonly used manpower models in the UK and prove to be extremely useful in practice.

216

However, other types of manpower models, as described below, have been developed to meet particular sorts of requirements.

Steady state or equilibrium models   Equilibrium models are based on a mathematical theory that if the recruitment, promotion, retirement, and growth assumptions about a manpower system are kept unchanged and its wastage patterns remain constant, then over time the system will reach a steady state or equilibrium position in which the promotion of people at each age within each level will remain constant. In effect, the organization has reached a state where it can maintain its preferred manpower policies indefinitely from one year to the next and is, therefore, sometimes described as having an 'ideal' age distribution, e.g., retirement bulges or promotion blockages are avoided. By comparing the current age profile of a manpower group with the corresponding steady state profile, users of equilibrium analysis believe an indication is given of the likely extent of future manpower problems.

Unfortunately, while such a model may have attractions in theory, when used in practice it presents a number of problems of analysis and interpretation. For instance, uncertainty and change in any organization make the requirement of constant growth, loss, and replacement assumptions that are necessary to achieve the equilibrium state very unrealistic. Also, because the model calculates the 'ideal' age profile by solving mathematical equations rather than 'simulating' the passage of the manpower system through time, there is no way of estimating how long it would take, even if constant operating assumptions were possible, to reach the 'ideal' in practice.

While difficulties make equilibrium models of much less practical use than an 'aggregate deterministic simulation' model, they can be of some benefit in providing a reference aid to judging change in the structure of a manpower system over a period of time.

Individual stochastic simulation models   Modelling for small groups of employees presents particular problems for the manpower planner. In this sort of situation, individual behaviour and chance become much more significant than with larger groups and the use of aggregate analysis with exact deterministic flows is no longer appropriate; when such models are applied to small number groups, resulting flows will often, unhelpfully, be in terms of fractions of people. Because of the more significant individual component within the smaller group, it also means that a greater level of detail has usually to be included within any modelling process.

To meet this kind of need, stochastic models have been developed which, against the background of a manpower system as previously described in terms of stocks and flows, simulate individual movement within the system allowing for the stochastic or chance element present. In these models, the rules govern-

217

ing movement are no longer applied as precise proportions and rates, but rather as probabilities, with each event within the operation of the model treated as a trial for which there is either success or failure governed by the level of probability applied to it, e.g., an individual leaves or stays, or is promoted or not, but movement of fractions of people is never possible!

Stochastic simulations are often highly sophisticated and complex in design and are perhaps the closest of the supply models to simulating reality. Promotion rules, for instance, may reflect a complex interaction of selection criteria, e.g., age, sex, potential rating, tenure in current job, etc.

This degree of complexity, however, creates a major problem when these sorts of model are employed in practice. First, their requirement for input data is very demanding, because information is no longer recorded on an aggregate basis but must be recorded against every individual within the system. Further, because of the large number of variables interacting at any point in the operation of the model and the underlying stochastic element, it is often extremely difficult to assess how a change of policy affects the behaviour of the underlying system. At a more fundamental level still, there remains the question, 'if one is unable to comprehend the real world as it is without a model, how can a perfect model of reality improve one's understanding?'

Generally, individual stochastic models are expensive to set up and run and the volume of output makes interpretation difficult. Experience suggests that these kinds of models only really contribute when they relate to extremely small groups and, more importantly, some broad aggregate analysis has been undertaken first to map out the general behaviour of the manpower system.

Optimization models   All the types of models discussed so far operate on the principle of identifying the implications for the behaviour of the manpower system of a given set of assumptions. Any manpower planning enquiry, therefore, probably requires a number of parallel runs to be undertaken to evaluate alternative options as a basis for subsequent decision making. In contrast, the body of optimization models set out to establish, for a given set of manpower goals, what the optimal manner of achieving them is.

Most of the work on optimization models has centred on the application of mathematical programming techniques. At the heart of such techniques is the 'objective function' which defines in mathematical terms the manpower goal to be achieved. The objective function is essentially a 'cost' function to be minimized, where cost is used in a number of alternative senses, e.g., salary bill, cost of employment policies, cost of not meeting target complements. Against the objective function, a number of constraints can be defined which express features of the manpower system and its behaviour over time. So, for instance, constraint equations can be used to express the promotion rules of the system.

Given an objective function and associated constraints, mathematical pro-

218

gramming analysis can be used to solve the equations and identify an optimal set of employment policies, if one exists.

More recently there has been considerable development in the United States of goal programming models. These models set out to minimize the discrepancy between future specified staffing levels and those actually achieved. Complex sets of constraint equations describe the structure and operation of the underlying manpower system, often with a stochastic element to them.

In practical terms, optimization models have met with mixed success. Their complexity, sometimes running into thousands of variables and equations, makes them formidably expensive to design and implement. While they have been used to analyse manpower strategy in relation to large manpower systems with many parallel job streams, the sophistication of the underlying mathematics makes them difficult to comprehend and properly interpret. Too often they have been utilized as no more than a report writing mechanism.

Generally, optimization techniques have been little used to date in the UK.

Summary

In this chapter we have attempted to de-mystify one of the most critical areas of manpower planning work – the use of manpower models.

Manpower models are our key to looking into the future to see the consequences of the policies and actions open to us and thereby help ensure more informed, sensitive decision making. Manpower models can be simple yet powerful, flexible yet easily comprehensible in their logic. We hope we have shown that manpower models need not be the preserve of the expert.

A 'Major' crisis

An example of using a manpower model – Generals and Privates – has been given to you and the implications of certain rules and policies have been worked through for one year. It is worth first reading through that example again.

Wastage levels and the recruitment needs are a major cause of worry to the Generalissima and her junta. The body has decided that the army must be restructured to make it more effective in fighting battles; we are to work through the implication of its decision.

A new rank is to be created – Majors. Only the bravest and least intelligent Privates will be eligible for the position. They will lead the Privates in battle, guiding and controlling them.

The following facts/opinions/requirements are relevant:

1. The expectation is that Privates' wastage will be halved. Wastage of Majors will be higher, equal to that previously sustained by the Privates.
2. Ratio of Majors to Privates 1:3.
3. At the end of the first year following the events described in the General and Privates example, 15 Majors will be created – 10 to be chosen from existing Privates and 5 recruited from outside. These proportions will remain for the foreseeable future.
4. Promotion to General will only be from Majors.
5. Generals to be reduced to 65 by the end of the fourth year.
6. Criteria for promotion to General as at present.
7. Promotion to Major 40 per cent 20–34, 60 per cent 35–49.
8. Recruitment of Majors 100 per cent 35–50.
9. Number of Majors to be increased by five each year.

Now draw the new manpower system. (See Fig. 7.21 for the answer.)

We know what happened in year 1. Now work through what happened in year 2. (See Fig. 7.22 for the answer.)

Your answer may be slightly different depending on how you have decided to 'round' numbers. Small variations are not of critical importance providing you have been consistent in applying your rules.

Most importantly, we have assumed that the total numbers in each age band are evenly distributed. In the absence of any other information, we must do

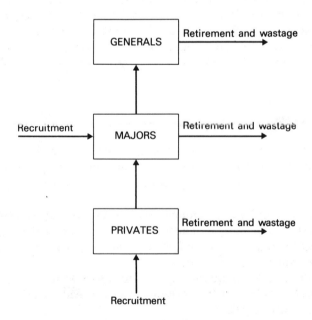

Fig. 7.21. A 'Major' crisis – the manpower system

	20–34	35–49	50–65	Total
GENERALS				
Start-year stock	10	54	32	96
Retirements			2	2
Wastage	2	8	3	13
Numbers left	8	46	27	81
Target				65
Promotions in				0
End-year stock	8	46	27	81
MAJORS				
Start-year stock	4	11	0	15
Retirements				0
Wastage	2	4	0	6
Promotions out				0
Numbers left	2	7	0	9
Target				20
Promotions in	3	4	0	7
Recruitment	0	4	0	4
End-year stock	5	15	0	20
PRIVATES				
Start-year stock	36	6	6	48
Retirements			0	
Wastage	9	1	1	11
Promotions out	3	4	0	7
Numbers left	24	1	5	30
Target				60
Recruitment	23	6	1	30
End-year stock	47	7	6	60

Fig. 7.22. A 'Major' crisis – year 2 calculations

this. Thus 1 in 15 of those in the top age band retires each year and when we age our army at the end of every year 1 in 15 moves up from one band to the next.

We have presented the calculation in its logical form:

– How many of our start-year stocks will retire in the year?
– Of those remaining, how many are expected to waste or leave?
– How many need to be promoted to the next level?
– What are we left with?
– How does this compare with what we want?
  Shortfall or surplus?
– If shortfall, how many shall we promote from below and how many recruit direct from the prairies?
– What does the end-year stock look like?
– But we have gone one year, we must age our workforce.

Now, try and work through what will happen to the army in years 3 and 4. Our answer is given in Figs 7.23 and 7.24.

Well done. Of course, faced with the analysis, the Generalissima moves to the difficult job: evaluation and interpretation.

She looks at the considerable turnover of Majors and the large recruitment of Soldiers. Her 'order of the day' is 'we must soldier on through this major crisis'.

	20–34	35–49	50–65	Total
GENERALS				
Start-year stock	8	43	30	81
Retirements			2	2
Wastage	2	6	3	11
Numbers left	6	37	25	68
Target				65
Promotions in				0
End-year stock	6	37	25	68
MAJORS				
Start-year stock	5	14	1	20
Retirements			0	0
Wastage	3	6	0	9
Promotions out				0
Numbers left	2	8	1	11
Target				25
Promotions in	4	5	0	9
Recruitment	0	5	0	5
End-year stock	6	18	1	25
PRIVATES				
Start-year stock	44	10	6	60
Retirements			0	0
Wastage	11	2	1	14
Promotions out	4	5	0	9
Numbers left	29	3	5	37
Target				75
Recruitment	28	8	2	38
End-year stock	57	11	7	75

Fig. 7.23. A 'Major' crisis – year 3 calculations

	20–34	35–49	50–65	Total
GENERALS				
Start-year stock	6	35	27	68
Retirements			2	2
Wastage	1	5	3	9
Numbers left	5	30	22	57
Target				65
Promotions in	2	5	1	8
End-year stock	7	35	23	65
MAJORS				
Start-year stock	6	17	2	25
Retirement			0	0
Wastage	3	7	0	10
Promotions out	2	5	1	8
Numbers left	1	5	1	7
Target				30
Promotions in	6	10	0	16
Recruitment	0	7	0	7
End-year stock	7	22	1	30
PRIVATES				
Start-year stock	53	14	8	75
Retirement			1	1
Wastage	13	3	1	17
Promotions out	6	10	0	16
Numbers left	34	1	6	41
Target				90
Recruitment	37	10	2	49
End-year stock	71	11	8	90

Fig. 7.24. A 'Major' crisis – year 4 calculations

223

8.

Planning careers

Developing and practising this approach to manpower problems has revealed one area of application where further work is needed. An approach that uses statistical techniques will break down when small numbers of employees are the subject of study; for example, when attempting to manage career streams. Here the patterns used to look at wastage and promotion are difficult to detect because of the small numbers involved. What do we do when a 10 per cent leaving rate has to be applied to a group of five people? 'Waste an arm or leg!'

Over the last five years this issue has been closely studied. The answer is unequivocal support for our basic approach to manpower planning, that of adding knowledge into the decision-making process.

Managing career structures

Nothing could be more individual than a career. If any given individual were reincarnated, the probability of that individual *suffering* the identical career to that of his previous life cannot be recognized on the probability scale of nought to one; so near is it to zero point. One has to go to the more evocative measure of the 'odds against'. In this case, millions to one.

A career is unique and, therefore, presents a major problem to statistical techniques. Not only is there an infinite number of outcomes, not only does the problem involve long time periods bringing into its compass the problems of extrapolation, but also the data problem is acute. Generally speaking, data are recorded about careers; the problem is that they are recorded in such a way – in correspondence, in files – that they are difficult to analyse. Many hours of clerical time would be required to analyse the career patterns of marketing people in a medium-sized organization, for example. It is not even as simple as analysing the records of the people currently in marketing; leavers cannot be ignored, neither can people who, as part of their career, have moved on from marketing to other functions.

Computerized personnel information systems are beginning to provide a solution to the data problem, but they have only been in existence for 10 years and careers, by definition, are at least 30 years long.

The large number of outcomes, the lengthy time periods involved, and the problems relating to data seem to indicate that the scope for techniques for planning careers based on a statistical approach is likely to be small, yet the need to plan careers better is a growing one.

The education system teaches people to aspire, it emphasizes goals and, as far as possible, guides its pupils to seek jobs which have a career structure, constantly stressing the desirability of a 'career'. At the same time the behavioural scientists' work on motivation indicates that people have needs which have to be satisfied. One of the more important of these is the need to realize one's full potential.

It is not surprising that individuals in companies show keen attention to the chances of promotion, their potential assessment, and the openings there are in their organization. There is considerable and increasing pressure on manpower planners in organizations to evaluate career prospects.

Current practice

Most organizations will, when asked, state that they plan careers. It has been our experience, gained from advising many companies, that there needs to be distinction between career planning and succession planning. Most organizations find it possible to plan succession to the next career step with a good deal of certainty, but the planning of subsequent career steps becomes increasingly difficult.

Consider the following hypothetical organization, which has a departmental manager, A, who is due to retire. Reporting to him are three group managers who each control the work of a section of people consisting of two or three section managers who, in turn, lead sections of a number of officers. The departmental manager now has to be replaced by one of the group managers who in turn will be replaced by a section manager, and one of the officers will be promoted and somebody recruited to join the organization. The factor which makes career and succession planning so difficult is the fact that each decision taken affects subsequent decisions.

Let us suppose that the man most suitable to fill the departmental vacancy was a group manager, B, aged 48. Let us further suppose that he was replaced by the section manager, E, who was 45 and in turn one of the officers, L, aged 33, filled the section manager vacancy, a policy of always promoting the youngest. The next promotion to departmental manager, assuming no untoward event happened, would not take place for 14 years. If this policy was then followed, four promotions would in fact take place in 29 years. It is worth commenting on the fact that neither of the other two group managers, C and D,

225

could become departmental manager since both would have retired before the next vacancy occurred. On the other hand, what would have been the case had the policy been to promote the oldest of the people in the level below? The outcome of that strategy is that the next promotion will take place in seven years, and in total four promotions will take place in only 11 years, and each of the group managers could become departmental manager. Neither of these promotion policies is realistic, but the point is that future promotion decisions are dependent on present decisions. In this example there are 210 different ways of replacing the departmental manager about to retire (see Fig. 8.1).

Perhaps a more realistic policy is to promote the ablest, and there is a general feeling in organizations that such a policy is always successful.

Consider the following case. Group managers B and D are judged to be the most able of the group managers with B exhibiting a marginally better performance than D. At the section manager level, the most able is manager K and he is considerably better than the rest of the section managers. If, following our policy of promoting the most able, we choose B as a replacement, then K, because he is older than B, will never be promoted to departmental manager.

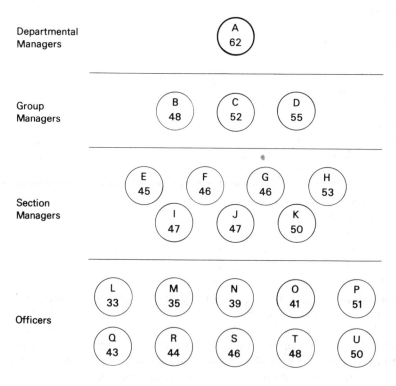

Fig. 8.1. A hypothetical organization chart

The organization may have to promote someone who is not capable of adequately fulfilling the role of departmental manager or else perhaps promoting an officer with high ability but much less experience. A simple example, it illustrates the point that organizations will sometimes accept a marginally worse solution in order to safeguard the longer term. This problem can be handled visually and manually without the use of sophisticated techniques because the numbers are small. It is not difficult to imagine how complex the problem becomes on examining the career opportunities of the officers where the average age is 40 and there are 25 years to go to retirement.

Simulation techniques

The first response to the complexity involved in forecasting succession was to use the computers. In a few tenths of a nanosecond a computer could examine all possible ways of replacing Mr 'A' and point out the best way of organizing succession policies.

Statisticians in organizations began to produce complex stochastic simulation models, attempting to get as near reality as possible, in which the individuals and their characteristics would be represented, together with the criterion for promotion.

This type of model recruits, promotes, wastes, and transfers whole people. The model used in Chapter 7 from the San Lavoro Generalissima operates by multiplying a stock by a rate, and when it tries to promote 3.2 or 4.8 people they round off to 3 and 5 respectively. A stochastic model uses probabilities instead of rates to generate flows. If the chance of a person leaving aged 25 with three years' service is 25 per cent, the model spins an imaginary roulette wheel marked in divisions 'STAY' or 'GO'. Of the 100 divisions, 25 are marked 'GO' and 75 are marked 'STAY'. The computer spins the wheel, flips in the ball, and waits for the wheel to stop. Oh dear! The ball has come to rest in 'GO' and that individual is randomly wastaged, simulating head-hunted by competitors or falling under a bus.

Since the wheel has no memory, each time it runs it may indicate 'GO' or 'STAY'. On average if it is run often enough it will waste a 25-year-old with three years' service 25 out of every 100 times. Similarly, promotion flows and indeed all flows are generated using these 'Monte Carlo' methods.

Many models of this kind have been built, varying in detail, but most of them have three disadvantages:

1. They are extremely costly to run. If you are using entity simulation techniques on the career structure of an organization with a few hundred people in its management streams; if you want to represent functional divisions and allow for such phenomena as high flyers and cross-functional promotions; if

you want to put potential indicators on people, to define the best age/length of service/length of time in job criteria for any promotion; if you want to run it over a number of years and a number of times in order to assess the sensitivity to individual movements: then your model has an enormous amount of work to do.

2. The second of the disadvantages can best be stated by using the analogy of the signal to noise ratio found in hi-fi terminology. The more complex the simulation model, the more it represents reality; the more features that are built into it then the more difficult it is to discern the policies which should be operated in order to control it. In other words, there is a very low signal to noise ratio. Much information is produced about the individuals and their likely promotions from such a model, but little can be deduced about the policies which should be followed in arriving at the optimum balance between the needs of the individuals and the organization.

3. The third disadvantage arises when, having run a simulation programme, the policies represented in the run have not produced the desired effect. It is often difficult to see how the policies must be changed to achieve the objective. A second run of the model could result in moving further from the goal, necessitating a third and perhaps fourth run.

After a flurry of activity using these models in the mid-1960s on succession and career problems, most organizations decided that they were ineffective and quietly put them on one side.

Fortunately, the problems of career planning of that period were to develop employees quickly enough to fill the jobs in the expanding organizations. The best career management strategy was to identify more than one successor for each job and put considerable effort into identifying people with potential and to develop them. In general the increasing technical demands of manufacturing processes, and the use of more sophisticated management techniques leading to a growth in the service organizations, created opportunities within organizations at a rate that strained the organizations' ability to develop managers.

The problem

Around 1970 there was a subtle change in the degree of confidence with which managers spoke about these policies. The rate of expansion of management staff began to slow and stabilize in the late 1960s and early 1970s. Research at IMS has shown that the rate of progress of individuals in organizations is fundamentally related to the growth in the number of opportunities. A reduction in the expansion rate from 4 to 3 per cent will have a significant effect on promotion opportunities.

The oil crisis of 1973 and its aftermath turned this slackening in the degree of confidence into a deep pessimism; it became difficult to provide adequate career opportunities for managers when organizations were rapidly cutting staffing levels to reduce costs and partially offset cash crises. Many organizations found that career management development policies which appeared to be effective and appropriate were heavily dependent on a high rate of opportunity creation. In the new contracting situation they were quite useless.

The responses of organizations to the cash crisis tended in addition to make things much worse: banning or reducing drastically the level of recruitment of graduate staff, the future managers of the organization; using 'voluntary' early retirement schemes to reduce numbers in the organization; the easy option of the 'equitable 10 per cent cut all round in staff achieved by natural wastage'; all these had made the problem of management career and succession much worse. Opportunities were slashed by the reduction in staff, by the non-replacement of retirees, and future problems were created by the total ban on recruitment.

The deep concern of organizations developed interest in methods of controlling management career structures. Fundamentally, the problems of controlling the management career structure can be classified into broad groups, those concerning the career structure, those concerning the rate at which opportunities are created in the organization, and those concerning how control is achieved.

CAREER STRUCTURE

The uniqueness of careers is a major obstacle to the development of methods for controlling career structures. Examining a sample of managers within similar functions over a number of organizations shows how diverse career paths can be. Using patterns of experience to help in forecasting the type of person likely to reach the management level in different functions is, therefore, difficult.

Careers involve long time periods. By definition a career is 25 to 30 years long. Who is to say that policies that are developed now and thought to be appropriate to getting young, inexperienced people into the management stream will still be appropriate in the conditions of 20 years from now when they will reach higher levels of management?

The raw material of any control system is information. Information about people, age, length of service, time in job, the number of jobs, and the pattern of promotion previously, all are items of data that are necessary for the control of career structures. In the management career structure this problem is particularly acute, as we noted at the beginning of the chapter.

OPPORTUNITIES

The second part of the problem of managing the career structure arises from the difficulties of creating opportunities within the organization. Opportunities are a function of three factors, the growth or contraction in the number of jobs in the management career structure, the wastage from the jobs, and the way that vacancies are filled.

Growth or contraction of the number of jobs in the organization's career structure is more than difficult to predict. Influenced as it is by random world events, by the oil crisis, by economic policies, and by the actions of competitors, the number of jobs an organization will have in the future is difficult to predict. It is, however, fundamental to the control of the management career structure. Each time a new job is created within the career structure, unless the vacancy is filled by external recruitment, a promotion or a series of promotions will occur. By the same token, the impact of a reduction in the number of levels in the career structure will be felt throughout the whole of the structure.

We have seen that the wastage patterns of an organization are as strongly affected by the pull exerted by the labour market as they are by the organization's internal manpower policies. A sudden expansion of a particular occupation, as is currently the case with the technological demands of the microprocessor, will cause organizations that have had previously stable wastage patterns to lose people. The general economic situation and the way that it creates vacancies will have a similar effect. Both the rate of technological change and the future economic situation are difficult to predict.

The organization's replacement policy will significantly affect the management career structure and its control. Filling a vacancy at a high level in the management's structure by external recruitment will affect the careers of managers below that level.

Singly, each of these three factors is important to the control of management career structures; together they increase the difficulty. The change from expansion to contraction that affected many organizations in the early 1970s created such a situation.

The expansion raised the expectations of employees to a high level by creating opportunities within the organization at a high rate. To fill vacancies the organization moved employees quickly, often with minimum experience. Managers found that they had not long to wait for promotion. They were highly motivated by the chance of promotion and this was reinforced when promotion occurred.

The move into contraction reduced opportunities. Promotions within the management career structure result from vacancies being created at the next higher level. Rarely will organizations promote individuals simply because they are ready for promotion or have been in their posts a long time. Organizations are very concerned about drift at senior levels and pay particular attention to preventing this. Opportunities, therefore, arise when there are vacancies.

Vacancies arise from two sources, when additional jobs are created or when wastage of incumbents from existing posts occurs. The move into contraction brings a reduction in the number of jobs and promotions result increasingly from the replacement of wastage, but unfortunately, contraction in the organization is often accompanied by a reduction in wastage rates.

As contraction of the organization continued, the problems intensified. One of the ways in which organizations attempted to cope with their cash problems was to reduce numbers of staff. Wastage was too low for reasons mentioned previously to achieve the reduction. Organizations sought other reduction policies. Early retirement was often used. This was effective in reducing numbers but it had a disastrous effect on the creation of future opportunities in the management structure. Since the 'early retirees' were not replaced, the overall effect was to cut future wastage with significant reduction in opportunities over the next five to seven years.

CONTROL

The third part of the problem arises out of the methods of controlling the career structure. Since the career structure is made up of individuals, changes in the individuals making up the structure affect it greatly.

Take the example at the beginning of the chapter. If the departmental manager who is due to retire is replaced by the older of the two candidates for the post (the two candidates are aged 55 and 48), barring accidents, the next promotion will occur when he reaches retirement at age 62 in 7 years' time. If the younger is chosen, the next promotion is likely in 14 years' time. A simple decision to promote one or the other significantly affects promotion prospects of managers at lower levels. A well ordered career structure with few problems can be wrecked by a few individual decisions.

Equally, the bringing about of a desired change to the career structure is difficult. Suppose it is desired to increase the amount of experience in the lower management levels before promotion to senior management: how is such a change implemented? Only by decisions to promote one individual against another. For a promotion board to deny what it feels to be greater ability for the sake of more experience consistently over a period of time is taking human nature to the ultimate. Yet it is the only way to bring about the desired change.

The approach developed

Fundamentally, the management career structure is under control when it is in balance and remains in balance in the future. Successful methods of control must be able to detect when the structure is out of balance, the type of imbalance that has occurred, what circumstances cause particular imbalances, and the remedies that help to achieve a new balance.

The imbalances that occur are of two kinds. The expectations of employees and the opportunities within the organization to satisfy those expectations get

231

out of balance. One of the problems of the 1970s was that the expectations of employees were very high resulting from the high rates of promotion experienced during the 1960s and the opportunities to meet those expectations had been much reduced during the 1970s as a result of growth rates in organizations falling considerably.

At the same time, the imbalance can be considered from another viewpoint, that of the organization. The organization needs to fill its jobs with people of the right calibre, experience, and ability. It can be said, therefore, that there is a need to balance the needs of the organization with the availability of people to fill them.

CAUSES OF IMBALANCES

The first step in the approach is to identify the circumstances that produce severe imbalances in the management career structure. Twelve circumstances, divided into four broad groups, have been identified:

Group 1 – Change in the size of an organization
– Rapid expansion
– Steady contraction
– Short-term growth not equal to long-term growth
Group 2 – Internal reorganization
– Change in number of levels
– Change in skill requirements
– Improvement in career prospects of a specific category of employee
Group 3 – Labour market pressures
– Many opportunities exist for employment outside the organization
– The outside world is very unattractive to employees
– Significant improvement in the pay and conditions of a specific group of employees
Group 4 – Problems of the age distribution
– Recent growth creates a young age bulge
– Growth 10–15 years ago creates a middle age bulge
– Post-war growth creates an old age bulge

The second step in the approach is to consider the consequences of the imbalance. In one way or another the consequences impinge on the organization's effectiveness. Where expectations exceed opportunities, the major problem will be to offset the behavioural responses of employees. Frustration at the lack of promotion and staleness produced by staying in jobs too long, are two examples. Where the needs of the organization exceed the supply of suitable managers the consequences are often poor performance. The approach de-

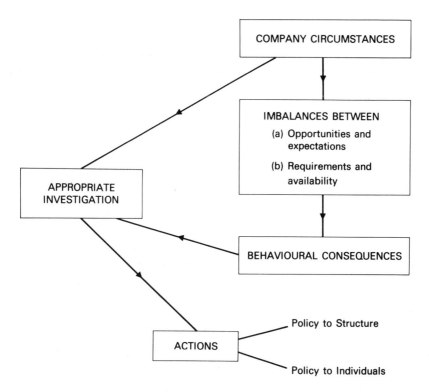

Fig. 8.2. Diagrammatic representation of the approach to career management

mands that for each circumstance the consequences, particularly the behavioural consequences, are thought through (see Fig. 8.2).

CONSEQUENCES OF THE IMBALANCE

The final step in the approach considers the practical actions that can be taken to offset the consequences and perhaps restore balance in the control of the management career structure.

There is available throughout the approach a set of tools and techniques that help in the analysis of the problem, by either describing data, or postulating the consequences of allowing the imbalances to carry on unchanged, or investigating how the implementation of different policies can reduce the behavioural consequences, in which direction, and by how much.

A case example

To illustrate how the approach is used in practice, one of the circumstances which can create grave career problems has been chosen. Within group two of the circumstances is one which concentrates on the difficulties caused to the career structure by changing the number of levels in management.

Probably two distinct situations occur which will cause an organization to decide that the levels in the existing management structure are no longer appropriate and must be changed.

The reason for the change could be economic. A company's expansion has been so rapid that the existing levels of management are too few to control the organization. A new level must be created to cope with the increased workload.

Economic circumstances, too, may force a company to contract its levels. Despite the fact that the present organization is an efficient one, it simply cannot afford to retain the number of levels in the less profitable situation.

The reasons for the change could be organizational. Recent work by organization developers has focused on the need to keep levels of management appropriate to an organization's objectives and management style. Perhaps the organization developers have diagnosed that the managment structure has too many levels to allow the freedom for managers to develop the creativeness that might be needed in an organization that is in a rapidly changing market. On the other hand, the conclusion could be that a large number of levels in a management chain have created communication problems.

Behavioural reasons, too, could spur an organization to increase its levels of management. An organization that has grown might find that too much power and authority have been concentrated in too few people with inadequate delegation, a stultifying effect created and opportunities missed.

Three circumstances should be considered:

- A rapidly expanding company increasing its management levels to cope with the added number of people in the organization.
- The removal of a level of management in a company that needs to economize to reduce costs in a declining market situation.
- Under the impact of some kind of organizational review, a company may increase or reduce its levels of management to make itself more efficient regardless of its economic situation.

Naturally such situations can and do go together. A company contracting for market reasons may also have good behavioural reasons for reducing the levels of management. Thus, these circumstances may interact with each other.

IMBALANCES

The main feature of the imbalances is that changes in the levels of management have an immediate effect on careers by affecting the opportunities available.

An organization that is expanding slowly, creating one or two management posts a year, is one situation, but the decision to create a completely new level of management in a short space of time is a much greater problem. In general, whatever difficulties an organization has in the control of its career structure before changing the levels of the management structure, these difficulties will be rendered much more acute by such a change.

An organization that has been expanding will have had little problem in meeting the expectations of its employees but its needs for managers will be great and it may already have problems in finding successors with the right qualifications, aptitude, and experience. Typically, a 1 per cent expansion in jobs creates a 10 per cent increase in promotion prospects. An additional level of management will greatly exacerbate those needs. Filling the new level of management by internal promotion, as the organization will almost certainly have to do since it is difficult to bring in a complete level of managers, greatly enhances the promotion prospects of managers immediately below the new level.

The contracting organization that decides to increase its efficiency and reduce its cash problems by reducing the number of levels in its management structure is in for a very difficult period. It is probable that reducing staff is one of the last remedies to be tried. Previously it may have cut back on recruitment. It will not be replacing vacant jobs, and will have been combining jobs together. There will already exist problems, imbalances, in its career structure; opportunities to satisfy employees' expectations will not be present. Whether there is a significant imbalance between the expectations of employees and the opportunities will depend on how long the company has been contracting and whether it has attempted to change employees' expectations. When the company, therefore, decides to remove a level in the management structure, it will widen the imbalance between expectations and opportunities considerably. The employees who felt they were on the verge of promotion would find that the chance disappears or recedes for a considerable time. To offset this there may be a reduction in the expectations of the employee caused by the company adopting such a radical approach to its problem.

QUANTIFYING THE ISSUES

Building on what we have seen in the example above, for each circumstance it is important to assess the size of imbalance and how this might change in the future.

This demands quantification of the expectations of employees, the opportunities available in the organization and the availability of suitably qualified candidates, and a method of assessing how these factors affect the imbalance.

Expectations of employees are difficult to quantify. If one is prepared to make the assumption that expectations of managers will be strongly influenced by the current and immediate promotion rates, then the techniques of career progression diagrams pioneered by Roger Morgan at the University of Cambridge offer a good way of quantifying expectations.

In practice, the opportunities available in the organization, even in the immediate future, are almost impossible to forecast and it is better to examine possibilities ranging around a likely estimate. The important factors to be considered are the organization's rate of growth and the levels of wastage from management jobs.

Although there is much that is subjective in all organizations' attempts to assess the availability of suitably qualified candidates, it has been our experience that a sufficiently accurate estimate can be aimed at and is usually available within the organization.

The means of bringing these issues together to quantify the imbalances is the CAMPLAN suite of manpower planning techniques. The suite was developed at Cambridge by Roger Morgan and is currently being made available for use through the Institute of Manpower Studies Models Advisory Service. CAMPLAN can be used to assess how the three factors will balance under different conditions of growth, wastage, and replacement for a number of years ahead.

BEHAVIOUR OF STAFF

The behavioural consequences resulting from the likely imbalances can now be assessed.

In the expansionary situation, the biggest problem is that people with inadequate experience and ability are promoted to fill the gaps. In this way, individuals get a higher regard for their abilities than they should, and although this does not necessarily affect the organization immediately, it will be a problem when the expansion eventually stops, since it will then have inadequate managers in jobs.

In the contractionary case, the behavioural consequences will depend largely on the external job markets. If this change takes place when the external economy is depressed there could be little effect on the organization in terms of the wastage of its managers. The desire and willingness to leave the organization of those whose expectations have been reduced will be substantially neutralized by the lack of opportunities in the external environment. The organization must look for behavioural consequences of a less obvious, more muted kind – absenteeism, the pursuit of personal activities and interests while at work, aggressive denigration of colleagues, lack of cooperation and overdue possessiveness in managers in asserting their span of control and the marking of territory.

If a level in a management structure is removed when the external economy is booming, then the company will probably face very high rates of wastage among its more able staff, since they will have seen their already poor career prospects diminished drastically by the change. Opportunities outside will be particularly attractive and plentiful.

ACTIONS

The actions required to offset the imbalances will differ between the expansionary and contractionary cases. The reasons for the change in number of levels, behavioural or market orientated, will only affect actions in so far as more time will be available in the behavioural case.

Expansionary
- Detect people with potential at an early stage and use good development and training schemes to accelerate development.
- Explore unusual career paths into the management level, organizations tend to restrict their look for successors to the most obvious routes when there is no shortage of likely candidates. Many other routes are possible with a degree of training and allowing a longer period for the new manager to settle into the job.
- Using external recruitment to fill specific vacancies will alleviate the most difficult situations. Providing that the reasons for the departure from the normal policy of internal replacement are explained, any disgruntlement should be minimal and short lived. The expansion will create enough opportunities for this.
- Redesign management jobs to be less complex and demanding. This will enable the organization to choose successors from a larger pool of potential promotees.

Contractionary   In the contractionary case, the imbalance is that the expectations of employees are greater than the likely opportunities. To reduce the imbalance, four possible strategies are possible.

1. **Create more opportunities**   Where the contraction of the organization is part of a general economic recession this will be very difficult. Where the organization's contraction is against the general trend the possibilities are increased.
   (a) Use managers and senior technical staff to launch new speculative ventures.
   (b) Second staff to other organizations. Many public institutes, technical, managerial, and political, have been lent experienced senior employees in the past to help them for two or three years. Customers of organizations have often been the recipient of a secondee from one of their major suppliers.
2. **Reduce expectations**   Realistic counselling of employees, making plain to them how their expectations will be affected by the new situation, is too

237

often ignored as a useful policy. Experience indicates that managers, once they feel that the organization is facing up to reality, will accept quite marked reductions in expectations. Realistic counselling has an added benefit; it will result in increasing the chance of really good performers staying if they are told that, despite the contraction, the organization has plans for their future.

3. **Alleviate the behavioural consequences temporarily** Allow grade drift, payment of special allowances, and redesign the pay structure. Quite big changes in status and lifestyle can be acceptable if the alternative would be redundancy and if time is allowed to adapt and the manager is protected against too big a loss of earnings too quickly. If such policies are carried on into the long term a new level of expectation is created and the only lasting results are higher costs.

4. **Reduce surplus staff** Three policies can be tried before outright redundancy is resorted to as a means of reducing the surplus managers.

    (a) Running down the number of managers by natural wastage will only help where the level of surplus staff is low. Wastage, excluding retirement, is usually very low for managers. A rundown of this type is non-selective and losses could be ill-balanced.

    (b) Early retirement with generous payments to those who accept it is an option. It can be very successful in reducing surplus staff very quickly in the year in which the policy is applied. However, the cost to the pension fund can be very high, more than the organization can afford. Early retirement has the effect of significantly reducing the outflow in future years by bringing future retirements forward to the current year. If the contraction is expected to carry on over a number of years, early retirement will be less helpful.

    (c) Voluntary severance schemes are very effective in reducing surplus management staff. Managers between the ages of 35 and 45 who feel that their present careers do not meet their long-term aims, and who have no capital to succour them while they make a major change in their career, are attracted by these schemes.

Managers of these schemes must control the loss by exercising the right to refuse the option to individuals who are felt to be essential.

Evaluating maintainable career policies

This is the crucial step in building aggregate policies which attempt to optimize careers for individuals. Too often organizations wish to follow career policies which do not take into account the constraints surrounding them. In a recent case, the head of an engineering function defined the criteria he wished to apply in choosing promotees within his function. It was found that no one in the function fitted the criteria.

An organization which had a policy of rapidly promoting people into senior positions at an early age suddenly found itself without room for manoeuvre when all the senior jobs were filled by managers in their early forties. It should be remembered that the only way one can have young managers at the top of an organization and still maintain rapid promotion is when rapid expansion is creating jobs. As soon as the expansion stops, another way of creating vacancies must be found to maintain that policy. Too often such factors as the age of promotion, the percentage of people being promoted at that age, and the number of people in grades, are treated as completely separate and independent factors. Of these three, if two are fixed, the third must follow. For instance, a policy which promotes 10 per cent of people aged 45 into the top grade has no control over the numbers in the top grade. It will be determined by the current age distribution. A bulge in the age distribution occurring immediately before the average age of promotion, will swell the numbers in the top grade for a period of time.

It is at this point that the need for quantitative analysis of the problem begins to show itself. Take a company that is facing a sudden increase in demand for its products. Establishing the facts of the situation shows that the organization currently has 40 managers and that it will need 50 managers by the end of 1982 to meet its expansion plans. Its career policies aim at developing potential managers by age 40. This has sufficed to fill its needs in the past. Using techniques for analysing the future, it calculates the number of managers that would be available from the current development scheme. Putting the demand for managers and the availability from the current development scheme together produces the picture in Fig. 8.3.

The number of managers likely to be available is going to remain fairly steady for the next few years at about 37 and then it falls quite rapidly till by 1985 only about 27 managers are likely to be left. There is a sizeable imbalance.

The approach developed considers possible ways of overcoming the imbalance and the effect that they would have on the problem quantified.

The company is losing managers to its competitors. Could it reduce the loss by paying more? This is a likely first response. The relationship between paying more and the subsequent effect on reduced turnover is very difficult to quantify. It is possible to quantify, however, whether reduced turnover, if it could be achieved by paying more, would help to solve the problem. The assumption is made that it is possible to raise salary levels and cut turnover by half, and the availability of managers is recalculated as shown in Fig. 8.4. In this example we can see that the impact of this policy is marginal, producing at best a few extra managers by 1982. The organization might take the view that it must pay more to retain its present staff but paying more is unlikely to make more managers available.

239

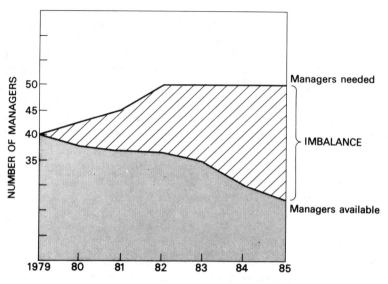

Fig. 8.3. A case example – 1. How many managers will be available from the current development scheme?

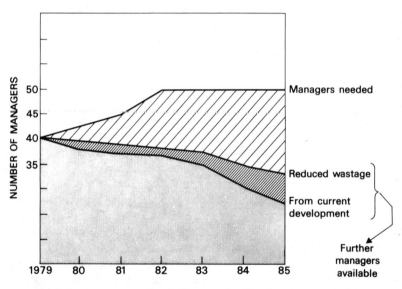

Fig. 8.4. A case example – 2. How much will reduced wastage help?

Could the availability of managers be increased by accelerating their development? Current policy is to prepare them for promotion by the age of 40. The basis of the policy is historical; it has provided enough managers to meet the organization's needs in the past. On examination, the organization finds that by adopting a specific programme of development and training, it should be possible to prepare people for management by age 35, some five years earlier. Implementing such a policy immediately would give an additional seven managers almost from the outset. It can be seen in Fig. 8.5 that by 1981 the problem is reduced by half.

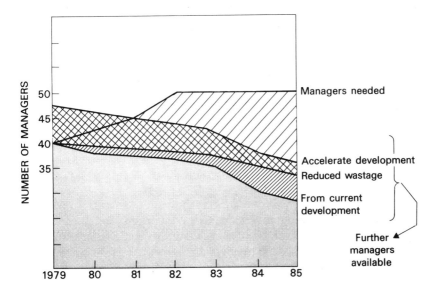

Fig. 8.5. A case example – 3. How much will accelerated development help?

What else could be done to increase the supply of managers to meet this short-term gap? One way of increasing availability is to do the opposite of accelerating development, namely, to delay retirement. Supposing, in addition to accelerating development, the organization has a temporary policy of asking people to stay on for two years after their normal retirement age. Figure 8.3 shows how much these two policies together would help the imbalance.

The problem of having 50 managers available by 1982 is probably solved and the short-term crisis can be coped with. Figure 8.6 shows, however, that there is a long-term imbalance and after 1982 there will still be insufficient managers.

Longer term solutions such as restructuring jobs, possibly appointing assistant managers to reduce the need for as many managers, recruiting managers direct from competitors, and finding new sources within the company could be

241

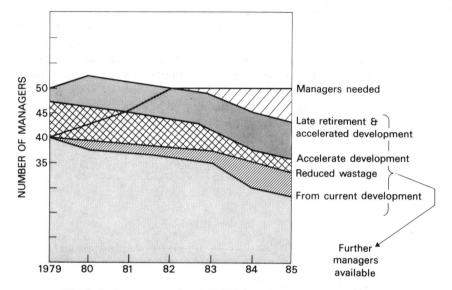

Fig. 8.6. A case example – 4. Will delayed retirement bridge the gap?

a possible solution, as in Fig. 8.7. Clearly, the delayed retirement policy cannot continue indefinitely.

The framework developed for managing the career structure shows there is a major imbalance between the demand for managers and their supply. It indicates that short-term solutions of accelerating development and introducing late retirement can be used to cover the immediate problem but there is a need for a longer term look at the career structure to cope with the likely problems of the next 10 years.

Real improvements in the control of management career structures will only come about from a considered analysis of the imbalances between the expectations of employees, job opportunities, and the availability of potential managers. Many organizations limit their work to assessing and developing potential managers. They are at risk when circumstances change.

Simulating the effect on individuals

The final step, having determined maintainable career policies for the organization aggregate, is to turn once again to the question of individual careers. So far, career policies have been defined in terms of age or length of service and proportion of people to be promoted. Such important factors as qualifications, experience, length of service in the current job, early retirement policies, etc., have been omitted. It is at this point that simulation techniques come into their

242

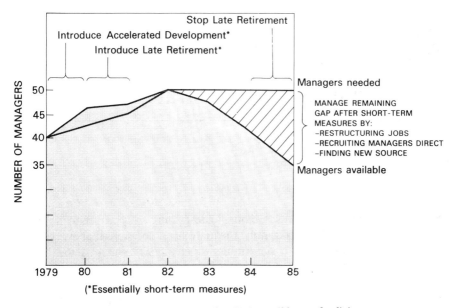

Fig. 8.7. A case example – 5. A possible set of policies

own. The previous aggregate evaluation of careers policies has defined the decision space and the direction to point the simulation model is known from the outset. Now, when the model is run a number of times the variation that will be produced will not affect the basic dynamics of the career policies, but reflects the additional factors which have been brought into play. The organization will be in a better position to separate cause and effect.

Summary

The approach to evaluating career management policies is basically the same as that used to evaluate manpower planning policies, i.e., bringing together information to help an organization explore how decisions on career policies must change as the organization's circumstances change.

243

9.

Developing manpower strategies

So far, this book has concentrated on: (1) describing an approach to manpower planning that depends on examining the manpower decisions that every organization faces, attempting to determine which factors, such as the level of demand for manpower, the rates of outflow, or the replacement policies, are important in those particular decisions; (2) gathering together information about the way the factors change in different circumstances; and (3) by quantifying the influence of the factors, building a picture, a map, of the decision so that the decision maker not only sees their impact on his immediate objective but also their effect on the surrounding circumstances of the decision. This enables a much more pragmatic approach to be taken to the development of manpower policies, but it leads to a problem.

Suboptimization is one of the immediate dangers of an approach that focuses on a particular decision. By concentrating too narrowly, a first-class job can be done on the decision of the moment and practical policies can be recommended, yet the decision that is taken on this manpower problem might have quite the wrong effect on other problems in the organization. An engineering function that has in the past taken on considerable numbers of graduate engineers to fill its supervisory posts might decide that this is an expensive luxury, and that it can manage adequately by reducing the graduate intake and promoting more people from the craftsmen ranks. It may fail to realize that a significant proportion of the production department's managers are graduate engineers who transfer from the engineering function to the production function when they have gained some experience of engineering, have probably passed through the supervisory ranks and become first line managers within the engineering function.

By drawing up the manpower system before any work is started, one hopes to gain an understanding of the interrelationships between manpower systems and it may be possible to spot the fact that graduate engineers do transfer in large numbers to the production function at that stage. For instance, in the Chapter 1 example on graduate recruitment, an attempt was made to relate

244

levels of recruitment with the training capacity available to induct and train them when they arrive.

Despite these precautions, however, it is not always possible to avoid sub-optimization and the long-term lasting solution is for the organization to begin to think strategically about its manpower. A major difficulty experienced by many organizations is relating overall manpower levels to levels of business in the long term. This problem we have already noted in the chapter on estimating the future manpower requirements when, having defined the objectives of the organization and estimated the manpower required by communicating those objectives down to the units and adding up the units' estimates of the manpower resources required, these estimates were compared with the manpower levels that the business parameters suggested the organization could afford to employ, there was a gap between the two. This gap expresses the difference that often occurs between the state of managers' thinking about the business and its manpower consequences and that which is being reviewed by the financial estimates. The only way to deal with this gap in the longer term is again to consider manpower strategically, elevating manpower policies to the position of a prime resource of the organization and not a tap to be switched on and off to control the organization's profitability.

Tactical suicide

It is all too easy to see what happens when an organization thinks of manpower policies tactically. Let us take the situation where a profitable organization meets a setback in its growth. The first response will be to cut back on stock levels of both raw materials and finished products and to indulge in cost-cutting exercises of the type where the organization bans all first class travel, substitutes brown envelopes for white, and reduces its subsidy to the recreation club. If the setback is sharp enough it may also decide to alleviate the effects by improving staff's performance in their jobs. The 'staff development programme' attempts to get responsibility down the organization to lower levels by making jobs more interesting and varied and encouraging a higher level of motivation among employees. The expectation is that the individual's effectiveness will be greatly increased and in time this better performance from the manpower will work through into increased profitability by allowing the organization to reduce its manpower levels. Such programmes are very worth while and do have a long-lasting impact on the organization but they need time to operate, and it is unlikely that the organization will see the results of the project in terms of increased profitability in anything under two or three years. In general, these attempts to offset the decreased profitability will not be sufficient unless the setback to the growth rate is a very shallow and short-lived one. At the end of the year the organization will find that the cost-cutting exercise has had very little impact and that nothing has yet been gained from the staff development programme.

RECRUITMENT BANS

A glance at the balance sheet and next year's profit forecast convinces the chief executive that something more must be done. 'Stop all recruitment immediately!' For a time the policy works well. Until this point the organization has been recruiting, and has a lot of people with short length of service and so leaving rates are high. There are, however, increasing complaints from managers that they are losing too many essential staff. Attempts to transfer people from departments that have surplus staff into these vacancies have failed. The problem is that wastage rates are highly variable between occupations and some of the occupations that the organization most needs may be ones with the highest rates, the organization, therefore, finds itself slowly forced into the position where it has to replace some of the staff who have left by recruits. The cynical view is that the demise of this policy is marked by the chief executive losing his own secretary and having to replace her.

A subtle twist is now added to the recruitment ban. Replacements will only be allowed if the director of the function has given his direct permission for it to take place and this is approved by the chief executive. This is a much more sensible policy with two immediate benefits, not only can essential people be replaced but also the fact that senior people are vetting the need for the replacement causes managers to look much more critically themselves at vacancies and only to ask for replacements that can be justified. The longer this policy is held on, unfortunately, the more difficult it becomes to reduce manpower numbers. The organization, in reducing its numbers, cuts back on its recruits and so the numbers of people in the organization with the highest rates of wastage are also reduced and, as we have seen in Chapter 5, the rate will fall quite rapidly.

THE 10 PER CENT CUT

Suppose that the setback in the growth rate continues and there is still pressure on profitability. The restrictions on recruitment have succeeded in cutting numbers in those departments with high wastage rates, but it is not enough and more must be done. One of the advantages of the bans or restrictions on recruitment is that they are policies that do not require positive action on the part of the managers apart from saying yes to one or two requests to recruit. When an organization has to cut its numbers further it meets a problem. The senior people now have to take decisions on *where cuts* will take place. This may mean that the board or the chief executive's committee must begin to discuss this question. These discussions are extremely difficult, especially if they are being conducted for the first time in the organization, when generally speaking there will be little information.

Defensive reactions are produced since board members may feel the need to defend their own function's existence for the sake of the people in it, even though they feel that some reduction is justified. Can you imagine the problems of the board member for research when he reports to his subordinates the results of the board meeting saying that he has agreed that the research function should be cut by 15 per cent while other departments have a less severe level of cuts?

When this situation is met for the first time, the tendency is for the board members to take the easy way out and declare that each department must reduce by the same percentage. 'The 10 per cent cut all round' is the cynic's name for this policy. It appears to be equitable and certainly avoids any odium being heaped on to a particular manager. Whether the 10 per cent cut can be reached in each of the functions will depend on wastage patterns. In general, there will still be sufficient wastage in some of the groups to allow the function as a whole to drop by 10 per cent but serious distortions are likely to occur within the manpower of each of the functions. In the manufacturing department it would be the general workers and possibly technically qualified staff responsible for improving production efficiency who would be lost. There may be some attempt to move people from one function to another and this may ease some of the distortions but is unlikely to cover them all. Probably the policy peters out after one year when it is realized that some departments can achieve the 10 per cent without too much difficulty, but at the risk of increasing overtime working, etc., while other departments may not have enough staff because of the high wastage rates.

EARLY RETIREMENT

Now all the easy options have been used up and, if the setback in growth is still continuing and profitability has not improved, the organization must begin to consider ways of reducing manpower by inducing outflow from the organization. Again the response is probably predictable. The organization needs to find a group of people who can be easily persuaded to leave and on whom the social consequences will not be too difficult. The natural candidates meeting this criterion are those in the organization who are about to retire. The organization dusts off its early retirement provisions, which were probably devised originally to cope with breakdowns in health of employees, and are generous enough to attract healthy members of staff to retire early.

The response to the enhancement of the early retirement provisions surprises most organizations. It seems that there are quite a number of people in organizations who are not fully fit but not ill enough to justify failure of health retirement. There are others who feel that they have reached the end of their career and do not get a lot of satisfaction out of their current jobs. Neither of these groups would volunteer to take early retirement since that would mean admitting failure in themselves. When, however, the organization makes a general appeal to people who wish to retire early and offers enhanced terms, the sense of personal failure is much reduced.

Of course, the effectiveness of an early retirement policy in reducing manpower numbers is greatest immediately after it is introduced. If it is open to all above the age of 50 (the minimum age for a pension in the United Kingdom) and the normal retirement age is 62, then a considerable proportion of the employees could be in that age band. Next year, the only new people who are likely to take up the early retirement option in any numbers are those who become age 50 during the year. Early retirement brings wastage that could be expected in any case in the next few years forward into the current period and so its continuing effect as a means of reducing manpower numbers is limited. It must be said, however, that once the option is offered it is difficult to take it away again and the long-term effect is to increase the outflow from the organization above the age of 50.

VOLUNTARY REDUNDANCY

Voluntary redundancy is the next option on the list for the organization in trouble. A package is produced to compensate people who decide to leave the organization early. The main components of this package are a lump sum payment together with protection of pension rights. The main criterion for deciding the amount of payment will normally be the length of service the employee has with the company. Typically, schemes will start offering a lump sum payment of two years' salary for employees in their mid-fifties, and will be reduced somewhat for those people who are very close to retirement. Indeed, over the age of 50 the early retirement scheme and the redundancy scheme would purposely be made to pay the same amounts of money. When these schemes are first offered, employees wishing to explore taking up the option are guaranteed anonymity. An office is established to which anyone enquiring their terms can telephone. Having got this approximation of their lump sum payment and the pension implications, the employee has to decide whether to approach his manager and ask formally to be allowed voluntary redundancy. Normally this will be at the discretion of his manager who has to assess whether the company can do without the employee or not.

There were two unforeseen effects of the voluntary redundancy schemes. In many organizations it was felt that the most immobile group, the 35- to 50-year-olds, would not be attracted. Heavy commitments at home, children settled in schools, and possibly wives starting on second careers, would mean

248

that it was much more attractive for these employees to stay in jobs for the security and stability. It turned out, however, that a significant number of the 35- to 50-year-olds were attracted by the terms. The ones most likely to be attracted were ones in middle management positions or in the higher ranks of the professional occupations, who had by this time decided that they were in the wrong career. In normal circumstances they would not risk changing. The lump sum payment that would go with voluntary redundancy might just be the amount of capital that an employee felt might help him to risk a change to a career that he had always wished to follow. An employee with a technical background who wished to start his own business might be able to use the lump sum to generate more cash from banks to help him set up his business. Other employees return to universities to take further degrees using the lump sum as salary during the period of training. The high number of people in this age range who left was especially beneficial to the company since it unblocked a number of promotion ladders which resulted from the reduction in manpower.

The second unforeseen impact of the schemes was felt in the secretarial and clerical ranks.

The scene is a Friday about 2.30 pm. A telephone rings and the personnel officer manning the confidential telephone prepares to calculate the lump sum and pensions implications for the enquirer. 'Is that the office where I can find out how much you will give me if I leave?' 'Yes' responds the personnel officer. 'How much then?' the voice asks. The personnel officer smiles wryly to himself, 'If you will just give me your name I can give you the information', he says, 'Oh No', interjects 'the enquirer', 'they said it was anonymous!' With a hint of resignation in his voice the personnel officer assures soothingly, 'Yes, of course, you have that option to remain anonymous but I can only give you approximate terms, which will have to be confirmed later. Now, how old are you, how long have you been employed by the company and what is your current salary?' A moment or two's pause and the information is passed to the enquirer with the reminder that the next step before accepting the terms is to discuss it with his manager.

Perhaps the enquirer was a young draughtsman, encouraged to enquire by his mates after a liquid lunch, or perhaps one of the more extravert secretaries in a typing pool. A typical amount for such an employee with a couple of years' service would be three to four months' salary, £1200–£2000 at today's prices. The personnel office could hear the brain working when he passed across the information. 'That's just the deposit I need for that sports car I saw in the local garage.' A quick assessment of the labour market for draughtsmen or secretaries is made and the manager is approached. Often such an enquiry sparks off a series of enquiries from the other occupants of the office. In many cases it is sad to record that a manager under pressure to reduce numbers will support such cases, risking future shortages or gambling that he will be able to recruit again in a month or two. The lesson is that a secondary sanction should be built into such schemes that can be imposed to stop managers following this type of short-term thinking.

It is interesting to note that many of the organizations that first introduced these schemes during crises have since continued them as part of their normal personnel and manpower policies.

Finally, if none of the options described so far is successful in getting the organization out of its problems, it must have recourse to what should have been done at the beginning. The senior managers will have to sit down and consider where any further cuts should take place, from the point of view of the organization. They will have to begin to consider the business that they are in, what its objectives are, and how they can best adjust the business to the new conditions. At the end of the process they will have to make people redundant. The unfortunate part of it is that if the organization had had a manpower strategy throughout this whole period, the chances are it would not have followed one short-term expedient with another, gradually being pushed deeper and deeper into trouble. It would have seen the need to consider manpower from a much more strategic point of view from the outset.

The tactical trap in the expanding organization

The ritualistic adoption of one short-term policy after another is not confined to the declining organization. It is equally evident in organizations which are expanding. Let us follow through the sequence of events in that case.

An organization that is fairly stable and has been for a number of years begins to expand. Perhaps it is a basic change in the market that has increased demand for its products. Having been a stable organization for a number of years, it will have developed good manpower controls and will meet the upsurge by increasing the level of overtime working, rather than taking on staff. The high demand continues and so do the high overtime levels, but the policy seems to be counter-productive. The high earnings of employees are generating a demand for leisure time which shows itself in an increased rate of absenteeism. The increased absenteeism means an even further increase in the overtime level, and so on. This phenomenon was much commented on in the 1960s among miners and car workers.

RECRUITMENT AND WASTAGE

Continually high market forecasts convince the organization that the high level of demand is a continuing one: it begins to recruit staff. The recruits arrive and the percentage of employees with short service increases and so wastage begins to rise. It may be that this company is experiencing its increased expansion as part of a general increase in economic activity which also increases wastage rates and it finds that it has to recruit more and more people, not only to meet its expansion plans but to cover the losses from the recruits. Recruitment standards will have had to be lowered as the labour market is exhausted. Poor quality recruits, which may be all there are available at a time of economic expansion, add to their problems as they tend to have even higher wastage.

Many organizations do not understand the relationship between length of service and wastage and treat the additional leavers as a symptom of increased dissatisfaction among employees. This type of organization often panics and responds by increasing its recruitment rate to allow for the wastage that should have been expected in the first place. Secondly, it investigates the reasons why people are leaving. As we have seen in the chapter on wastage, these reasons are often inconclusive as they do not allow for the length of service effect. Finally, the attention focused on wastage by the investigations the organization conducts tends to highlight the high rate of wastage among its present employees, and employees who are normally stable begin to question whether they should join the leavers and go for the better jobs outside that other people are going to, and so the wastage spiral increases.

TRAINING BOTTLENECK

The training capacity within the organization is quickly exceeded. Not only has it failed to anticipate the additional wastage caused by the recruitment but it is placing tremendous demands on its training department. The training department has fixed resources and cannot cope with the expansion and finds that it is unable to train the new recruits. Three choices are open to the organization in this situation. It can move the new, partially trained, recruits into jobs and risk the errors in manufacturing that will undoubtedly result. It can keep them hanging around doing odd jobs until the training capacity is free; unfortunately, there is a high correlation between induction into the organization and wastage. When there are good induction practices in the organization that seem purposeful to the employee and efficient, wastage levels are low. When employees are not given adequate training and are not sure what is going to happen to them, wastage rates tend to be higher. Finally, the organization can cut down or stop its highly organized recruitment campaign.

LABOUR MARKET RESPONSE

By this time, the labour market itself is beginning to respond to the expansion that is taking place. Employees with a particular professional discipline that is in high demand observe that it is possible for them to command a better price by offering their services on a contractual basis rather than being paid employees. The company has little option but to accept because there are few people on the labour market who wish to be permanent employees.

The high rates of recruitment create a demand for labour in the local area.

251

Other employers, to avoid losing employees, may increase rates of pay and the price of labour in the area is bid upwards. The organization recruiting may have to adjust its rates to attract recruits, with subsequent pressure to readjust the narrow differentials by increasing pay for its other staff. It may avoid this or try to hide its existence by paying the recruits allowances that are specific to them, i.e., clothing allowance, training allowance, stability bonuses, etc. Additional pressure on the pay structure often comes when experienced men are moved from their existing jobs to staff the new plants. There may be claims for additional pay for responsibility; indeed, many organizations' pay structures specifically allow for the payment of job allowances for this reason.

HOARDING STAFF

Managers in the organization begin to be affected by the difficulty of replacing staff. They become less willing to allow their staff to move to other career opportunities within their own organization. They feel that if they release a good performer then the person they will get as a replacement will be of much lower quality. In any case, they can offer good inducements to their own staff to stay since the expansion, within time, will probably create vacancies within their own chosen career.

GROWTH OF SERVICE FUNCTIONS

As the expansion continues, the organization begins to meet difficulties in attaining its business objectives because of the manpower shortages. It feels that a sensible strategy is to ensure that no obstacles are put in the way of the departments that form the bottlenecks. It, therefore, begins to augment its direct line departments with technical support, with administrative back-up, in order to help them to concentrate on their essential work. The feeling is that if we can only release the production and manufacturing people from the administrative chores this will enable them to improve productivity and obviate the need to get more staff.

The pressure to expand manpower to satisfy profit targets seems to induce a short-term approach in the minds of managers. Any problem can be solved with enough money. Recruitment requests for 150 fitters by next Monday are common. Buying machinery at great expense, to cut out jobs and reduce the demand for manpower, leads to high rates of expenditure and many of the solutions are impractical because insufficient thought has been given to them. Fast expanding companies are littered with white elephants rotting away in a corner of the scrapyard.

Obviously, when organizations are rapidly expanding and when they are part of a labour market which, in itself, is expanding, there are going to be enormous difficulties in the way of recruitment of people into the organization. These

252

difficulties will be made much worse by the sort of tactical thinking that has just been described. Attempts to think about the problems of expansion and their impact on manpower at the beginning will lead to longer term solutions being adopted, i.e., the expansion of the service functions much earlier, more considered efforts to improve productivity, the building-in of adequate training capacity before it is required.

Breaking out of the short-term thinking cycle

Organizations that have shown themselves to be successful in weathering the crises described and organizations that avoid getting into them in the first place appear to have one thing in common: an appreciation of the need to think strategically about manpower. Many of them have found the act of breaking out of the cycle extremely difficult and most of them have had to use some systematic way of thinking about the problem to help them to do this. In nearly every case, the breaking out has involved a systematic attempt to improve the organization's productivity. Where an organization is undergoing a crisis of expansion it concentrates on improving productivity to cut out the need to take on more staff but not necessarily to reduce manpower numbers. Where the organization is going through a crisis of contraction, the techniques that are used focus on increasing productivity by trying to cut out activities and improve the existing way that jobs are done and thereby reduce the manpower levels rather more quickly.

PRODUCTIVITY COMPARISONS

Organizations have found difficulty in assessing their levels of productivity objectively. It is not the absolute level that is the concern. It is fairly simple to measure productivity by taking the inputs and the outputs of the business and relating one to the other. The problems organizations have are answering the question, 'Is our level of productivity sufficiently high to allow us to compete with other organizations in our area of business?'

The use of global ratios   Comparison of the different productivity ratios available between organizations usually proves fruitless. It is not that the commonly used productivity ratios are not readily available, since most are to be found in company balance sheets. First, attempts to use one single parameter to compare organizations are valueless. It is only when a number of ratios are used to reflect different aspects of the business, and the relationship of manpower to those aspects, that something like a true picture begins to show itself.

Consider the following example. An organization wished to compare itself with its competitors across Europe and the USA in terms of manpower performance. To eliminate bias or problems of comparison, it chose first of all only those companies which were in similar lines of products within the total chemical business. It looked first at numbers employed, but since the organizations had different total levels of manpower, it concentrated on how quickly manpower levels were changing. By comparing indices of number of employees, it showed that its increase in employees was much lower than those of its major competitors. Indeed, one of the competitors had increased its number of employees by almost two and a half times over the 10-year period (see Fig. 9.1).

However, its low growth in number of employees might simply be due to its lower expansion rate compared with its competitors, and so a ratio that reflected and related sales to employees was looked for. The level of wages and

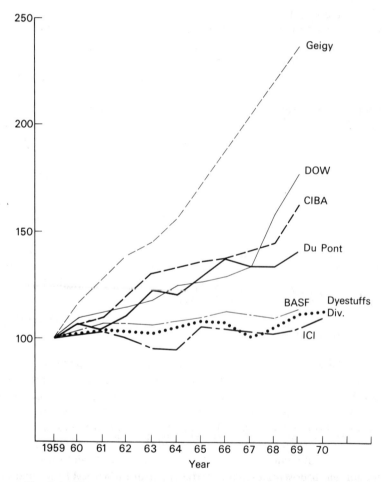

Fig. 9.1. Using global productivity ratios – 1. Indices of total employees

salaries as a percentage of total sales revenue would be a useful measure to reflect this.

In Fig. 9.2 it can be seen that the amount spent on wages and salaries as a percentage of total sales revenue was much lower than most of the other organizations. Whereas on average it spent £23 out of every £100 of sales revenue on its people, one of its competitors had to spend some £35 out of every £100 of total sales revenue on its employees. Surely, it concluded, our level of productivity is much better. Not only was it increasing its numbers of employees at a much lower rate than its competitors but a much smaller proportion of its total sales revenue had to be spent on people. If the total sales

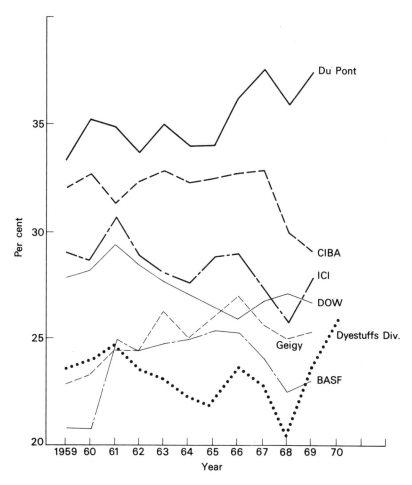

Fig. 9.2. Using global productivity ratios – 2. Wages and salaries as a percentage of total sales revenue

255

revenue represented output and the wages and salaries represented the amount of input, its productivity was vastly superior.

The nagging doubt that there was a fallacy in the reasoning was sickeningly confirmed when the third ratio was added to the other. The analysis of sales per employee of these same organizations showed that this company was also the lowest in terms of sales per employee (see Fig. 9.3). The reality was that the other companies were increasing their numbers at a higher rate, were paying their employees much more and also were generating a much higher level of sales from those employees, and, therefore, in terms of overall productivity were vastly superior. The diverse interpretation that can be generated from

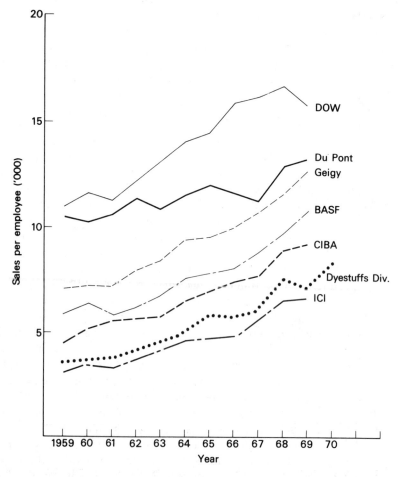

Fig. 9.3. Using global productivity ratios – 3. Sales per employee

different sets of productivity ratios makes it difficult to use them authoritatively within the organization to make a judgement about the need to improve productivity.

Productivity ratios can be used successfully to highlight the relationship between inputs and outputs within an organization and the relative importance of labour, capital, and materials in productive improvement, but are difficult to use at this global level to measure the relative performance of organizations.

The joint study team approach   Part of the problem in the interpretation of overall company statistics is that, although companies may be in the same business, they may manage that business in different ways especially in the groups of people that they employ. A simple example is the way that organizations man their engineering maintenance activity. Some employ their own fitters, others contract out this activity to organizations that specialize in it. Manpower costs generally exclude payments for contract services and so the organization using contract maintenance appears to have low manpower costs. Some attempts have been made to eliminate this from productivity comparisons by the use of joint study teams. An organization would select another organization that produces the same product and agree with that organization to establish a joint study team to visit each other's plants. A number of such studies have been done and the results, although interesting, are hard to use in improving productivity. In almost all cases they show that the historical development of the company has determined the manpower configuration and organization structure. Many of these decisions are lost in history as to why they came about, and even if the answer is found, they prove not to be very helpful. For instance, a study team finds that on one chemical plant the numbers employed are higher than on the similar chemical plant in another organization. The reason is that the first organization tests the quality of its products in laboratories that are in the production plants, with staff that are part of the production department. In the other organization, it was decided to do the quality control testing in a research department where there were people with expertise and equipment already established to do the job.

How does the study team responsible for making the comparison judge the relative merit of these two ways of organizing the manpower? Is it better to minimize the delay that would occur if the tests were done away from the plant by buying additional equipment and locating it on the plant or is it more worth while to save on the cost of additional equipment and possibly use staff in the research function who are really expert and who might have unoccupied time to do the tests?

The usefulness of this technique is limited by its expensive, time-consuming nature and by the fact that it is almost impossible to generalize the lessons learned from the two plants and apply them to the improvement of productivity across the whole organization.

Middle-way productivity comparison   The McKinsey organization has pioneered a method of productivity comparison that attempts to steer a middle course between the global assessment of productivity as typified by the example shown in Figs 9.1–9.3 and the joint study team.

The process starts by breaking the organization down into manpower categories. It is important not to get too many categories since the resulting work in assessing their productivity levels will be too great, but it is also important not to combine together two manpower groups whose productivity is dependent on different factors. Clearly, considerable skill and experience are needed for this part of the task.

Let us suppose that we are applying the method to a bus company. The productivity of the bus drivers will be dependent on the number of miles driven, the type of route covered, and the number of stops on the route. Their productivity is only marginally dependent on the number of passengers carried, unless of course their company has negotiated one-man buses in which the drivers collect the fares.

The productivity of the staff who man the ticket offices will be dependent on the number of passengers carried, the fares structure, and the routes the company runs. A complex fares structure involving lots of concessionary fares, season tickets, discounts for return journeys, etc., will slow down the time taken for a ticket clerk to handle a passenger. On other routes, a higher proportion of passengers might pay for their journeys by season tickets and so the productivity of the clerks on these routes will be lower. The productivity of the general manager of the bus company will be much more difficult to define and part of the McKinsey philosophy is that the organization should concentrate on maximizing the productivity of the direct workers, i.e., in the bus company example the drivers, and minimize the number of people required in the last category which it somewhat euphemistically describes as the burden, the general manager. In between these, there is a group of indirect or support staff whose productivity is measurable but whom the organization needs to minimize since they are adding to the cost and not to the value of the operation. McKinsey suggests that the manpower categories be grouped according to this classification: direct, indirect, and the burden, and the analysis is carried out in that order.

Measures of productivity must now be determined for each of the manpower groups isolated. For drivers of one-man buses we might decide that the best measure is the number of miles multiplied by the number of passengers carried. For the ticket clerks we might take a weighted average of the types of tickets issued, reflecting the complexity of the work involved in each type of ticket. For the general manager, the comparison might have to be some overall global measure of the performance of the organization. Essentially, the measure chosen must be meaningful to that group of people whose work it represents.

Since the McKinsey corporation has such a wide experience over many countries, over many industries, it has been possible for it to arrange for a group of organizations to undertake the comparison at the same time and to use the same measures for the categories of employees. In this way reasonably good productivity comparisons are possible. The organization has a choice of how it chooses the particular comparison. Does it go for the average of the other organizations in the comparison? It may do this if, say, for its bus drivers, it found that the productivity ratio per passenger mile was much below that of other organizations; it might feel that setting a higher target than to reach the average of the other companies would be too disheartening. Not only has it to pick a comparative target but it also has to indicate when it feels that this target should be achieved. For companies that are conducting this exercise, outside the McKinsey organization, there are greater problems, since it is unlikely that they will have access to direct measures of comparison. Such a company has two choices: either it can agree unilaterally with a number of other companies to make an exchange of this sort, a task which will involve it in considerable negotiation and management time, or, alternatively, it can choose to compare its current level of performance with some level in the past and, looking at that rate of growth, to accelerate the rate of change of productivity to a higher level.

Now the final column of the analysis table in Fig. 9.4 can be filled, the 'Action plan'. It is only when the organization has sat down and considered the level of productivity target to be achieved by the manpower group and *the practical steps it will have to take to achieve it*, that the exercise will begin to bear fruit.

Manpower category	Productivity measure	Target for improvement	Action plan
Drivers – one-man buses	No. of miles × no. of passengers	1540 passenger miles per shift	Install coin-operated ticket machines on the bus
– with conductors	No. of miles × no. of stops/route coefficient	–	Negotiate one-man buses for all routes
Ticket clerks	No. of tickets weighted by ticket type	10% improvement in two years	Reappraise fare structure and consider reducing number of ticket types
General manpower	Profit/capital employed	Actual level of x by 1985	Replace outdated buses with ones with better fuel economy

Fig. 9.4. Productivity comparisons

259

If this stage is omitted or done casually, productivity improvement is unlikely to be generated and the exercise will be a waste of time. It is at this point that many issues will arise in which the organization may have conflict with its workers. These must be faced up to and negotiated with employees.

Now another problem emerges: the search for an increased level of productivity in one group of staff can, at worst, reduce the ability of another group to achieve its targets, or at least make it very difficult for it to do so. To take a silly example: the productivity of the ticket clerks could probably be increased by getting the drivers to issue season tickets, but the productivity of the drivers would become disastrously low. This is a serious disadvantage of this approach. Unless there is very good coordination in the choice of target levels and unless deep consideration is given to how the achievement of one target will affect the organization as a whole, suboptimization can often occur. It might be very easy for the commercial department of the bus company to improve substantially its productivity by operating more routes for the buses, but the problems of scheduling those routes for the buses and providing drivers on those routes might be so difficult that the savings achieved in the commercial function are easily outweighed by the losses on driver productivity.

It is like building the perfect car by analysing all the cars that are currently in production, and taking each component and selecting the very best component to be found, and trying to assemble a car from among them. When assembled, the vehicle might not run at all.

This approach has one major advantage. It is a positive attempt to improve. It takes what is and attempts to generate more productivity and is particularly useful for organizations that feel that their productivity is lower than competitors but not so disastrously low for them to be uncompetitive or in trouble. To work well, an organization has to have time to do the exercise, to choose manpower groups, to establish productivity measures, and to build and achieve the action plans. It is probably not so appropriate for an organization that is in deep trouble where more immediate attention must be given to reducing activities.

Questioning the basic manpower assumptions of an organization

Organizations that are in a crisis, or where productivity is falling rapidly, need a more immediate and more direct way of concentrating minds on the reduction of activities to achieve a higher level of productivity. Two techniques seem to have been used with differing degrees of success.

ZERO BUDGETING

As its name implies, the zero budgeting approach is one which forces managers

260

to justify their total operation from zero. At the beginning of the budgeting period, they are told to assume that there is nothing allowed in their budgets and that everything that they wish to do has to be justified. The expectation is that managers will think deeply about their current activities.

The truth is that in many organizations, activities grow over time and are barely questioned. Too often, current activities are unnecessary, resulting from a change in the past. A typical case frequently occurs in manufacturing plant maintenance. Because of the importance of maintaining high plant occupation levels, a fitter or maintenance craftsman is allocated to a group of plants and his job is to wait until a breakdown occurs, mend it, and get the plant back on stream as quickly as possible. Often, there are long periods of inactivity when there is nothing to be done and the plant is running well. The plant operators become dissatisfied, they are working hard operating the plant and are being paid less than the skilled craftsmen responsible for the maintenance of the plant who seem to have nothing to do. The dissatisfaction may rise to such proportions that it is felt important to give the maintenance craftsman something to occupy his time when the plant is operating normally. A preventive maintenance schedule of tasks for him to do is issued in the hope that it will lead to improved plant performance. Too often, this set of tasks is selected more in hope than in expectation. Too often the list of tasks is simply brought together to give him something to do.

The level of plant breakdowns may begin to increase, perhaps because the plant is getting older, or because the production and throughput levels are increased. The maintenance craftsman soon finds that he cannot complete his preventive maintenance tasks and complains to his supervisor. The word goes up the management chain and soon we find the engineer arguing for an additional maintenance craftsman because the level of plant breakdowns has increased and, of course, there is substantial preventive maintenance to be done. The original reason for providing the preventive maintenance tasks has been fogotten.

The hope is that the zero budgeting approach will make managers question the basic reasons why people are employed or why thèy perform activities within their function, and is subject to challenge probably by a committee of higher level managers. Experience seems to indicate that this approach works the first time that it is applied. If it is then used on every subsequent year, the effect very quickly wears off as the whole exercise is not given sufficient thought: the managers simply take out last year's submission, reword it, alter it marginally at the edges, and resubmit it. In truth, the process becomes a charade.

A number of organizations realizing this have made a slight change to the zero budgeting system. They start the process off by going back to zero in the initial year and then in subsequent years they use a zero change philosophy in their handling of the budget. In this case the challenge of zero change to the budget is applied. The manager, in submitting his budget, can make quite a lot of changes within the budget itself so long as it does not affect the total. For instance, if he wishes to employ an additional person to start a new activity that he believes is important, it will not be challenged provided that some other activity equal to the suggested one is given up. This zero change approach is often used for a number of years immediately after a zero-based budget exercise has been gone through, but it does need the repetition of the zero-based budget from time to time to make managers again question their total activities.

A fundamental contradiction exists within the zero-based budgeting approach which becomes apparent when it is used in an organization undergoing rapid contraction. Managers who are asked to apply the approach realize only too well that any activities which they reveal as unnecessary will be cut out. As the organization is contracting, manpower savings will result from the approach. The more zealous and free thinking a manager is in applying zero budgeting, the more likely he will have to follow it up by getting rid of employees. Since few managers are eager to make people redundant there is a constraint on their use of zero budgeting as a means of reducing manpower levels.

THE BASE CASE STUDY

The base case study not only attempts to help the organization rethink its total manpower levels but begins with a deep and rigorous questioning of the organization's other strategies. The basis of the system is the question of a business profile and its associated manpower for two or three years into the future around which new manpower philosophies can be built. The process begins by understanding that a deep and fundamental change in manpower practices cannot be instituted in a very short space of time, and that manpower strategy in an organization will fundamentally be dependent on the nature of the business. First, therefore, it is necessary to define the type of business that the organization expects to be in in two to three years' time. This gives the opportunity for a fundamental deep questioning of a number of organizations' strategies, allowing them to be defined and for the managers to consider the manpower requirements in the light of those changes. There are three main areas of questioning, the products, the markets, and the manufacturing rationale. The process is best explained by the use of an example.

Questioning the product strategy The organization's range of chemical products was very large, over 2000 products, and had grown up over the years, primarily because the marketing strategy of the organization was that it should make every product within its general business sphere thus allowing it to offer its customer a complete product range. The feeling was that gaps in the product

262

range would allow other manufacturers not only to sell products to fill the gap but also to compete with the organization's own range. Consequently, many products were being made solely for that strategy and were uneconomic when considered in their own right.

The products were analysed and questioned under a number of headings, as follows:

- Products that were made in high volume and had a high rate of return. By definition the organization did not have many of these products: if it had, it would not have been in trouble. For the few that it had, it decided to increase investment to maximize the return.
- Products with a high rate of return but low volume of production. It could be that these products were speciality products or were products that were just beginning their market cycle, had come out of the research function and were beginning to grow. Again the strategy was to increase investment in such products.
- Products made in high volumes, but with low rates of return. These were known as the cash flow products because they contributed a large proportion of the organization's working cash. It was impossible to stop producing them immediately because of their contribution to cash flow, but in the long run they would either have to be made more profitable or the organization would slowly have to get out of them.
- Products that were currently profitable but if substantial reinvestment was required would become unprofitable. In other words, products that had a limited life. One of the organization's small factories made high quality products on plant that had been built many years ago. The products competed with an alternative range that were cheaper but of poorer quality. If the time came for that plant to be replaced, the price that would have to be charged for the products would rise to the point where the trade would switch to the slightly inferior but now much cheaper product.

Another example was a small plant that produced a requisite for the fashion trade: deep blue dye with an unusual property, it faded when it was washed. The organization knew that when the fashion trade stopped concentrating so much on denim and jeans, then the viability of that plant would be suspect.

Questioning the market strategy The strategy that the organization used to market its products was also strongly challenged. Over the years the organization had built up marketing and sales departments staffed by its own expatriate employees in most overseas countries. Consideration of the expenses of this operation and the value of the markets led to the conclusion that a major change should take place. It was decided that only in the major centres should company expatriates head the marketing operation but that increasing use should be made of local agents in other markets, particularly where marketing products and sales customs were very different from those employed in the United Kingdom.

Questioning the manufacturing strategy   Finally, the production and operational strategy of the organization was analysed. Currently the organization had 11 plants, the largest employing about 3000, the smallest about 100, spread from the centre of Scotland down to the Midlands of England, covering areas from the east to the west coast. The product rationalization allowed further reconsideration of the way products were made on which plants. It was decided that one of the organization's middle-sized plants should be closed and production transferred to more modern sites that already existed.

Establishing the basic level of manpower   The result of the questioning process was to establish a new business profile that the organization felt it could achieve in two to three years' time. This was now communicated to all departmental and functional heads with the instruction to prepare a case arguing for the basic level of manpower needed to achieve the business profile, i.e., the BASE CASE.

In the direct departments this was an easier task than in the indirect departments. The objectives had been specified in business terms and were easier to quantify in terms of tonnages of different products to be produced on different plants. Each manager, in putting forward his base case, was told that he would be rigorously questioned and the only additional manpower that would be allowed would be where there was a safety reason or legal reason or because company policy at the centre demanded this. Each function plan was examined by a deputy chairman and two members of the board. In the case of the overheads or indirect departments, an unusual twist was added. The heads of these departments were asked to justify their cases to the works managers; in other words, the overheads department or the level of service in the organization should be related to the direct departments' needs.

Once a manager had had his plan approved by either of these two processes he was then allowed to add in additional manpower where he could justify it. A similar process of questioning was invoked for this second round. At the end of it the organization had a completely new manpower profile, a 'realistic case' to set against the business profile, and could, therefore, set about attempting to achieve it over the two or three years that remained before the profile date.

Observations on the process   Clearly, 'BASE CASE' study involves a lot of the management's time and energy. Initially it was a highly secret exercise because it was feared that there would be strong reaction against management if it were known that major manpower reductions were being considered. In the event, the secrecy fell at the first hurdle.

Collecting data on profitability of products proved to be a more difficult task than was imagined. Although the organization's accounting information system was a good one and contained detailed information, an unforeseen problem occurred. In an organization whose products are interchangeable, where one product can be used as a raw material in the process of manufacturing another product, where different products are built on the same plant, and where the same products are manufactured on different plants, it is essential that the costing of energy, manpower, and materials be rigorously done. The allocation of these costs is done at the shop floor level by supervision.

Sometimes costs are wrongly coded in error. Other times, costs are wrongly allocated in order to hide problems. It is often the case that products which are highly profitable are used to hide such problems.

A number of such cases occurred in the examination of the product strategy of the organization. It became essential to go to the supervisors and discuss with them the coding, and from that point on secrecy was no longer possible. Instead of the outraged reaction of the workforce there emerged a much more positive one than had been expected.

It seemed that the staff of the organization recognized that a positive attempt was being made to sort out the organization's problems instead of the series of short-term idiosyncratic measures that had taken place before. There were demands for guarantees of no redundancy and these were rejected. Instead, the organization's plans were made much more widely known and, assurances were given of a rather practical nature. Instead of a 'no redundancy' guarantee which could not have been kept to if the profitability had reduced radically, the more realistic assurance was given that when a plant was closed down, its workers would get the first opportunity of jobs on other plants. Other organizations that have attempted similar strategic discussions with their workforces have found the same, more positive, reaction than expected.

Again, this approach is very time consuming and cannot be repeated year after year.

THE 'IDEAL MANPOWER' APPROACH

An unusual way of rethinking manpower strategy is to use the 'ideal manpower' approach. Instead of attempting to cut back manpower levels by questioning current manpower assumptions this approach starts at the opposite end. It attempts to establish the ideal manning levels of the organization. Subsequently, this theoretical level is made practical. Getting started in implementing such an approach is usually difficult; where should a start be made and how searching should the rethinking be? A practical way of overcoming these problems is to consider ways of removing all those patently obvious barriers to manpower efficiency that currently exist in the organization and to conceive new ways of organizing manpower when those constraints are no longer present.

Some time ago the Wellington Chemical Company went through such a process. It was expanding its plant and a completely new plant on a 'greenfield' site had been sanctioned. The managers destined to operate the plant had operated similar plants in the organization before and had come to the conclusion that they were most inefficiently manned if traditional practices were adhered to. Much thought was put into rethinking the whole manpower philosophy.

Process workers   A major problem on the existing plant was the company's recruitment policy of taking untrained people from the labour market and using them as process operators. This had worked reasonably well in the past when the plants were much simpler with much less electronic control and the processes were relatively unsophisticated. Plants were becoming increasingly complex. The task of observing changes in pressure and temperatures in the modern control room was becoming too demanding for the existing operators who were recruited from the labour market with no previous experience. The company trained them in process plant operation. Since they had no technical background the first job had to be very simple. As they gained experience they moved up a ladder of jobs established within each plant, each job becoming more responsible and demanding more of the operator, but inevitably the amount of responsibility entrusted to the most experienced operators had to be limited because of their total lack of technical knowledge.

In the manning of the new plant the naïve question was asked, 'Why should we not recruit people with a higher level of intelligence and train them thoroughly in the technical requirements of the plant?' The immediate reaction of some managers was to fall about laughing, saying that the wastage would be enormous as people with technical skills would not stand the boring nature of the process operator jobs. The retort was that the boring nature of the process operator jobs derived from the fact that they were designed for people with no technical skills. If technically trained people were to operate the plants, the jobs could be totally redesigned. In particular, if supervisors were recruited with technical qualifications manpower could be reduced and instead of having a technical expert on each shift, as was current practice, to assist the supervisor and the operators, both of whom were usually unqualified technically, the new process teams would be much more self-sufficient, and so manpower savings would offset the higher rates paid to the new type of process operator.

Plant maintenance   The problem of having maintenance fitters on a continuous plant has already been referred to earlier in this chapter. This, too, was questioned. Would it not be possible to contract out maintenance and call in the maintenance team as and when the plants required? Two practical difficulties had to be overcome.

First a safety consideration, contract workers might not be as familiar with the hazards of the plant and the safety regulations as they would need to be. Secondly, they would not know the technical details of the plant as well as the maintenance craftsman normally assigned to that plant.

The solution was to establish on each plant a highly trained shift fitter. He would deal with the minor maintenance requirements that occurred during the shift, leaking pipes or the changing of a motor, but if anything major occurred the contract maintenance team would be brought in and he would act as a supervisor to the contract fitters. He would know the plant, be able to direct and assist them in the technical nature of the work, and also be fully aware of the safety hazards.

Workshops' manpower On its other chemical plants the Wellington Chemical Company had workshops employing a variety of tradesmen to handle the major breakdowns that occurred. This was rather inefficient in that it did not have sufficient work for all the trades involved and consequently in many cases, to keep the men occupied, work had to be sought from outside customers. At times, this created a conflict of interest within the workshop, between the needs of the plant and the outside customers. Management proposed that a new grade be created, multi-trade craftsmen. Clearly it would be impossible to expect every man to have equal levels of skill in all trades as in his own. It was recognized that there would have to be two basic groups of workshop craftsmen, mechanical based and electrical based. Within these two groups, in order to make sure that they could perform the jobs as skilfully as a fully trained craftsman, it would be necessary to back them up with better workshop machinery. This, too, was instituted. Substantial savings on maintenance manpower costs were witnessed even after allowing for the payments to the contract maintenance company.

Works administration The manpower structure of the works was almost a microcosm of that of the Wellington Chemical Company. There was a line or operational department and the headquarters functions were also represented on the works in the form of a personnel department, an accounts department, and so on. Divided loyalties between the works operations and the responsibility to the head office function often occurred. An alternative way of organizing these service activities of the new works would be to establish on each plant an administrative department which would handle the more simple and clerical tasks of the accounts, personnel, and commercial functions. The supervisor and his staff would be responsible for the time sheets for the men, basic accounts recording, ordering materials, and recording finished goods, etc. In this way the total number of support staff was reduced since on each plant in the traditional manned works there were support staff who had free time which could be used for these other functions.

In this way, the Wellington Chemical Company adopted a completely new manpower structure for its new 'greenfield' site. Pessimists held that the new practices would be impossible to negotiate. That view was proved to be quite unfounded, even though the 'greenfield' site on which the plant was to built was next to another of the company's plants in which the manning practices were, to say the least, archaic.

Clearly this approach is much more useful for organizations that are building new units. It is much more difficult to incorporate into an existing plant since the manning structures are already established.

Information – the key to strategy

The techniques that have been described in the previous section attempt to focus the attention of the organization on to its manpower problems and relating those manpower problems to its objectives as an organization. Having used them, there is a temptation to sit back and recover from the exhaustive nature of the exercise. All too often the gains are lost simply because the organization does not ensure that manpower issues are considered in the ongoing situation.

Some organizations find that the sources of manpower information are incapable of supporting the integration of manpower and organization planning. Manpower information, in many organizations, is (a) not readily available and (b) insufficiently detailed for this purpose.

MONITORING MANPOWER LEVELS

A case in point is the control of the number of people employed in the organization. Statistics about the manpower levels in an organization are often crude. In most cases numbers are reported in rather broad categories on a monthly basis. Often they are not related to the budget or target level to be achieved. Perhaps the organization has successfully identified a manpower strategy that is consistent with its business objectives. It may have translated this into specific actions to achieve its purposes and communicated these down to the managers. All too often these objectives are not achieved. The system of monitoring is inadequate. Reading the papers that managers produce in support of their arguments as to why they have not reached their budgeted target figures is very instructive.

The arguments used are often detailed and extremely convincing, pleading new situations have occurred that the manager could not ignore and that resulted in an increase in his manpower strength. These submissions from managers often quote situations where jobs were allowed to become vacant because, perhaps, there were no candidates of the right standard, and such jobs have been left vacant for some considerable time, but now the manager claims

268

in his submission that the right man has been found, but the vacancy was authorized some years ago and was not included in the current target. In large departments the opportunity for this type of camouflage is ever present for the managers to use.

Comparing results with promises   The key is to look at managers' submissions over time and to compare actual performance with what is suggested would be achieved and to track the increases and decreases in manpower back to specific reasons. The manpower planning manager of an organization was explaining to his visitor on a tour of the testing department that a major increase in productivity had taken place. The testing of the company's products was an extremely complex operation requiring a lot of manpower to observe the performance of the machinery, to record details, and to analyse the observations in order to evaluate fully the performance. Some nine people continuously observing the test took 20 minutes to complete the set of observations required to analyse the performance. A team of highly skilled performance engineers spent two to three weeks analysing the data and produced a report on the piece of equipment that had been manufactured.

The company installed an on-line computer which took a complete set of readings in 30 seconds, analysed the results in a further 30 seconds, and provided minute-by-minute reports on the machine's performance at any time during the test for the engineer responsible for the testing, either on a visual display unit or on a printout. A considerable saving in productivity. But was it? Only if the people who used to do the testing and analysis of the machine's performance were employed on essential activities, or were used to fill vacancies in other parts of the organization, or were allowed to leave, was the productivity gain really achieved.

It is interesting to think of the parallel during the 1960s when the manpower savings of computerization of the accounting function were very little. The size of the accounting departments hardly changed. The computers themselves contributed greatly to a reduction in the number of people who were book-keepers in the organization but in most accounting departments this spare capacity, the manpower released from book-keeping by the computers, was then used to create management information systems, to revamp the costing systems. Only if the management information system and the revamp of the costing system were really necessary was there a gain in productivity. All too often the manpower released by the implementation of new methods is employed on the manager's own latest pet idea and not one essential to the organization.

Realistic recording   One works manager had an excellent system for ensuring that this did not happen. The works was small, employing about 1000 people. In the office of the personnel department's general foreman was a very large blackboard. On the blackboard were ruled lines producing a table. The columns of the table were the departments within the works. Rows across the table depicted the type of manpower within the departments. In each cell of the table were recorded the number of people that were agreed in the manager's budget and the actual numbers at the end of every week. If a person left this was shown as a vacancy in the same cell on the table. Every Monday morning the works manager came down to inspect the table and to consider whether vacancies should be filled or not. When the new packing plant was finally commissioned reducing the number of people employed in the warehouse, he made it his business to decide where the displaced workers should be used within the organization. This represented a true saving in productivity. Many American companies pay great attention to the control of jobs in this way.

'The nutcracker suite'   One British organization has developed an excellent suite of forms for recording manpower levels that force the subunits within the organization to be realistic in setting manpower targets and in achieving them.

Figure 9.5 shows an example of the form. The company operates a four-year planning cycle, the current year and three years into the future. A different form is used for different groups of manpower and the manager has to fill in the stock of people at the beginning of the current year, and to show reasons for manpower increases across a number of categories; the level of business activity, the amount of capital expenditure, the reorganization of the structure of the company. This block of data is followed by similar data on reasons for manpower reductions and finally, the sting in the tail, the manager has to

	Current year	Forecast year 1	Forecast year 2	Forecast year 3
Stock at 1 January				
Manpower increases				
– Business activity				
– Capital expenditure				
– Takeover/mergers				
Manpower reductions				
– Business activity				
– Capital expenditure				
– Divestment				
– Productivity improvement				
Stock at 31 December				

Fig. 9.5. Monitoring manpower levels – the 'nutcracker suite'

270

indicate how he expects productivity to improve in addition to these manpower increases and decreases.

By taking the stock at the beginning of the year, adding on the increases, deducting the decreases, and reducing the number for the productivity improvement level, we get the number of people at the end of the year. This stock at the end of the current year is carried forward into the opening stock of the forecast years and the whole exercise is repeated.

Most managers have two opposite temptations in putting in the productivity improvement target. Either they enter first the manpower levels they think they can achieve by 31 December and then calculate the productivity improvement as the result or they put in a target for productivity improvement that they feel their senior manager will demand. Rarely do they consider what they could achieve or how it will be reached.

The forms are filled in for the first year and the manager sits back. At the end of the year the forms are returned to him and he has to bring them up to date showing what actually happened in the current year and how he feels the targets for years 1, 2, and 3 should change now that they have become the current year and years 1 and 2, and finally to add a completely new forecast for the new year 3. In looking at his achievement, the chances are that the productivity improvement target will not have been met and that the manpower numbers at the end of the year may be higher than anticipated.

The natural tendency in reworking the forms for the new situation is to maintain the overall level of productivity improvement because it would be difficult to admit to a lower target, but to spread this so that although it was not achieved in the first year, by the end of the third year the total level will have been achieved. Most managers are tempted to do this; the forms are filled in again in the appropriate way and we wait for the third year to come round. Now the manager has to say what has happened against current year, which is of course his original year 1 and so the person reviewing the forms can see what the manager said he would achieve in year 1 when the forms were originally completed, and how he revised that forecast after one year's actual data had been collected, and now what was actually achieved against that revised forecast.

It becomes extremely difficult for managers to argue away an underachievement of the target. These forms and the organization in which they were used became known as the 'nutcracker suite', because of the way that they gradually tightened their hold on the managers. They were a very effective way of making managers face the reality of their situation.

MANPOWER COST INFORMATION

Most business decisions involve costs. It is imperative, therefore, that adequate strategic information on manpower costs is available. It is useful to look at the way manpower costs are generated and the way they relate to other business costs. Many organizations are in fact different businesses, and the products of the different businesses have different cost structures and require resources in different proportions. In Fig. 9.6 the organization has three businesses. Business A is the manufacture of a wide product range but within the product range four or five of the products are made in large volume and account for a large proportion of the manpower. In business B the products are made in a highly capital-intensive plant. Very little manpower is used and the products are made in large volume. Business C, on the other hand, is a business which is specializing in the making of five products of high quality in low volumes. It is highly manpower intensive.

	Business A	Business B	Business C
Direct costs	$\dfrac{\text{Manpower costs}}{\text{Business costs}}$ % 30	10	50
Site overheads	20	12	10
Organization overheads specifically allocated	35	65	16

Fig. 9.6. Relating manpower and business costs

It will be very difficult to take decisions about manpower and business objectives unless these three businesses are considered separately.

Sources of manpower costs The manpower costs of an organization are generated from three sources. The volume of production has an effect on manpower costs. As the volume of production rises there may be a need to increase manpower to a greater or lesser extent. This organization isolated those costs which moved in direct proportion to the volume of production and called them direct costs. We can see that in business A the direct manpower costs as a proportion of the other direct business costs are some 30 per cent. In business B, because of its capital-intensive nature, the direct manpower costs are only 10 per cent of direct business costs, whereas in business C, because of the speciality nature of the products, half of the direct business costs are manpower costs. A big rise in the volume of business B will have little impact on manpower. A big rise in the volume of business C will require many more employees.

Manpower costs are incurred secondly because of the way that the business is organized. Wherever an organization establishes a site then additional man-power costs are incurred. Often the site will need a personnel officer, and usually there has to be a safety officer: perhaps there has to be an accounts function. If the organization were only on one site then there would be opportunities for savings on these 'site overhead' costs. The only way of saving these manpower costs would be to close the site. In the decision to pull out of a particular business all too often the organization only saves the direct costs involved, yet it should make some attempt to save on the site overheads allocated to that business otherwise the site overheads are spread over the remaining businesses. This is particularly difficult if, for instance, the organization has each of its three businesses located across each of its sites.

Finally, to function as an organization there are overheads, the third source of manpower costs. It is possible to allocate some overheads directly to the different businesses particularly in those organizations where there is a strong business management flavour in the design of the organization structure. In this case the marketing function and the research function were both organized on business bases and their costs could be directly attributed to the businesses. The remainder have to be allocated across the organization. In each case it is interesting to isolate the portion of these total overhead costs that are man-power costs. In closing down the business, therefore, we can see the equivalent manpower savings that would have to be made to avoid spreading the costs and increasing the burden on the other businesses. The organization used the table when looking at levels of business activity to try and derive the necessary productivity improvement figures that were needed to make each business viable.

INFORMATION ABOUT CHANGING MANPOWER STRUCTURES

In assessing the way that the future strategies of the organization will affect manpower, there is a need to be able to define the group of manpower that is likely to be affected and assess the consequent results. In attempting to do this, organizations find that they have a need to look back over the way that their manpower structure has been changing. Often the key to the future can be found in the movements of the past. Organizations run into two problems at this point:

1. The data are just not available. In the past no one could see the benefit of storing information about numbers in different departments or holding information about losses from the organization over the past few years. Consequently, no information at all might be available.
2. If an organization has had the foresight to store the information, it finds that historical information can be quite difficult to use in this respect. Perhaps the organization is considering, as part of its future strategy, the need to

increase staff who have a background in computers or with computer-related skills. It feels that this change has been going on over a number of years and that it would be interesting to see how fast numbers of such staff have been increasing in the past. Currently, all such staff are to be found in the management services department. On asking the question, how many people there were in management services in each year for the past five years, the response is that the data are only available for two years since the management services department was only formed two years ago. Before that, such staff were employed in the operational research section of the statistics department, some staff were in the accounting function operating the computers used to mechanize the accounting procedures, and others were to be found in the research function where again there was a need for statistical work. To overcome these problems, organizations have had to change the way that they classified their manpower. The basic problem is that the organization's structure changes fairly frequently. Hence, the management services function was formed out of two of the departments two years ago. There is need to be able to classify manpower at a level that gives information as to what people do in a way that does not change very often.

The activity and role axes   The answer that has been found is to look at manpower from two viewpoints. To what end does an organization employ a person? In manufacturing organizations there are people who are employed because there is manufacturing to be done, products to be produced, others are employed to maintain the machinery, yet others are employed to sell the produced goods, others because the organization feels it ought to have a function that relates particularly to people employed, i.e., the personnel function. We call this the activity axis.

The second piece of information required is what does a person do to achieve the end for which he is employed? The production function employs operators of the machinery that produces the products, others are clerks who are responsible for helping the information flow that is necessary to record production, others will be needed to control and direct the function – the managers, whose roles are different but whose activity is production. Using these concepts of activity, the end to which people are employed, and the role, and what is done towards the fulfilment of that activity, a very useful table can be produced (see Fig. 9.7). Across the top of the table we list the basic activities of the organization. It has been found useful in the manufacturing type of organization to put the production activity on the left-hand side, moving through to what can only be described as organization administration on the extreme right-hand side. Down the left-hand side we list the various roles within the activities.

Using concepts derived from the IMS system of occupational classification, IMSSOC, five basic groups of roles have been defined. At the top the convention is to put the people who actually perform the activity, the direct workers. In the case of production these are the process workers; in the case of personnel these are the personnel professionals; in the case of marketing these are the marketing professional staff. Moving down the table the next group would be the support staff, i.e., drivers, cleaners, clerks, etc.

Organizations are continually seeking ways to improve what they do and again in many activities there are to be found people whose role it is to improve the way that the activity is performed: the OM analyst, the technologist on the production line, people whose responsibility it is to look at new computer systems within the management services function. Slight semantic problems can arise if the organization employs a research activity. In this case the people who do research come under the doers of that activity and not the improvers' or searchers' column of the production activity. Finally, there is the need to control activities and at this point we can include the managers and supervisors of the different activities.

Activity / Role	PROD	CONST	R&D	MARK	--------	FINANCE	PERS	LEGAL	ORG CON	TOTAL
Doers										
Supporters										
Planners										
Searchers										
Controllers										
Total					--------					

Fig. 9.7. Activity/role table

275

Strategic decisions   The table (Fig. 9.7) can be produced at a number of different levels within the organization. It is best used, however, wherever strategic decision making takes place. It is unlikely to be a great deal of use at the level of the plant or the site, but where an organization is divided into divisions or businesses such a table would be a very useful way of looking at the manpower structure of the organization. It is used primarily to help the strategic planner get a quick understanding of the consequences of some of the strategic decisions that they are considering taking.

For instance, if the company is deciding to equip its clerical staff with word processors it wishes to know the impact on its manpower. A way to assess the maximum impact will be to look along the row section headed supporters where all the clerks and typists are to be found in each of the activities. A quick assessment of the rate of saving in terms of clerks or typists of the word processor can then be applied across the whole of the clerks and typists in each of the activities to get some idea of the overall effect on the organization.

Perhaps the organization is considering increasing its marketing activity. It will be able to see that the current level of support, in other words what supporters, planners, improvers, and controllers are needed to back up its marketing offices (the doers) and in assessing the additional marketing staff required will be able to make some estimate of the need to increase the support to the new staff.

Summary

Undoubtedly this is a particularly difficult area of manpower work. Much more work needs to be done in the estimation of productivity in finding ways to concentrate management's attention on the problem and in developing better ways of linking manpower policies to the medium-term planning of organizations.

Areas under study at the moment are the use of linked sets of productivity ratios to help an organization see the interrelationship between the returns it gets from capital, materials and labour and to help it decide how to improve manpower productivity. Processes are being developed to help organizations look at the value they get from the overheads and services functions.

10.

Data needs and handling methods

If the authors earned £1 for every day that elapses between an organization's realization that its manpower planning activities will require considerable information about manpower stocks and flows and the day when the resulting computerized personnel information system whirrs into action, they would be very rich men.

The definition and creation of computerized personnel information systems seem to rank in degree of difficulty with the labours of Hercules. Working parties to define the information required and how it shall be kept are created and disbanded with gay abandon. Feasibility studies by computer and management services specialists suggest sophisticated data-bases, rings of mini-computers talking to each other, links with payroll, etc., in terms incomprehensible to the personnel manager who only wants a few data to investigate his graduate recruitment or wastage of senior executives. Research in the United States some years ago suggested that only one-third of all attempts to computerize personnel information come to fruition satisfactorily.

This chapter considers this question from two viewpoints and suggests a practical way of overcoming the problems. Defining the information required for manpower planning is not too difficult now that there is considerable experience of it in practice. It is emphasized that this section of the chapter will only consider the information needed for manpower planning reasons and does not attempt to define that required for other personnel objectives. The striking thing is that with the exception of one or two items, most of the data are required for many of these additional objectives.

The structure of the computer file to be set up has a significant impact on the success of the system created. The personnel man should not shrug his shoulders and leave it to the computer experts, he should attempt to get them to explain to him in layman's language how different file structures work and what impact they will have on the use of the system. A section of the chapter will consider the experience of other organizations and put forward practical suggestions for file structures.

The alternative to long feasibility studies leading to endless debates on system design is to create a personnel information system by stealth. A small-scale trial reveals very quickly the real needs of the personnel function and the limitations of systems, and the results obtained can be shown to other managers to help justify the system. Such an approach is described in the third section of this chapter.

This approach to manpower planning is based on using information to help manpower decisions. Reporting manpower information effectively and simply contributes significantly to effective planning. In the last section of the chapter, consideration is given to the reporting activity.

The information needs of manpower planning

The need for a particular piece of manpower information will not be argued from an academic standpoint. The starting point is experience gained in a wide variety of organizations during projects designed to help organizations create a manpower planning capability. In essence it will be biased; if there is a choice or even a contention as to whether an item of information is needed for manpower planning or not, then the advice of the authors will be to include it, subject to considerations of cost. An information system created by including all the items of information suggested in this chapter will be the most comprehensive that could be required for an effective programme of manpower management.

The task of managing manpower has been divided into three broad areas as far as defining its information needs are concerned, matching the subjects covered in earlier chapters.

ESTIMATING MANPOWER NEEDS AND DETERMINING MANPOWER STRATEGY

How many branch managers do we have and could you divide them between large and small branches? What was the ratio of computer staff to normal bank staff five years ago and what is it now? How has the number of employees changed since 1973, and could you give me the numbers by region and by two groups of staff, above chief clerk, and chief clerk and below? I want to look at the ratio of headquarters staff to total sales turnover and compare our south east region with the rest of the United Kingdom. I have the number of accounts year by year since 1975, could you produce the numbers of people employed for the two areas and produce me an analysis by grade? I am trying to compare the spread of resources used in a typical branch serving a large city with the resources required to staff a quiet country area. The departmental organization does not help, since there are more departments in the city branch, could you produce me a listing by activity?

These are the sorts of questions that senior management ask when taking decisions about the number and type of employees required to meet business objectives over the next five years. Relating manpower to an organization's needs and determining its manpower strategies is largely a question of looking at the resources used by the organization and the way that these resources have developed over a period of time.

In the first place the numbers of employees currently in the organization will largely determine the activities that it can perform in the near future since, by definition, it is impossible to change radically the personnel of a large organization. Overnight, computer programmers cannot be switched to investment analysts, assistant branch managers cannot be turned into taxation specialists without training and the building up of experience. In short, considerable information is needed about the disposition and type of resources currently employed. The following items of information will be needed:

1. **An organization code** This code represents the administrative grouping within the organization, reflecting the lines of responsibility and accountability for staff. Typically a three-level code is required. In the case of a bank, the region could be the first level, the second level could be the branch within the region, and the third level could be used in the case of large banks to break down departments into groups. Similar coding structures are required in other organizations; a conglomerate's first level code could be one identifying the separate organizations making up the conglomerate.

2. **Location code** In organizations which are spread geographically across the country, it is normal to keep a location code. Since the banks are organized regionally, this code is in part catered for by the organization code, but in other organizations it would be necessary to create one for all employees. It may be useful from the point of view of answering government statistical returns to produce a further subdivision of the geographical location code that links the organization with the government standard regions.

3. **Occupation classification** The next area of information has proved to be one of the most difficult to describe. Occupation classification is the name that is commonly given to this area. Many schemes have been attempted and, in general, the experience of organizations has been that the systems that have been devised have been disappointing. The opinion of the Institute, having spent many man-years in the study of occupational classification, is that two items of information are needed.

Organization activity code In managing manpower policies, information on how manpower is deployed to meet the changing needs of the government, and how this deployment changes over time, is essential. Complex, large or small organizations, seem to need to reorganize departmental structures; abstracting analyses of manpower deployment and how it changes over time then becomes very difficult.

The solution to this problem is to establish a new code which represents the activity to which a person's work is directed. Experience shows that in a reorganization, employees' basic activities do not change but that the activities are grouped together in different ways.

This code attempts to collect together all the people who are needed to support a particular activity within the organization, i.e., a computing resource. In the decision to have such a resource, an organization is implicitly accepting that it not only needs staff associated with the computer itself – systems analysts, programmers, machine operators, punch card operators, etc. – but the additional staff that are needed to support these people. Typists, clerks, possibly a security man, and maintenance people for the machinery are required. If the organization were to decide, as part of its manpower strategy, that it would no longer have its own computing activity but rely on external services, then it would need to divest itself of these support staff as well as the computer professionals. The organization code may sufficiently describe people to allow this to be done but there are cases where for administrative reasons, for example, all the typists would be located in the central pool and coded under an appropriate heading. Yet these same typists are needed to support a number of different activities.

Below is an example of an attempt to derive an activity code for a Civil Service. Ministries are constantly changing but civil servants perform the same activities.

First level		Second level		Third level	
A	Security	AA	Relations with foreign states and international agencies		
		AB	Armed Forces	ABA	Army
				ABB	Navy
				ABC	Air Force
		AC	Border services		
		AD	Immigration		
		AE	International security	AEA	Criminal
				AEB	Civil
B	Management of the economy	BA	Natural resources	BAA	Food
				BAB	Minerals and water
				BAC	Forests
		BB	Wealth creation	BBA	Industry
				BBB	Trade
				BBC	Tourism
		BC	Services	BCA	Financial
				BCB	Employment
				BCC	Coordination and planning

First level		Second level		Third level	
C	Management of the Environment	CA	Physical infrastructure	CAA	Roads, bridges, tunnels
				CAB	Maritime installations
				CAC	Aviation installations
				CAD	Energy installations
				CAE	Parks and gardens
				CAF	Public buildings
				CAG	Urban development and planning
		CB	Cultural infrastructure	CBA	Museums and archives
				CBB	Monuments
				CBC	Academies
				CBD	Libraries
				CBE	Entertainment
				CBF	Sport
		CC	Regulation of the mass media		
D	Fiscal management	DA	Raising revenue	DAA	Customs
				DAB	Direct taxation
				DAC	Company taxation
				DAD	Lotteries
				DAE	Government bonds
				DAF	Justice revenue
		DB	Coordination planning and control	DBA	Audit
				DBB	Price control
E	Education and training	EA	Primary		
		EB	Secondary		
		EC	University		
		ED	Vocational		
		EE	Special and research institutes		
		EF	Student services		
		EG	Equipment		
		EH	Staffing		
		EI	Planning		
F	Health	FA	Hospitals	FAA	Municipal
				FAB	District
				FAC	Central
				FAD	Special
		FB	Preventive medicine		

First level		Second level		Third level	
		FC	Mental health		
		FD	Mother/child health		
		FE	Blood transfusion service		
		FF	Convalescence units		
		FG	Research units		
		FH	Administration	FHA	Coordination
				FHB	Planning
				FHC	Equipment
				FHD	Inspection
G	Welfare and social security	GA	Welfare groups	GAA	Children
				GAB	Women
				GAC	Old people
				GAD	Handicapped
		GB	Rehabilitation		
		GC	Social security payments		
		GD	Coordination		
H	Justice	HA	Supreme courts		
		HB	Registration	HBA	Civil
				HBB	Building
				HBC	Land
				HBD	Motor vehicles
		HC	Notary services		
		HD	Courts	HDA	Local
				HDB	Labour laws
				HDC	Family
				HDD	Civil
				HDE	Criminal
				HDF	Juvenile
				HDG	Police courts
		HE	Forensic services		

Job role code   In managing manpower policies, the concern is not only with the ends to which people are employed but what they do towards that end. This is known as 'job role'. Manpower efficiency is often gauged by examining the ratio between the direct employees and those who are needed to support them in their tasks. In a large hospital, for instance, only a proportion of the employees will be directly concerned with the patients' health; doctors, nurses, physiotherapists, etc. There will be some who support these direct workers; clerks, drivers, etc. Also, there are those whose function is to manage, plan, and coordinate activities. The study of these ratios over time can be helpful in determining the direction which manpower policies should take. The activity code and the job role code are used in conjunction with each other and offer a very powerful tool to help the understanding and control of manpower policies. Chapter 9 discusses their use in greater detail.

Job knowledge A fundamental problem of manpower management is to ensure that the supply of people in the organization meets the needs of the jobs that the organization has established to meet its objectives. Over the years jobs have become more complex and demand a higher level of knowledge than in the past. A useful way of monitoring manpower policies is to compare the level of knowledge required by the jobs within the organization with the level of knowledge of the people within the organization. If the general level of the employees' experience and knowledge is below that required by the jobs, then there is a significant training problem.

This type of assessment can be made only if there is some way of relating the knowledge required by the job to the knowledge of employees. Two items of data are required to create a job knowledge code, the subject or discipline, together with the level to which it is required.

Costs Manpower cannot be related to business needs nor effective manpower strategies developed without bringing in cost. People cost money, and decisions to change the composition of the workforce will have their financial consequences. As a basis for estimating these, the salary level of an individual and any job-related payments must be included.

The importance of historical information At the start of this section of the chapter a number of questions were posed. Historical information about the composition of the workforce was needed to answer the majority of those questions. The key to developing effective manpower strategies is the ability to look back in time over the way that the composition of the workforce has changed. Commercial needs, the labour market, and the rate of technological change will affect the composition of an organization's workforce, and the ability to trace such changes in the workforce over the past few years will often provide the clue to the policies needed to fulfil an organization's manpower needs in the future.

There are two ways of meeting this need for historical information.

1. Some organizations have been extremely comprehensive and have recorded every change in an individual's circumstances, whether it be the activity, the location, the job, or his place in the organization that has changed. In this way a complete picture of the composition of the workforce can be obtained for any time between the start of the information system and the current date.
2. Other organizations have decided that year-end snap shots are quite sufficient. Instead of recording every change, they record the position of each employee at the end of the year. The loss is that there will be no record

of the situation for employees who have more than one change during the year. Later in this chapter the file structures needed for holding, storing, and manipulating manpower information are examined in detail.

There is a set of questions, issues, and considerations often cynically described as the 'numbers game'. It relates to the need to answer such questions as: How many graduates should we recruit this year? What will be the promotion rate for qualified accountants during the next five years? Do we have enough people at the assistant branch manager level of the right experience and age to fill the vacancies that will occur in the branch manager jobs this year? How fast can we run down the organization when profits fall?

Such questions, and the need to answer them form the majority of the work of the manpower planner. They are typically questions concerning the supply of manpower, starting with the people that the organization has, and relating them to the likely demands to be made on them. In determining the information needed to answer these questions, it is sensible to break down the area into the subdivisions of the earlier chapters.

Defining the manpower system The majority of the information needed for this process is already needed to relate manpower needs to the business objectives. The main items are the organization code, the location code, the activity code, the role code, and the job knowledge code. To this must be added information on the level of the employee in the organization, i.e., the grade, the educational qualification (the job knowledge code can in fact be used as an education qualification code by applying it to the individual).

Recruitment source Some organizations have found it valuable to record the source from which an employee is recruited, i.e., school, university, other employment, even going so far as to record the type of previous employer. Recruitment is one of the more fundamental of manpower policies and as the education system changes and as the labour market adapts to changing conditions, an organization may have to change its recruitment policies. A useful measure for monitoring the need for change is to look at the source of recruits to the organization over a period of time. Judgement is required here as to the usefulness of such information, and it should be noted that difficulty has been experienced with coding this sort of information in a satisfactory way.

Assessing the outflow from the organization

Reason-for-leaving code The rate of loss from different occupational groups within an organization is one of the most significant factors in the development

284

of appropriate manpower policies. Rates of leaving vary from occupational group to occupational group with the state of the economy and are strongly related to the length of service of an individual. In calculating rates of outflow it is necessary to compare the leavers during any period with the number of people who formed that group at the start of the period.

The reason-for-leaving code should be simple. Experimental evidence derived from behavioural science studies indicates that information about the subjective reasons for leaving is unreliable. Individuals, whether they are interviewed at the time of leaving, or some time afterwards, either find it hard to state the real reason, or feel inhibited from doing so. The general pattern of those organizations which have developed computerized personnel information systems is to record leaving under such headings as voluntary, redundant, ill-health, death, early retirement, dismissal, etc., without any attempt to split the voluntary leavers down and isolate the source of 'dissatisfaction'.

Inflow into the organization

Replacement policy   This forms the third of the subdivisions under the general heading of the 'numbers game'. Information about recruitment and promotion becomes important in determining these policies. In order to be able to examine recruitment patterns for any given period of time, it will be necessary to have dates of joining. Some organizations have broadened this to exclude all sources of entry. In a large organization it is useful to indicate when an employee transfers from one function to another. If there is a tradition for employees who have left the organization to return some time later, it is sensible to hold 'date of re-joining' the organization.

The main reason for separating these categories of people is that new starters to an organization tend to have much higher rates of wastage than people who have previous experience of the organization. Since length of service is used in the estimation of wastage rates, then it is important to separate those people who have previous experience from those in the organization who have not.

In case of promotion, all the necessary information has been suggested under other headings. The basic need is to be able to isolate all movements up the organization structure and relate them to age, length of service, and/or time in job. The need for job history is, of course, reinforced under this heading.

CAREER AND SUCCESSION PLANNING

The two previous areas of manpower planning have in fact provided the majority of items of information that will be needed for career and succession planning. Obviously, historical information is extremely important if one is attempting to assess the pattern of promotions, the right type of experience for a particular type of job, and so on.

The additional pieces of information that are required are a source of contention in most organizations – performance and potential appraisal information. Clearly, it is of great importance, if one is assessing whether the supply of junior managers will be sufficient to meet the needs of the organization, to make some judgement as to what proportion of the junior managers are promotable. Indeed, it is the potential assessment data that are needed for manpower planning purposes. Whether or not this information is recorded on the file is a matter for the organization. Little advice can be given, organizations appear to be equally divided as to whether it should or should not be kept.

SUMMARY

The considerations behind keeping any particular piece of information for manpower planning work have been set out in the above section.

Excluded from the list are items of information that are needed for other tasks of the personnel function, i.e., personnel administration, salary policy, development, and a host of other activities that the personnel function has to perform. If this manpower planning information system is to stand alone, then it must, of course, include some means of identifying individuals. Usually a unique number, often a pension fund number, is chosen to identify the individual and his name, initials, and title should be kept in addition.

The following items of information should be kept:

1. Organization code
2. Location code
3. Activity code
4. Job or role code
5. Salary
6. Grade
7. Date of birth
8. Date of joining
9. Date of re-engagement
10. Reason for leaving
11. Date of leaving
12. Job knowledge/education qualification code

System design

There are many issues to be considered in designing computer systems and only those which affect manpower information are considered here. The objective of this section of the chapter is to help the personnel man understand how system design affects his ability to get and manipulate manpower data. The intention is to help the dialogue between systems analyst and user, not replace the analyst.

Five years ago a major consideration was whether to go for on-line processing or to remain in the batch mode. Computers and software have developed so rapidly that only on-line processing needs to be considered in today's conditions. All the points about system design that follow are made with on-line processing assumed.

RAISING AND VALIDATING DATA. *GARBAGE IN, GARBAGE OUT! AN OFTEN REPEATED MAXIM!* The quality of any information system rests on the quality of the data. The following points should receive consideration.

1. **Use of payroll**   Where possible, an existing computerized payment system should be used to generate personnel data. Data that are used for payment systems tend to be kept to a good standard of accuracy since a mistake is easily noticed. The complaints that follow errors in pay motivate those operating the systems to get them right.
2. **Properly designed input forms**   If the organization is one in which the personnel administration is done from manual records, then a specially designed set of forms should be used to record each change in personnel circumstances. These will be filled in by the clerks when notified of changes in personnel. All other forms that had previously been used to record personnel changes and initiate such things as promotions should be superseded by the new forms, since to have two systems in parallel is a major source of confusion and inaccurate data.
3. **Linking computer and data clerk**   It is helpful in getting accurate data in the first place, and keeping them accurate, if the link between the computer and the point at which data are raised is kept as short as possible. The ultimate is to use the clerk who is responsible for recording the change in the person's circumstances, whether it be a new starter or a promotion or a leaver, to instruct the computer directly through an on-line terminal. In this way the basic record is changed immediately and the change can be seen to have taken place. This is expensive and demands a complex system. Clerks in a small unit, however, may not get enough experience of changes that happen infrequently and inaccuracies can arise.
4. **Validation routines**   A lot can be done in even the simplest system to check the data that are being entered on to a computer file. Bad or inconsistent data should be looked for under the following headings drawn up originally by Vivian Bowern of ICI when he was with IMS.
   Missing data are the easiest kind to deal with. Providing missing data are

drawn to the attention of users and there is a will to find and re-submit, the problem can be resolved. However, the identification of missing data may prove a problem. A nil entry in a field may mean that it has been missed or it may mean that there is no valid value applicable. As far as possible, a value indicating 'not applicable' should be specified for fields where there is such a possibility. Fields left blank on the coding sheet will cause the computer to reject the entry.

Technically erroneous data are comparatively easy to deal with by program check, provided users re-submit correct data. They are of two kinds:

(a) format – alpha characters where numeric digits are expected and vice versa;

(b) code errors – use of a code which does not exist, e.g., when M = male and F = female and W is submitted.

Numeric data which are out of range are again easy to deal with provided the admissible ranges are clearly specified. A combination of program check and user re-submission will be capable of dealing with the problem, e.g., when a shift disturbance allowance higher than the top negotiated rate is submitted, or when 31/04/73 appears in a date field.

Data which are inconsistent with data in other fields Relationships between data fields are less easy to specify and may be complex but a program check is desirable. One should not be afraid of indicating 'possible inconsistencies' in the case of situations which are rare though valid. e.g.:

(a) a date of birth which implies age over 21 yet the individual is assessed as a juvenile;

(b) a date of birth which when compared with the date of joining implies age of joining of less than 16;

(c) a date of leaving which implies a different number of weeks paid to that entered and associated with the pay field.

In the accompanying error message the inconsistent fields could be underlined by the computer.

Data which are submitted which are inconsistent with data already submitted Data which are submitted with dates associated may be apparently at variance where the changes, in pay rates for example, pre-date changes already submitted. Where records are regularly updated with fresh data being submitted for some (or perhaps all) fields, a program check is possible to ensure that all records for which no leaving data have been submitted are actually updated, e.g., in a system holding cumulative earnings and hours data, the control program expects these fields to be updated on every normal update run. If no leaving data are (or more accurately have previously been) submitted, then the absence of fresh cumulative data is picked up and an error message is generated.

These five types of data error are capable of being subjected to validity checking by computer program. When an error or apparent error is detected it is possible for the record containing the error to be regarded by the system as 'incomplete' and, until corrected, passed over in any enquiry.

The remaining two types of error are more difficult to cope with for program checks will not identify them.

Data which are incorrect but plausible, e.g., if a date of birth is a year or two out it is unlikely to be picked up unless it is in some sense at the margin of consistency with some other description. The only way to correct data which, so far as the system is concerned, are plausible, is by exposure of those data (this means most, if not all data held) to the people who know the reality. Who better than the individual himself?

Data which do not satisfy the intended interpretation of the field definition, e.g., gross pay means different things to different people who handle it. The identification of these kinds of bad data is only possible through analysis of the file itself. The solution is careful definition.

5. **Using audit files** Validation to check incorrectly input data can be done at this stage and the amended copy of the file, together with the changes that have been applied, are stored until the end of the day or the end of the week, whichever frequency is desired, and then the current master file can be updated. In this way, if something goes wrong, by storing on an audit file of all the changes that have been input, it is possible to correct the master file.

File structures for personnel records

This is a difficult and complex subject in which to give specific solutions. Indeed, specific solutions are not possible until the data to be stored have been specified, the data system subjected to a full analysis, and consideration given to the ways in which the data on the files will be used and the reports produced. The problem is that the demands are conflicting. Usually, retrieval from a file can be made easier and quicker but only at the expense of increased storage costs. Storage costs can be reduced but only at the expense of inefficient and slow retrieval of data. The balance can only be drawn when experience is available of the way that the files are used. This presents an impossible situation since we cannot use the file until file structures have been designed.

Experience of other organizations allows some judgements to be made which will help to establish the practical boundaries within which the file structures can be designed.

DATA-BASE CONCEPT

Theoretically, the best solution for an information system is the 'data-base' concept. This is a term which is frequently misused and applied to computer systems which are not a true 'data-base'. In a true data-base information is held once and once only, no matter what the application. Whether an item of personnel information is required for a payment system, for pensions' calculations, for medical records, or for manpower management records, it is only held once. Items of data are related to each other for specific purposes for specific systems.

To create a personnel information system within a data-base, embedded pointers are included in the computer system that allow the relationship between different items of data to be specified according to the end purposes for which they are needed. For example, in a personnel information system, salary, grade, and job would be linked together since those three items of information could be the subject of a report from a personnel information system. On the other hand, in a payment system you are much more likely to find salary, grade, and special allowances related together since these will often be the subject of a report from the payroll system.

Data-base technology is still in its infancy and in many instances design work has started and had to be abandoned because the relationships have been too complex to specify or are taking so long to do that the cost becomes prohibitive. Attempts to use data-base solutions for personnel information often involve too great a concentration on computer technology at the expense of creating a practical personnel information system.

SEQUENTIAL FILE

At the opposite end of the spectrum is the simple sequential file. While it may be a very convenient, cheap, and efficient way of updating records in a batch system, since the changes can be sorted into the sequence of the file before they are applied as a transaction, and while it may be suitable for the production of standard reports which never vary, the time taken to retrieve data on an *ad hoc* basis is prohibitively expensive for systems covering large numbers of employees.

In between these two extremes lie a range of solutions which use concepts of master files, sub-files, and coordinated files using direct access as a method of operation. The data are broken down into groups in which they would normally be updated and used. These are established on files which stand alone but which are capable of being coordinated with other similar files to produce much more complex output.

INVERTED FILE

A particularly useful concept which facilitates this approach and speeds up the access is the concept of an inverted file. In the British Civil Service system PRISM all the files are inverted thus making access to any piece of data for any individual extremely easy and simple, but the storage costs are extremely high. Experience indicates that the 'full inverted file' solution is not necessary.

A possible solution to the file structure for most personnel information systems can probably be found on the following lines, although a detailed final structure may vary according to the circumstances.

LINKING FILES

The system should consist of two basic files, a personal file and a job file, which are linked together by a series of linking files.

The personal file   The purpose of this file is to hold and relate together all the information that concerns an individual. On it will be, for instance, name, identity number, address, qualifications, and training record.

The job file   This file should hold all the jobs that are done in the organization. The file would hold the department in which the job is located, the geographical region, the activity code, the job role code, the job knowledge code, and the status of the job code. This will necessitate the organization raising a unique job number for every job that exists. The creation of such a job file will enable a major step forward to be taken in manpower management. It will enable complete analysis of all the jobs that are done, whether the job is vacant, whether it is filled by a permanent employee, or whether it is filled by somebody who has been temporarily promoted from below.

The 'linking' files   Frequently the system would need to output details of people together with the details of their jobs. Other circumstances would require analyses by job detailing the people that are occupying those jobs. In order to be able to link these two files together and provide such reports, there will need to be a series of files holding the key fields of the separate files. There will be a number of files, some of which will, however, need to be created from the outset.

'The current job link' file   Many reports require the linking together of people in the organization with their current positions. This file would hold as its key field the personnel record number and the record number of the current job from the job file.

'The job/current people link' file   The previous link file will have to be reversed in order to enable the retrieval of information by groups of job together with the people who are currently in them. In this case the key field for this file would be the unique job number and the personnel record number of the person currently in that job will be held as its subsidiary information.

'The job history link' file   One of the most important pieces of information facilitating the development of good manpower policies is the job history that

291

individuals build up during their career. A 'link' file should be created with the personnel record number as its main key field linked to the unique job number of all the jobs that the individual has done in his time in the service. This will enable the tracing of career histories. With each unique job number should be linked the date at which the individual was appointed to that job.

'The manpower flow link' file   One of the more difficult pieces of information to use and to retrieve from a computerized personnel record is the changes that happen in manpower during a time period. This task can be facilitated by the creation of a link file which links together manpower movements, jobs, and people. The file would be keyed on a 'Reason for job change' code and consideration should be given to setting up a subsidiary key on the date of the change. The information that is linked to these keys would be the personnel record number. This would enable a full analysis of new starters, people who have been promoted, and leavers to be easily obtained.

'A reason for change/job history link' file   This file will contain as its key the 'Reason for change' code with a subsidiary key on the date on which the change takes place. The secondary information linked to it will be two job record numbers. The first will lead to the job situation immediately before the change takes place (if the reason for change is recruitment this will be blank) and the second will contain the information about the job immediately after the change has taken place (in the case of a leaver, this will be blank).

During the course of implementing a new system, careful monitoring should be done if requests for information and the type of reports that are produced to test whether the 'link' file structure suggested is sufficient. It may be necessary to invent further 'link' files as experience shows the need. It may even be that some of the 'link' files suggested are not necessary.

The use of sub-files   One of the more useful assets of a personnel information system is the ability to explore a problem by selectively asking questions. Perhaps an organization has a problem concerning its salary structure. It may first want to ask a question about the average salary by grade. Having got the answer to that question it may see that its problem lies only in one group within one or two divisions. It will now want to ask further questions about that small group of people. If the information system is set up in such a way that the whole of the file has to be searched through to answer each of those questions, then the cost of doing so would be very great.

It is much more useful to be able to isolate small groups with their complete records and set these up as a sub-file which can be examined in the same way. The operating costs of the system and the time taken to do the retrieval are much reduced by this. Any system that is set up should be able to create such sub-files extremely easily.

292

A practical way of making a start

It is understandable that organizations have difficulty in coming to terms with the design, definition, and creation of a computerized personnel information system. The two problems, defining the data required and designing a suitable system, are difficult to overcome as the answers are dependent on the use of the system which in itself cannot be done until the problems are solved – 'Catch 22'. The most likely response is to commission feasibility studies. The hard reality is that most feasibility studies take a long time and do little to clarify matters. The computer department suggests the latest technology and software, because it is interesting to experiment, the personnel function wants to have maximum flexibility and power to store all data and retrieve them cheaply. Often the result of the feasibility study is to recommend the creation of a brand new system costing a lot of money. The personnel function finds difficulty in justifying the high cost because it has no experience and evidence of what it can achieve with the system. Stalemate results and the problem is referred to another committee or working party.

There is a very practical way out of this dilemma. A limited trial system can be produced covering a small number of employees at minimum cost but using very sophisticated software. This is possible because a number of computer time-sharing bureaux have built very comprehensive software systems designed to hold, store, and retrieve information. The user only pays for the time he uses on the computer and for storing his data, thus avoiding investment which could be wasted.

More importantly, it allows organizations the opportunity to set up a system covering a small number of employees with which the organization can experiment. Good hard evidence of the uses to which personnel information can be put is gathered, and experience is gained which will allow the personnel function to understand the nature of its requirements thus allowing the management services function to specify an appropriate system.

The personnel director of an organization of around 8000 employees was frustrated in his attempts to do manpower planning because data on employees were not readily available. The payroll system was an old one keeping only the data needed to pay people. The management services function to which he turned for help informed him that there was a backlog of three man-years' work needed to build and rewrite the systems needed for the organization's operations.

It was decided to set up a trial of the feasibility of personnel information using a computer bureau. A small but complete unit of 800 employees was chosen for the trial. What limited information there was on the payroll about these employees was copied from the master file on to punched cards and used to create a master file at the bureau.

The original objective of using an existing form which recorded changes in employee details could not be achieved and neither could the intention of using a new form to update both payroll and personnel information systems. This problem was referred to the organization and methods section within the organization.

Instead, a set of computer input forms was designed to cover the five main types of personnel movements the trial identified, namely new appointments, transfers between locations, resignation, promotions, and changes of name.

The trial commenced and the necessary updating and reporting programs were developed and written. Regular reports were kept to a minimum and the trial concentrated on providing information to line managers when they needed it to solve problems. Managers who were used to taking personnel decisions without information were pleasantly surprised by its ready availability from the system. Furthermore, they did not have to accept a close alternative to their ideal, but the ideal also was available by courtesy of the personnel system's powerful, flexible, but 'user-friendly' reporting language.

The proposal after six months trial experience was well received, indeed some managers, who had observed the service provided to their colleagues on the trial location, felt that the decision to extend it was overdue. Smoothly, one location at a time, the system was extended to cover all locations of the organization. Now the system could be tested in the operational situation.

A pay and grading review was reaching its final stages and data relating to the posts and the scores allocated to them by the new job evaluation system had to be analysed. The data-base was extended by the incorporation of an information system on the 'posts' within the organization and it was possible to record the scores and codes allocated to the job elements when making up the post.

The regrading exercise necessitated a new salary scheme and the organization had difficulty in deciding where to draw grade boundaries. The posts system was used to simulate the effect of drawing grade boundaries at different scores giving the organization detailed information on the costs of implementing the review and providing a sound basis for negotiations with the staff associations and trade unions. To do this effectively the new posts information system had to be linked with the personnel information system using techniques described earlier in the chapter.

The organization's head office was to move its location, it was decided, and the information system was to be used to control and facilitate the transfer of staff. The additional data on family circumstances, willingness to move, home ownership, and travel implications were collected by questionnaire. The information was coded and added to the data-base. Listing and reports could be produced detailing such things as the number of employees willing to move and the financial consequences to the organization emanating from the relocation assistance package that had been negotiated. The system was created, data entered, and the first results appeared within the space of a month. The

294

personnel sections involved were well satisfied with the information and pleasantly surprised at the speed of execution.

The system was specially extended to cover the 300 senior staff of the organization. Further fields of information were added detailing previous job history and pay and allowances held. Security of information and access was of paramount importance and successfully guaranteed. The chairman and managing director now receive regular information on their senior staff.

Some two years after the trial commenced, the organization was able to return to one of its original objectives, the design of an in-house system. Now, the discussion between the user, the personnel department, and the systems specialist is quite different. The systems specialist sees that the user has experience, knows the information he wants and why he wants it, and also understands the problems of data processing as far as they apply to information systems. The user appreciates the need to specify his requirements accurately and rigorously and also recognizes that the systems specialist cannot work miracles. The resulting design is usually achievable and meets the design objectives.

The key, of course, is the trial. Without that little would have been achieved. One can imagine the reception that would have been given to reports from personnel asking for an on-line computerized personnel information system for all 8000 employees, incorporating a specially extended section for senior staff and a compatible system recording details of all posts in the organization. The systems specialist would have laughed at their technical *naïveté* and the line managers would have dubbed it 'an irrelevant flight of fancy as far as running the business was concerned'.

Summary

Far from being the *bête noire* of the personnel manager's life, the data needed for manpower planning are by and large available in most organizations and are already kept for a number of different purposes by different individuals. The problem is that the nature of manpower planning demands that they be brought together for the first time. In all but the smallest organizations a computer is by far the most efficient way of storing, manipulating, and making available the information in the form that it is needed.

Currently the personnel function has been singled out by the computer manufacturers and software producers as the next area of the market to be satisfied. The average personnel manager can begin to pick and choose between purpose-built systems for the mainframe, for mini- and micro-computers, and in some cases for word processors. In making his choice the points made in this chapter should prove useful.

11.
Getting started. From theory into practice – the problems

This book has set out to describe the elements of a highly successful approach to manpower planning which the authors have employed in a wide variety of organizations, and seen other organizations use for themselves. It is one thing, however, to talk about manpower planning, 'the good idea', to accept that there is value in it, and to recognize its important contribution to management within an organization. It is another actually to turn this commitment into a credible and effective practical activity. Our experiences suggest that many organizations encounter a wide variety of problems and obstacles, both real and psychological, in trying to implement manpower planning. These difficulties are such that often they undermine the very will of the organization to do something at its most sensitive early stage. The end result is that a lot of talk goes on, but manpower planning stays 'the good idea', and the true benefits that can accrue from its successful implementation fail to be achieved.

The objective of this closing chapter is to highlight some of these typical problems and, where possible, identify and give some thoughts as to how they may be resolved. Observing what happens when organizations attempt to get started in manpower planning suggests that the barriers to bridging the chasm between theory and practice fall into three broad groups.

The first sort of area of difficulty may be summed up in the following plea for help:

> The board of the company recently took a decision that there was a need to improve the management of our manpower resources and that we needed an effective manpower planning activity. I was told that I was going to be in charge of this activity although I have no previous experience in this area. The trouble is, the board have said 'yes we are going to have manpower planning', but they have not told me what I am actually supposed to do, or how I am supposed to do it. Basically I am lost!

What we have here is a problem of knowing what is meant by an 'effective manpower planning activity', what the practical contribution of such an activity is, and the best, most effective way of achieving that end. Put another way – it's about 'getting the right orientation to manpower planning'.

The second type of problem cure may be summed up as follows:

The company has recently set up a manpower planning activity. We've been given clear objectives as to what we are trying to do and the contribution we're trying to make, and we think we have a reasonable understanding of the general approach that we should be adopting. The trouble is that when it comes to the crunch of looking at particular manpower problems, or dealing with key issues, we lack confidence on the practical details. For example: What sorts of information do we need and how good does it have to be? How detailed, and what specific analytical tools are available to us to, for instance, look at wastage analysis, or examine the future direction we're going in? Who can we turn to for advice when things go wrong?

We may describe the problem here as 'ensuring the right tools are available'.

Finally, the third problem area that faces companies getting started in manpower planning is one which usually affects those organizations where the manpower planning process has been active for a period of time. They would summarize their difficulty as follows:

We have set up a manpower planning activity and think we know what we're trying to do. We are clear in our approach, we have developed information systems to provide the information we need, and we have available to us the necessary analytical and data handling techniques. The trouble is that when we carry out investigations, produce reports and convey our findings to our management and board, nothing ever seems to happen as a result. The response is always: 'very interesting but . . .'

Here we have highlighted a rather different sort of obstacle. We are no longer concerned with concept or technique as such but much more with communication and commitment. We need to 'create the right climate' which will ensure that management understands what we are doing, is fully committed to the manpower planning activity, and takes seriously the contribution that manpower planning can make to the overall management process of the company.

Let us look a little more closely at these problems of getting started with manpower planning.

Getting the right orientation

Here we really have two fundamental sorts of issue facing the organization. Firstly, what practical function is manpower planning trying to perform: what is its role, its objectives, its contribution? Secondly, how is the organization actually going to go about this activity in a way which will maximize the chances of success. Now, if there was one key message which we wished to leave with the readers of this book, it is our firm belief that manpower planning is only an effective and successful activity when it is seen in the terms of the task of adding knowledge to decision-making processes within the company. Manpower is a resource which needs to be managed like any other resource, against a background of change and uncertainty. As a result there is an element of risk attached to the manpower decision-making process. If that risk is to be minimized and the decisions taken today in relation to today's problems are not going to create problems in the future, in effect, to mortgage future flexibility, then those decisions must be made on a properly informed basis. This then is our fundamental contention: that manpower planning's job is to provide that base of information on which such informed decision making can take place.

This view of manpower planning is very much in contrast to the traditional idea of a highly precise, technically based activity, which would deal with all the manpower problems and needs of the organization. A universal panacea. Many organizations have tried such an approach in the past and invariably failed, because it lacks the flexibility and responsiveness to deal with uncertainty. We must always remember that our ability to forecast the future is extremely poor and that the best we can do is to try and understand the key areas of manpower decision making facing an organization and the factors influencing the way any such decision should be made.

We have discovered, through our own practical experience, that a much more modest and pragmatic view of manpower planning, approaching it as a contributor to the management process rather than a replacement for it, is one that works, and it is the only concept of manpower planning that we would feel happy to recommend. It is also a concept we believe holds valid for all organizations, whatever their area of activity, however they are structured, and in particular, whatever their size. For in a small organization as much as a large one, there is a need to be continually looking at how best to manage what manpower resources are available and to make resultant decisions on a fully informed basis; a requirement in relative terms, as great, if not greater than for an organization employing many thousands of people.

Having defined manpower planning as a process for adding knowledge to decision making, what practical approach should be adopted? Again, our message here should be clear: there is no single 'right' way of approaching manpower planning, and certainly the traditional view of a highly rigid set of technical procedures is one which has been proved to be totally unworkable in reality. It is perhaps best to think of manpower planning as a loose assemblage of ideas, tools, and techniques, which can be applied as necessary to the individual needs of a particular organization, and reflect its particular circumstances. The key issue that faces it, besides factors such as its size and shape, are its stability, its area of activity, and the types of manpower it employs. So, for example, an organization which has a highly stable workforce has no need to devote a lot of its manpower planning effort to wastage and turnover analysis in the way that a firm with a highly mobile workforce needs to. Alternatively, any sophistication in career analysis and planning is of little value to an organization with a very flat organizational structure.

298

Different organizations will then gear their manpower planning at any point in time to focus on the issues and problems of most relevance to them. And even organizations with similar sorts of problems may well have legitimate variations in their approach. For example, in order for an organization employing a large workforce to monitor and analyse the pattern of wastage for its employees, it will almost certainly need to undertake some formal statistical analysis; without analysing losses on an aggregate basis it would be very difficult, because of the numbers involved, to quantify what level of turnover is taking place, and assess changes and trends. In contrast, a smaller organization looking at its turnover may well be able to get a good insight without any formal analysis at all. The managing director of a firm employing 20 people will almost certainly carry fairly intimate knowledge of each individual in his head. He will know that Fred and Jack and Jane are coming up for retirement in the next year, and that John and Mary are getting rather restless, and that there is a good chance that they will leave in the next six months to get other jobs. Without having to do any analysis at all, he can start to build a fairly clear picture of just how many people he can expect to lose over the coming months or year, and start to consider responsive action accordingly.

Having said this, even with small groups of employees some degree of statistical analysis can be useful, and certainly where one is looking at groups of more than a 100 individuals, structured analysis becomes very necessary.

In concluding this discussion on the right orientation to manpower planning, let us make two final observations.

First, whatever the organization, the issues of concern to it, and the circumstances in which it is operating, there are two components which seem to be present within any effective manpower planning activity. There is a need for a regular monitoring and control activity, by which the organization keeps in touch with the important details of the structure and behaviour of its workforce. It can identify trends and highlight emergent problems and issues which need to be dealt with. Complementing the monitoring process is the need for the investigatory, analytical process that can examine particular problems and concerns, can identify the factors affecting the resolution of these questions, and can weigh the options for action available.

The second observation is how critical it is to start looking at any manpower question in very simple terms and add detail as necessary later. There is always a natural temptation in our analytical work to seek to reproduce perfectly the reality of manpower in the organization by taking account of every item of detail and every nuance of behaviour. The result is invariably that we cannot see the wood for the trees. Start simple, and always recognize the importance of sensibly defining the manpower system as the base for any subsequent manpower analysis planning. If you cannot make sense of a very simplified, broad-brush view of the world, you will never make sense of the real thing!

Ensuring the right tools

Let us now turn our attention to the needs of those concerned with having the right tools available. And in talking about tools, we have in mind three things in particular: information, analytical techniques, and advice.

INFORMATION

As manpower advisers, we have often had the experience of being contacted by organizations wishing to get started in manpower planning. Time would be spent discussing their situation and their needs, and giving our views about the nature of the manpower planning process and how it should best be approached. At the end of the conversation though, the response from the organization would be, 'Well, that's very interesting, that's exactly the way we want to go. But we can't do it at the moment because we simply don't have the information available. We're going to have to spend the next couple of years getting our data sorted out and when we've done that we can actually get going and do a bit of manpower planning.'

Now the trouble with committing effort exclusively to developing information systems, on the presumption that manpower planning is not feasible without a source of detail and accurate historical information, is that such organizations find themselves, two years on, still struggling with the problems in getting their information systems working, and never confident enough that the data are sufficiently good to make manpower planning possible.

Too many organizations, coming into manpower planning, become obsessed with the deficiencies, as they see them, of their data-bases, without realizing that in view of the uncertainty and change within which manpower planning has to operate, this striving for perfect data is, in many ways, striving for spurious precision. Perfect knowledge of the situation now, or as it has been in the past, is rarely an accurate guide to what the future will bring. In addition, by delaying the implementation of their manpower planning activity until they feel their information will be right they lose the opportunity to learn from practical experience what data are in reality useful and those that are less so, how detailed the data need to be, how accurate and how timely.

We hope we have shown in this book that much can be achieved in manpower planning with the minimum of hard information. Much of the time the most valuable information available to us is people's perceptions of the manpower situation they are dealing with and their estimates about what changes might occur in the future, e.g., new employment opportunities, a change in replacement policies towards more buying in of staff. A few data go a long way and nearly all organizations are able, fairly easily, to compile details on each employee indicating location, occupation, date of birth, date of joining and, if the employee has left, date of leaving and reason for leaving. This is very basic information but sufficient to make possible most of the analysis we have described in this book.

ANALYTICAL TECHNIQUES

In parallel with their obsession with data, companies getting started in manpower planning often have preconceived notions about the need for sophisticated analytical techniques. This is another result of the traditional thinking about manpower planning as an essentially technique-orientated, rather than a decision-orientated activity. Again our firm and tested belief is that much understanding and illumination can be derived from the application of essentially very simple techniques and in many instances trends can be highlighted and problems identified merely by the sensible presentation of the manpower information available.

The use of complex techniques and models may impress some people, but more often than not they are expensive investment in time, effort, and money, for little real reward.

Clearly there are times when the application of more sophisticated techniques is justified and productive. In the past this usually meant the organization had to employ its own resources to develop those techniques and the result was a considerable amount of duplication of effort and reinvention of the wheel. Today an increasing range of powerful, generalized analysis and modelling techniques is available 'off-the-peg' for companies to use. In the main, these are computerized and usually available for the organization to put on its own machine or be accessible on a commercial time-sharing basis. There now remains little necessity for individual organizations to be developing techniques in isolation.

ADVICE

Finally, in looking at the problem of access to the right tools, let us not forget that good advice is as necessary a tool as data or techniques themselves. Advice is available to an organization getting started in manpower planning from a variety of sources. For example, an increasing number of organizations are willing to provide consultancy advice, and many institutions and bodies offer training and appreciation courses. Yet in our experience, the best source of advice is to talk to other companies and individuals engaged in manpower planning. The exchange of ideas between those actively engaged in applying manpower planning within their organization is no substitute for any amount of teaching or theorizing. In large divisionalized organizations, one development of this idea of sharing experience is that of the informal manpower planning club. Membership of the club is open to anyone from the company who has an interest in manpower planning and the club meets at periodic intervals, say, every six months, to share ideas and problems. Such an information network has been encouraged in a number of large organizations with great success and benefit to those involved.

Creating the right climate

Let us now turn our attention to the problems of creating the right climate in which manpower planning can grow and flourish. Here we are concerned not with technique so much as with how we organize and sell manpower planning to create commitment and credibility for this as an effective and important contribution to the management within the company and how we ensure we properly communicate the messages that manpower analysis reveals. There are a number of dimensions to be looked at.

LOCATING THE MANPOWER PLANNING ACTIVITY

First, where is the manpower planning activity itself most usefully to be located? People tend to hold very strong views on this question. Some would argue that manpower planning could only function if located within the personnel department in order that it can benefit from the general knowledge and experience of personnel matters to be found there. Others argue that, because it involves the use of mathematical techniques and statistical analysis, it is necessarily best placed within the management services area. Others would see it as one of the jobs of a computer department because the data techniques themselves may well be computerized. There are as many opinions as there are people involved.

Such arguments are invariably futile because they miss the essential point: that if we believe that manpower planning is about aiding those who must take the decisions within the company, then all that matters is that manpower planning be located in such a place that it can best serve their particular needs. So, in a small organization, the chief executive may well be best placed to be his own manpower planner. He will probably have neither the time nor inclination to apply more than the most rudimentary analysis to his manpower situation, but in a small organization this may well be sufficient. Where he is uniquely advantaged is in being able to look at manpower questions and considerations in the light of his knowledge of all other aspects of the business.

As the size of an organization grows, manpower planning will become identified as an activity in its own right, but whether this is located with personnel, corporate planning, management services, or wherever does not really matter so long as it effectively serves the needs and adds knowledge to the benefit of those charged with managing the manpower resources of the company.

302

Very large and diverse organizations will often see it as sensible to split the manpower planning responsibility. In such organizations the corporate or central manpower planning unit will often only have direct responsibility for planning and analysis related to corporate manpower resources, i.e., those individuals, such as senior managers, who are viewed as freely mobile between the constituent parts of the company. Its main task will be to standardize, encourage, and monitor the manpower planning activity across the company as a whole, with detailed planning for non-corporate resources resting with line management and manpower planning units within the individual locations and departments where the individuals are employed.

Whatever organizational arrangements are made, what is vital is that manpower planning does not devolve into a low level, technical backroom activity divorced from the management and decision-making process within the company.

PROVIDING THE RIGHT LEVEL OF RESOURCING

A complementary consideration to the optimal location for manpower planning in an organization is the initial level of resource and particularly manpower resource which should be put into getting this activity off the ground. The need now is to avoid one of two unsatisfactory extreme problems being arrived at: on the one hand starving manpower planning of any effective resources because it is a new, unproven area to which the organization has no established commitment; on the other as 'flavour of the month' creating, overnight, a manpower planning empire with far more staff than can usefully be employed in the first instance and serving only as a target for corporate 'in-fighting'.

Our own experience is that, in getting manpower planning started from scratch, a team of two full-time staff can be very effective, particularly if they have access to computerized personnel information. Even where collation of manual data is required this can often be satisfactorily dealt with by utilizing temporary clerical taskforces as the need arises.

And what are the characteristics of the 'ideal' manpower planner. Experience again suggests that what matters is to get a blend of intimate company knowledge with an appreciation of, and the expertise to use, the sorts of structured analytical techniques we have described in this book. Of these, company knowledge is perhaps the most critical, for someone with the right aptitude can acquire necessary technical skills much more easily than they can usually gain an in-depth understanding of an organization's structure and operation. Of overriding importance, however is that manpower planning is carried out by staff of sufficient seniority and influence in the organization that they will be listened to by the *key* decision makers.

The next issue to be dealt with in considering how best to create the right climate for manpower planning is to assess the extent to which manpower planning is purely a backroom specialist activity or benefits from the involvement of management and employees. There is growing support for the value of a participative approach to manpower planning. Involving management in the process is beneficial in that these are the individuals who will need to implement any resulting policies. Similarly, involving employees can help to gain their commitment to decisions and actions which may well be affecting their working lives. However, whether they are managers or employees, the workforce of a company is a fund of knowledge and experience which it would be foolish not to tap. Companies have found this particularly to be the case where they are involved in trying to improve productivity, or introduce new technology, and have discovered that the employees on the shop floor are often much better able, if properly motivated, to identify areas of improvement simply through familiarity with the job in hand in a way that management or manpower planners never could.

As an example, one manufacturing company decided to involve fully its shop floor employees in working out the details of introducing and manning new production equipment vital to its survival in a highly competitive market. The company recognized that a reduction of some 20 per cent in the workforce would be required to justify the capital investment but that the re-equipping exercise provided a valuable opportunity to develop improved working methods and more interesting and responsible jobs in the factory. In the event, through the active participation of the employees in planning the manpower aspects of the project – machine operators, for instance, not only drew on their experience with the existing machinery, but also were able to suggest and evaluate possible new manning arrangements on a test unit – manpower reductions in excess of both target and management expectation were identified while new production jobs with a much higher level of self-management were identified. A variety of unforeseen side benefits were also achieved, including supervisory staff being released from their traditional duties to concentrate on operator training and quality control, previously the concern of junior management.

One lesson that many manpower planners have learnt the hard way is that no matter what resources are applied to this activity and however technically skilled the planners are at their job, without good communications to those making relevant policy decisions manpower planning can easily be a non-event. In this respect it is no different from any other support activity within an organization. Unless as much effort goes into effectively presenting manpower planning and its outputs to the world as into the technicalities of the manpower planning process it will not get the serious consideration it deserves and a lot of conscientious endeavour is likely to be wasted.

Good communication and presentation, the whole art of 'getting the message across successfully' is a subject in its own right. However, drawing on the experience of practised manpower planners we can distil some basic common guidelines:

1. Manpower planning's contribution on any issue should be presented in as simple terms as possible with technicalities and jargon carefully avoided, detail kept to an absolute minimum, but key messages, findings, recommendations clearly highlighted. A summary of findings and recommendations at the beginning of a report quickly focuses the reader's attention and ensures maximum impact.

2. The assumptions underlying any analysis or conclusions should be stated, as should their sensitivity to change. One manpower planner could never understand why his company's management always commended his efforts but never seemed to progress his reports beyond the filing cabinet. His analytical work was sound and he put a lot of thought into presenting his findings. However, in his anxiety to keep things as short and simple as possible he invariably failed to state the assumptions on which he was working. The reaction of his management was to be uncertain as to how to evaluate what he was saying without knowing the base from which he started, and, as a result, his efforts, however clearly stated, were ignored. When he did, by chance, include a statement of his assumptions, his work received a much more positive response. In fact, his management disagreed with the assumptions he was using and sent him away to repeat his work with an alternative set. What mattered though was that by stating his assumptions he created a point of constructive dialogue and rapport with his management which previously had not existed and on which he could build interest and commitment.

3. Graphics and other visual aids can often convey information far more effectively than any tabular presentation of the data. Particularly where comparison, deviation from a norm, or the highlighting of a trend is concerned, a picture presentation, especially if enhanced by colour, will highlight the important messages much more quickly and with much greater impact.

4. Communicate in a language decision makers understand. It is a fact of life, good or bad, depending on your position, that most organizations are managed on the state of their financial balance sheet. It is, therefore, important that even though there are many features of the manpower situation in an organization which can only sensibly be described in qualita-

tive terms, where possible manpower planning should present its conclusions in cost-related terms to which management is naturally attuned. So, for example, the management in one marketing company was not unduly concerned to be told that 15 man-years of administrative effort would be required to implement a price control scheme saving an estimated £250 000 per year. When the 15 man-years was translated into a total manpower cost of £300 000 management quickly reconsidered its views on the proposed scheme!

Demonstrating the value of manpower planning by results not promises

The last key piece of advice we would give anyone or any organization starting manpower planning for the first time is to reach the point, as quickly as possible, where the benefits of manpower planning can be shown by a real-life demonstration rather than through theorizing and promises.

Do not just talk about manpower planning but do something. Identify a problem or concern, relevant to the organization, which is capable of being investigated within the limits of the immediately available data, techniques, and expertise. Tackle it speedily and well and put effort into effectively presenting it to those who might act on its conclusions. In this way, manpower planning can show what contribution it can make and, if justified, quickly gain the commitment and impetus needed for further development.

Getting started – an action plan

If you have reached the end of this book and are still apprehensive about launching into manpower planning for real, here are some suggestions for practical, first steps which could help 'break the ice':

- Try and assess the major manpower concerns of your organization by talking widely to line managers, personnel staff, and other employees with useful knowledge.
- Draw manpower systems for key groups of staff to help you understand better their internal structure and mechanics. Show them to relevant managers to get their reactions.
- If possible draw the systems to scale and try some simple 'key indicator' analyses – e.g., age profiles, career prospectuses – to see whether they highlight any obvious problems or discussion points.
- If there is not an existing personnel information system, carry out a rudimentary investigation to identify what data are available in personnel files, dossiers, etc., which could be easily collated for manpower planning purposes.

Guide to Further Reading

Since the objective of this book is to bring to the notice of managers a new approach to the problems of planning manpower which is based on the practical experiences of the authors, it does not draw specifically on previous publications. Equally, it is difficult in the chapters to point the reader to publications where a particular point is elaborated on from the same practical point of view.

Clearly the approach outlined in this book draws on the accumulated experience of researchers and the products of their research in a general way. John Bramham's book *Practical Manpower Planning* is a useful source for readers coming new to the subject, but the most practical way that the authors feel they can help readers develop their further reading is to point them to a series of bibliographies produced for the *Department of Employment Gazette*. These are the most up-to-date bibliographies that have been produced in the UK, but they are some seven years old.

There are four in the series:

- 'Manpower Planning Literature'
- 'Manpower Planning Literature – Manpower Demand'
- 'Behavioural Science and Manpower Planning'
- 'Manpower Planning Literature – Statistical Techniques of Manpower Analysis'

They are available from the Institute of Manpower Studies, Publications Office.

A very useful newsletter produced in the USA, the 'HR Planning Newsletter', published by R. B. Franztreb of Advanced Personnel Systems, 756 Lois Avenue, Sunnyvale, California 94087, telephone (408) 236-2433, carries, once a year, a review of the manpower planning (or human resource planning, as the practitioners in the USA prefer to call it) publications produced each year.

Index

Managers, future demand for, 23–24
Manpower assumptions, 260–68
Manpower/business scenarios, 104–12
Manpower categories, 28
Manpower costs, 1–2, 257, 271–73, 283
  relating to business costs, 272
  sources of, 272–73
Manpower demand estimation, 19
Manpower effectiveness, 4
Manpower efficiency, 282
Manpower flow link file, 292
Manpower flows, 41, 45, 61, 92
Manpower forecasts, 7, 103–4
  relationship between business and, 100
Manpower levels:
  aggregating to organization total, 126
  basic, 264
  building into corporate plans, 121–34
  estimating at the unit, 125–26
  forecasting future, 7, 103–4
  monitoring, 268–71
  quantifying techniques, 112–21
  too high, 27
  too low, 27
Manpower losses, 284–85
  (*see also* Loss rates)
Manpower management:
  early developments, 3–5
  long term approach to, 2
  objectives and nature of, 1–27
  pressures to improve, 2–3
  techniques available, 1
Manpower map, 10, 22–26
  example, 23–26
  graduate recruitment levels, 25
  use of, 26
Manpower modelling, 23, 24, 184–223
  aid to decision making, 209
  basic steps, 186–208
  case study, 209
  development of, 185
  example of, 186
  function of, 186
  logical sequence, 190
  other types, 216–19
  practicalities of, 214–19
  quantifying the key factors, 187–89
  real world applications, 209–14
Manpower needs (*see* Manpower
  requirements)
Manpower performance, 132

Manpower planning, 61
  action plan, 306
  advice sources, 301–2
  background to, 1
  creating the right climate, 297, 302–6
  demonstrating the value of, 306
  difficulties in implementing, 5–8
  ensuring the right tools, 300–2
  framework of system, 4–5
  getting started, 296–306
  getting the message across, 304–6
  getting the right orientation, 297–99
  information needs, 277–86
  involving others, 304
  location of, 302–3
  practical approach, 298
  problems of implementation, 296–306
  resourcing level, 303
  staffing needs, 303
Manpower policy, 2, 5, 6, 27, 60, 61
  assessing changes in, 197
  differences in assumptions, 210
  identifying major differences, 212
  tactical approach, 245
Manpower policy decisions:
  identifying, 9
  practical approach to, 8–26
Manpower problem indicators, 16–19,
  60–98
  case study, 90–98
Manpower problems, 27
Manpower profiles, 61
Manpower proportions, 117–19
Manpower ratios, 132
Manpower relation to business, 99–134
  conceptual problem, 99–104
Manpower replacement policies (*see*
  Replacement policies)
Manpower requirements, 4, 7
  estimating, 278–84
  future, 184, 187, 210
Manpower resources assessment, 124
Manpower Services Commission, 3
Manpower situation, 60
Manpower Society, 28
Manpower strategy, 'ideal', 265
Manpower strategy decisions, 276
Manpower strategy determination,
  278–84
Manpower strategy development, 26–27,
  244–76

311

314